T0328989

THE HUBRIS HAZARD, AND HOW TO AVOID IT

Hubris is something we've all seen in action and experienced all too often. It's a significant occupational hazard and a serious potential derailment factor for leaders, organisations, and civil society. Hubristic leaders—intoxicated as they are with power, praise, and success—behave in ways that, if left unchecked, invite unintended and unforeseen negative consequences which impact destructively on individuals, industries, economies, and nations.

Despite numerous examples throughout history of hubris' destructive consequences, it nonetheless appears to be an ever-present and growing danger. Many leaders seem to be blind to the hazards of hubris and oblivious to the lessons of history. Prevention is better than cure and understanding the nature of the hubris hazard and the associated risk factors will help leaders and managers improve their personal performance and avoid derailment and, even more importantly, protect the well-being of employees and the resilience of their organisations over the long term. This book explains the characteristics, causes, and consequences of hubris, and shows how to combat the significant hazard it poses to managers, leaders, organisations, and society. With contemporary examples, each chapter explores a particular 'hubris risk factor' and shows how the risk can be managed and mitigated and exposure to the hubris hazard minimised.

The Hubris Hazard, and How to Avoid It offers practical guidance and action points for managers and leaders on how to recognise hubris in themselves and others and what to do to combat it when it arises. It will also be useful for business and executive coaches and leadership trainers and developers.

Eugene Sadler-Smith is Professor of Organisational Behaviour at Surrey Business School, University of Surrey, UK. His research interests are hubris in leadership and intuition in decision-making. His most recent books include *Hubristic Leadership* and *Intuition in Business*.

"At last hubris compels attention at the core of business risk. This book is a splendid addition to Eugene Sadler-Smith's already formidable contribution to the academic literature on hubris."

The Right Honourable Lord Owen, CH, FRCP, *The House of Lords*

THE HUBRIS HAZARD, AND HOW TO AVOID IT

Eugene Sadler-Smith

Routledge
Taylor & Francis Group

LONDON AND NEW YORK

Designed cover image: Getty Images

First published 2024
by Routledge
4 Park Square, Milton Park, Abingdon, Oxon OX14 4RN

and by Routledge
605 Third Avenue, New York, NY 10158

Routledge is an imprint of the Taylor & Francis Group, an informa business

British Library Cataloguing-in-Publication Data
A catalogue record for this book is available from the British Library

ISBN: 978-0-367-62679-2 (hbk)
ISBN: 978-0-367-65221-0 (pbk)
ISBN: 978-1-003-12842-7 (ebk)

DOI: 10.4324/9781003128427

Typeset in Joanna
by Apex CoVantage, LLC

CONTENTS

FIGURES

TABLES

PREFACE

Hubris is a grandiose sense of self, characterised by over-confidence, arrogance, pride, and contempt towards the advice and criticism of others. Hubristic leaders tend to over-estimate the likelihood of positive outcomes and under-estimate the likelihood of negative outcomes, and in the absence of the necessary checks and balances they create the conditions which invite unintended negative consequences. The hubris hazard's potentially destructive effects extend beyond individual leaders and organisations and make hubristic leadership a societal-level risk.

This book explains why hubris is a hazard and suggests some ways in which the risks emanating from hubris might be mitigated or eradicated. One of the book's main ideas is that risk is the product of a hazard and the level of exposure to it (i.e. Risk = Hazard × Exposure). The corollary of this is that we can avoid risk by reducing our exposure to hazard; if the exposure to the hazard is zero, then likewise, the risk will be non-existent.

The Hubris Hazard's focal concept is 'hubris risk' (this is the title of Chapter 1), an idea first mooted by Dr Andrew Bailey, Governor of the Bank of England. The book explores how to minimise hubris risk by avoiding exposure to various hubris risk factors (i.e. intoxication of power; unbridled intuition; irrational exuberance; self-deception; narcissistic tendencies; excess; conducive context; complicit followers; and lack of checks and balances). The list of hubris risk factors covered in the book is not an exhaustive one. Other people will have different views about what the risk factors are and other factors will, no doubt, come to light as we learn more about hubris.

Following Chapter 1, which introduces hubris via the example of the global financial crisis of 2008, each of Chapters 2–9 deals with a specific hubris risk factor, for example: Chapter 2 looks at the risk of being exposed to a leader's intoxication with power as illustrated by, amongst others, Vladimir Putin, who at the time of writing is engaged in a long and costly war with his neighbour Ukraine. Chapter 3 explores the risks that come about when a leader's hubris is enabled by complicit followers in a conducive context as illustrated by the case Elizabeth Holmes, founder and CEO of the now-defunct medical devices company Theranos, and who at the time of writing is beginning an 11-year jail sentence in Texas having been convicted on several counts of fraud. The final chapter, Chapter 10, introduces the idea of the Hubris Health Check as a way to estimate how exposed an organisation is to the hubris risk.

There are numerous crossovers between the various hubris risk factors and the ways in which they manifest in practice. They're separated out for ease of explanation only, for instance in the case of Putin several risk factors are at work: he's intoxicated with power but has also been enabled by complicit followers and the historical and geopolitical context of the demise of the Soviet Union and relationships with the USA and Europe.

Donald Trump, who is discussed mostly in Chapter 1, is both a gift to and low-hanging fruit for scholars of hubris, hence I have resisted the temptation to over-rely on him and coverage of his case in kept to a minimum. That said, Trump's hubris illustrates some of the deeper structural issues that are at work in early 21st-century society including nationalism and populism. These are two of the main driving forces behind what sometimes feels like a hubris epidemic in politics as elucidated in Lord David Owen's recent book *Hubris, the Road to Donald Trump: Power, Populism and Narcissism* (Methuen, 2018). Barely a day goes by without a report in the press of some hubristic excess or other by a president or prime minister. The situation is no better in business and, even though the structural issues and driving forces are somewhat more opaque than in politics, there is nonetheless no shortage of CEOs to illustrate the potentially destructive effects of hubristic leadership in the corporate world. It seems as though many of our business organisations and political institutions have been infected with a hubristic 'tone at the top' thus making hubris an occupational hazard for CEOs, presidents, and prime ministers to be guarded against.

The examples used in the chapters are drawn more or less equally from business and politics. They are topical in the sense that they're drawn from a world which is a fast-moving 'living laboratory' of hubristic leadership. But being topical raised challenges for me in writing this book not least because some hubrists become quickly forgotten outside their immediate orbit whilst their legacy reverberates; for example, we're still living with the negative effects of hubris and the global financial crisis long after the main protagonists have left the scene. The effects of hubris can be nothing less than historic and monumental, for example the catastrophic impact of Russia's invasion of Ukraine will be felt for generations to come and will change the face of international geopolitics for ever.

A further issue with attempting to be topical in the writing of the book is the fact that that the examples can quickly be overtaken by events; for example, Sam Bankman-Fried (SBF) co-founder and CEO of the now-defunct crypto-trading firm FTX, discussed in Chapter 8, is at the time of writing beginning his trial in a Federal court in Manhattan on numerous charges including conspiracy and wire fraud; the outcome of the legal process is unknown currently but if things go badly for him he could face a very long jail sentence. Future readers will be in a better position than I am to judge the appropriateness of SBF and some of the other cases used in this book as examples of the destructive effects of hubristic leadership. Hubris has been around since at least the Ancient Greeks, and there is no reason to suppose that business and politics in the future will be a hubris-free zone. There can be little doubt that in the immediate as well as the longer-term future, new examples will come to light.

The choice of examples also illustrates another of the challenges in researching hubris and writing about it: hubris is something of a 'rear view mirror' phenomenon, observable only after the leadership accident-in-waiting and subsequent derailment has actually happened. To get round this conundrum the essence of the book's argument is that preventing hubris is better than curing it; this is the idea behind the Hubris Health Check (Chapter 10). The irony is that if this book were to have even just a scintilla of the much-hoped-for practical impact it might lead to less hubris and hence there'd be less for people like me to research and write about and less mess to be cleared up. That would be a very satisfactory outcome.

To conclude, my sincere thanks go to all those colleagues–too numerous to mention but who are acknowledged in the text and with requisite apologies for the inevitable errors and omissions–who have educated and supported me in my on-going endeavours to understand the hubris hazard. I would like to single out Dr Graham Robinson and thank him for kindling my interest in hubris in the first place and Dr Vita Akstinaite for her irrepressible enthusiasm and energy for the topic of hubris and leadership. I am very grateful to Lauren Whelan, Editorial Assistant at Routledge and copy editor Sue Cope, for their invaluable assistance in the editorial and production process. My particular thanks go to Rebecca Marsh, Senior Editor at Routledge, without whose support *The Hubris Hazard, and How to Avoid It* would not have seen the light of day. I hope you enjoy the book.

Eugene Sadler-Smith, University of Surrey, October 2023

FOREWORD

Edward O. Wilson, American sociobiologist, memorably noted in a debate that "the real problem of humanity is the following: we have Palaeolithic emotions, medieval institutions, and god-like technology."[1] That was in 2009. His view then that "it is terrifically dangerous, and it is now approaching a point of crisis overall" seems less and less like hyperbole, in a world facing the twin emerging challenges of how to handle artificial intelligence and cope with climate change.

If Wilson is right, *The Hubris Hazard, and How to Avoid It* really matters, because it's about what we do when we humans, in our still relatively simple institutions, interact with forces and opportunities for projecting and potentially misusing power on a scale or at a pace that is literally unprecedented.

First, Palaeolithic emotions. We are all, like it or not, still just Mark One *Homo sapiens*; human beings, aka 'carbon-based lifeforms' in the system. This means we are prone to all the limitations of creatures that evolved to survive and thrive in extended tribal groups, to hunt and gather for food to survive, but also–most interestingly–to engage in complex social rituals and hierarchies. Hierarchies and groupings for which our big brains developed and evolved to process the sheer complexity of our social relationships with each other and how they are inextricably linked to power. Those of us in the coaching world now often start our work in the somatic, helping our clients reconnect with their bodies, understand their feelings and how and why these are being triggered. We know more than ever before about how and why, for example, the amygdala's fight or flight response might be triggered in an executive. But we have yet to find a reliable way to turn it off, and indeed we know that without emotions we can't make decisions effectively or assess risks properly. There is much in this book to illustrate what happens when the emotions take over in the wrong way in decision-making, and Chapter 5 takes an in-depth look at some of the biology behind our irrational exuberance and the role of the endocrine system in hubris.

Second, medieval institutions. As time went on Mark One humans evolved myriad, culturally distinct, institutions to enable them to engage together in all forms of human life: churches and ceremonies to manage spiritual life (and priestly power); judicial courts (to dispense justice); royal courts (to advise and serve monarchs); parliaments and senates (to share power more widely with elected or selected power groups); armies and navies (to organise military power); universities and colleges (to study and share knowledge); guilds and clubs (to develop professions and trade); and many more besides, later on including boards of directors of the limited stock corporations and forms of cabinet government and professional civil servants with their own checks and balances. Each of these evolved its own rules and customs about how to wield power, how to run a hierarchy, and how to pass on power from one generation of leaders to another. The majority, it should be noted, were male only, at least initially, by design, and some explicitly to this day by their own choice.

Many of these institutions developed from ancient times (for example, the Athenian agora and Academy, the Roman senate and army). There was then massive change (we used to say 'progress') throughout what we now know as 'medieval' times in various parts of the world, with notable achievements in China (where a massive empire was run centrally via a disciplined, merit-based civil service); Africa (where even before the controversial times of 19th-century Empire there is evidence of a mercantilist era when wealth accumulated, trade routes developed, and great civilisations grew); Europe (the apotheosis of centralised religious power, the Enlightenment, and the growth of non-kingly power culminating in modern Republicanism); and the Middle East (the original cradle of civilisation, trading capability, and where religious empires met to fight for dominance); not to mention the rise and fall of civilisations in the Americas such as the Inca. So, Wilson's claim is well-founded; the origin of so many of our (no doubt flawed) institutions for politics and business lies in these centuries. And yet we scarcely even think about how many of today's issues stem from these origins. The tendency now is to see such institutions as flawed: sexist, racist, archaic, and hierarchical, we see their remnants all the time, like an oak-framed wall in a much-developed house. It would be the work of another book to explore their successes and failings and their fitness for purpose today, but clearly institutions have evolved, consciously or otherwise, both to enable and to contain hubris. When they still work well (e.g. when a board fires an errant CEO who has gone too far, or when a political party takes down its dangerously incompetent leader) we should recognise their efficacy. Their failures are perhaps better documented, but much of the time institutions can and do work well.

In the 19th century we modernised the old and evolved new institutions, to cope with the opportunities and social changes as power shifted dramatically in the Industrial Revolution. This was a time that saw the introduction of mass education and widespread literacy, a new rich class of non-landed gentry factory owners (and a new, poor working class), widening of the electoral franchise, and a (now fiercely debated) global mindset as new state empires, greater than ever before, could project power worldwide. These new empires evolved and started to fight for influence. But as well as a deepening of the influence of medieval institutions in Western societies, the 19th century also saw new institutions becoming more open and available to less elite groups, the growth of self-improvement (e.g. the Mechanics Institute) and sometimes violent uprisings against the (hubristic?) elites in revolutions in countries across Europe and the Americas.

The third element: God-like technology. All of these changes above have links to the technologies which enabled them, gave voice to leaders and their ideas (think of printing, or steam power, or the telegraph), and provided the means to turn ideas and dreams into reality. At every stage people worried that their generation was the one that was finally facing a level of complexity (but also of opportunity) which none had previously seen, or perhaps could have been anticipated.

So now we have Twitter and the atom bomb and electric cars and global supply chains. We have Deliveroo and online voting, and Instagram stories of our lives broadcast to the rest of the planet. And we already have ChatGPT and green hydrogen projects to give us a hint of the exciting, yet challenging, opportunities ahead. Each of these advances has required confidence and ambition and courage to launch and develop, yet each has also had major detractors, as discussed in the final chapters of this book.

One of the reasons for our ambiguity about the benefits of tech is that despite all this 'progress', we, the Mark One people, are still working with our largely original hardware (aside from a few who are able to benefit from bionics or other moves towards 'transhumanism'). Yes, there may have been a non-linear increase in our technological capabilities (with more soon to come), and we now have complex institutions such as multinational companies which enjoy legal personhood and have economies bigger than most countries.

Yet we remain people who would have been able to connect with our forebears, and through the medium of literature, still can. We do not struggle to relate to the heroes of Homer's *Iliad* (the film *Troy* was a huge hit), the female protagonist of the Euripides' play *Medea*, or the lovers of the poems of Sappho or Catullus. Being a human being is, to some, a limiting factor. But it's also a linkage to a common identity which connects us to all the achievements, follies, and learnings of thousands of years of history about how to cope with power and manage mankind's fallibility in the face of it. To ignore what the past can teach us, given our hardware remains essentially unevolved, seems to me rather foolish.

For many thousands of years, then, we have known the challenges of managing power in our social groupings. The concept which this book studies, and studies perceptively, is that of the concept of hubris, where power is over-reached and breaches the walls of the institutions designed to contain it, leading to disaster, harm to people and reputations, death, and dishonour. We might reasonably imagine that the ancient Athenians were not the first people to conceive of the abuse of power, but I've always felt it must be significant that the flowering of their literary and philosophical study of the problem began at a time when a newly created citizen democracy was still mindful of the challenges posed by kingship gone wrong. It's not for nothing that our word 'tyranny' comes from the Greek word for king.

So, although we may decry our medieval institutions (or even their classical forbears), the reality is that institutions (that is, the mechanisms for bestowing and controlling human power) are all we have between ourselves and either an anarchy or a crude form of totalitarianism. Faulty and failing they may be, but we need ways to manage power and those who wield it, and institutions remain our best way to do that.

If that claim is true, it means we should pay the greatest of attention to these institutions, and to what they can do to reduce the risks that are inevitable in promoting individuals to positions of power.

In some cases, the answers lie with company boards, universities, political parties, the press, and other existing institutions to do their jobs more effectively. However, it's clearly up to all of us as citizens to play our role, as the Athenians did (well, the male, property owning, free-born 10 per cent who actually had a vote), in containing and managing potential hubrists. This might be by not voting for clearly hubristic candidates, not falling for the charm of charismatic and manipulative leaders, or insisting on the separation of powers and independence of judgement in all our worlds. It might be by demanding real humility, valuing character over personality, and encouraging the normalisation of 'toe-holders' of real influence and courage to tell leaders difficult truths. For my own profession of executive coaching, it means not colluding with hubristic leaders or weak governance, but also to have the skills to let those at risk see their own issues and find ways to mitigate them, not leave them suddenly ruined and friendless after a hubristic episode.

Lord David Owen, the distinguished politician, psychiatrist, and author, has always advocated that it is as important for us to study and control hubris in business leaders as it is in politicians. This book is an important contribution towards that goal, showing how the problems of hubris are common problems of power, with examples from both worlds. Hubris, in short, is not confined to leaders in politics. The lessons from politics also apply to leaders in business (and, I would add, to leaders in the public sector, charities, and any other area where power is concentrated and can potentially be of real good or real harm to other people).

Each of the chapters of Eugene Sadler-Smith's excellent book provides usable material for anyone involved in governing, advising, or coaching leaders, and it provides a readable and practical way to put into action the lessons we have learned from literally centuries of thought and scholarship. He provides recent, relevant, resonant examples to help make that scholarship accessible, relevant, and urgent for today's readers.

It's vital that he does. Given we as Mark One humans are unlikely to contain the growth of technology, nor to massively upgrade our brains and bodies in ways which would make us notably more capable of better leadership, perhaps we should go back to focusing on institutions, governance, and the constraint of individual leadership power as the one thing we can–and must–change to enable Homo sapiens to continue to flourish on this planet.

The alternative is perhaps too chilling to contemplate. Hubris may yet cost us the earth ...

Matt Nixon, Executive Coach and Author, *Pariahs: Hubris, Reputation and Organizational Crises*, June 2023

Note

1 Debate at the Harvard Museum of Natural History, Cambridge, MA, September 9, 2009. Available at: https://www.oxfordreference.com/display/10.1093/acref/9780191826719.001.0001/q-oro-ed4-00016553;jsessionid=7BA97CBA7AA45B01A26658182F17F164

1

HUBRIS RISK

Pride goeth before destruction, and a haughty spirit before a fall.
— Book of Proverbs, Chapter 16, Verse 18

Blinding Over-confidence

Hubris is a societal-level risk which if left unmanaged can lead to calamitous consequences for individuals, industries, economies, and nations. This fact has long been recognised, but nonetheless hubris appears to be an ever-present and growing danger. If proof were required we need look no further than the spate of corporate, political, and geopolitical failings that have bedevilled the first two decades of the 21st century which were ignited and fuelled by the hubris of numerous chief executive officers (CEOs), prime ministers, and presidents.

Andrew Bailey, who at the time of writing is the Governor of the Bank of England, gave a speech in his capacity as the Deputy Governor in the City of London in May 2016. It was in this speech, entitled 'Culture in Financial

DOI: 10.4324/9781003128427-1

Services – A Regulator's Perspective', that Dr Bailey spoke about the relationship between hubris and risk and, to the best of my knowledge, was the first to introduce the concept of 'hubris risk' in banking and finance. He cautioned against the culture of hubris that had infected his industry and helped to precipitate the 2008 global financial crisis:

> Culture [in banking] has laid the ground for bad outcomes, for instance where management are so convinced of their rightness that they hurtle for the cliff without questioning the direction of travel. We talk often about 'credit risk', 'market risk', 'liquidity risk', 'conduct risk' in its several forms. You can add to that, 'hubris risk', the risk of blinding over-confidence.[1]

In the view of many commentators, one of the most famous examples of the 'blinding over-confidence' and hubristic culture that had infected some quarters of the banking industry was at the Royal Bank of Scotland (RBS) under the leadership of its CEO, Fred Goodwin (nicknamed by the popular press 'Fred the Shred' for his cost-cutting).[2] The bank's culture, which in the eyes of many contributed to the collapse, was described as an "alpha male culture of fear" in which staff were "in constant fear of losing their jobs"; the CEO's "lieutenants were said to have stopped employees speaking out about problems" and the traditional values of service and prudence had, according to many, been diminished.[3] Under Goodwin RBS Group grew to be one of the biggest and most successful banks in the world. At its peak it had over 200,000 employees spread across the globe, assets of $3 trillion, and a market capitalisation that was bigger than that of Coca-Cola.

The acquisition of the Dutch Bank ABN Amro was the inflexion point in Goodwin's meteoric rise to fame and fortune and his spectacular fall from grace. In the view of many financial experts by the time the acquisition took place ABN Amro had sold on to Bank of America its most prized asset (its Chicago-based La Salle unit) which left the RBS consortium with an underperforming London-based investment banking franchise and some small Asian operations.[4] In spite of this, Goodwin and RBS Chairman Sir Tom McKillop decided to press on with the ABN Amro acquisition on the presumption that 'bigger is better'.[5] The £49-billion price tag paid in October 2007 by the RBS consortium for ABN Amro has been estimated to have been three times its book value. The official report described the acquisition as "disastrous"; it was funded with short-term debt which eroded RBS's capital adequacy and increased its reliance on short-term loans.[6] The decision to acquire ABN Amro left RBS in a highly vulnerable position and was instrumental in its near-collapse when the full force of the global financial crisis hit in 2008. As a consequence RBS needed a Treasury bailout to stop it going under; it ended up costing the UK taxpayer £45.8 billion.[7]

This episode proved to be Goodwin's undoing, and his is a classic tale of decline-and-fall. In his rise to fame and fortune Goodwin was knighted in the Queen's 2004 Birthday Honours List for "services to banking". After his fall from grace Goodwin was defenestrated into mere 'Mr Goodwin' when in 2012 Her Majesty the Queen annulled his knighthood and his demise as banker was complete. In the words of a Cabinet Office spokesperson:

> The failure of RBS played an important role in the financial crisis of 2008/9 which, together with other macroeconomic factors, triggered the worst recession in the UK since the Second World War and imposed significant direct costs on British taxpayers and businesses. Fred Goodwin was the dominant decision-maker at RBS at the time. In reaching this decision [to annul], it was recognised that widespread concern about Fred Goodwin's decisions meant that the retention of a knighthood for 'services to banking' could not be sustained.[8]

Goodwin has been described as "a banker who always knew better than anyone else, was contemptuous of his competitors on the High Street and had convinced himself that when it came to takeovers there was no one to match his genius".[9] The evidence from 2008 is unequivocal and Bailey is correct: the time is right to add hubris risk to other already acknowledged sources of risk faced by individual leaders, organisations, institutions, and wider society.

Hubris

Her late Majesty Queen Elizabeth the Second visited the London School of Economics on November 5, 2008 to open the New Academic Building in Lincoln's Inn Fields. It was shortly after the near-meltdown of the banks and in the midst of the global financial crisis. The collapse of the American investment bank Lehman Brothers under its CEO Richard Fuld, which heralded the crisis, occurred less than two months earlier. During her visit the Queen asked pointedly, "Why did nobody see it [the credit crunch] coming?"[10] Later the following year the British Academy convened a group of experts from business, the City, its regulators, academia, and government to address this question and produce an 'unofficial command paper' that attempted to provide Her Majesty with an answer. Their conclusion was that as far as the "financial wizards" who firmly believed that they had found new and clever ways of managing risks were concerned, it is hard to recall "a greater example of wishful thinking combined with *hubris*".[11] The global financial crisis is estimated to have cost the US government alone well over $2 trillion, as a result of increased expenditures and decreased revenues.[12]

The global financial crisis has become the epitome of the destructive effects that hubris can have and serves as a warning that "those who cannot remember the past [and learn from it] are condemned to repeat it".[13] The hubris which produced these calamitous consequences, whether it be in business or politics, is defined as follows:

> Hubris is a grandiose sense of self, characterized by over-confidence, arrogance, pride and contempt towards the advice and criticism of others. In the absence of the necessary checks and balances, hubristic leaders create conditions which invite unintended negative consequences because they over-estimate the likelihood of positive outcomes from their decisions and actions and under-estimate the likelihood of negative outcomes.[14]

In short: bad things can happen when leaders get too full of themselves and the necessary checks and balances aren't in place. Hubris often develops when a person gains a position of significant power. It is a consequence of an intoxication with and the misuse of power. Analogous to an "acquired [medical] condition", hubris is an illness of position more than of the person.[15] This makes it an occupational hazard for leaders in all walks of life where power is on hand as a potential intoxicant. Lord David Owen, author of *The Hubris Syndrome: Bush. Blair and the Intoxication of Power* (2007) and ex-UK foreign secretary who trained originally as a doctor, has argued that it's in the public interest that we know more about the state of mind of leaders such as RBS's Fred Goodwin, Lehman Brothers' Richard Fuld, US Presidents George W. Bush and Donald Trump, and UK Prime

Ministers Margaret Thatcher and Boris Johnson who succumbed to hubris, and whether their states of mind changed during their time in office and, if so, why. In Owen's view it is imperative that we learn more about the transformative effects of power and success on leaders' personalities and behaviours and how any such changes can be predicted and managed.[16]

Owen and his colleague, psychiatry professor Jonathan Davidson, argued that 'hubris syndrome' is an acquired personality change brought on by the intoxication of power and success. They proposed 14 symptoms of hubris syndrome (HS), for example, "Excessive confidence in the individual's own judgement and contempt for the advice or criticism of others" (HS Symptom 7) (see Chapter 2 for a full description). Of the 14 symptoms, several were shared with other psychiatric conditions, such as narcissistic personality disorder (NPD), for example, "A disproportionate concern with image and presentation", HS Symptom 3), but five of them were unique to the syndrome (for example, "Restlessness, recklessness and impulsiveness" HS Symptom 12). For a positive diagnosis three or four of the symptoms should be present and at least one of these should be unique to hubris syndrome. Owen has informally diagnosed several political and business leaders as having developed the syndrome, including Tony Blair, George W. Bush, Vladimir Putin, Margaret Thatcher, and Donald Trump. The hubris syndrome approach provides a systematic and comprehensive framework for the analysis of the personalities and behaviours of hubristic leaders in business and politics.

Psychological and psychiatric approaches take us some way to understanding the characteristics, causes, and consequences of hubris, but as hubris researcher Graham Robinson has noted, hubris is a phenomenon that is likely to come about as a consequence of a combination of neurological, psychological, organisational, social, and cultural factors rather than being a "single disorder, acquired or otherwise, of the personality of a particular individual who happens to occupy a position of leadership and power".[17] An implication of Robinson's argument is that it can be an over-simplification to always put the blame for the failures in business and politics squarely on the shoulders of CEOs and heads of government. In many of the tales of hubristic rise and fall, whether in business or politics, there's seldom a single factor at work. In keeping with this view, leadership scholar Dennis Tourish, found that five factors intermingled to create the conditions for hubristic leadership to emerge in the global financial crisis:

(1) intense pressures for success in a culture that required results and in which individuals convinced themselves of the "spectacular value" of the work they did and their own "extraordinary importance" in achieving it;

(2) high levels of reward and a determination to achieve ever greater rewards accompanied by the certitude that such exorbitant remunerations were merited;

(3) the acquisition of and intoxication with power which bred a sense of entitlement and privilege;

(4) the perks of office that came with power and success signalling a growing detachment from the body of the organisation they led and ultimately from reality;

(5) institutional failures to punish transgressors but instead often encouraging and rewarding "out of control individuals with a with a strong sense of self-importance, and the status to have their behaviours tolerated".[18]

In the global financial crisis, structural conditions in the industry helped to create conditions that contributed to the catastrophic consequences that followed, including the multi-billion RBS bailout price tag for UK taxpayers. It wasn't just in the UK: a system-wide lack of proper checks and balances created the ideal environment for hubris to flourish which exposed the global financial system to the risk of meltdown. This created a fragile, high-risk situation that turned sour eventually in 2007 and 2008. The aftershocks reverberated for years afterwards at enormous cost to shareholders, taxpayers, and wider society. The global financial crisis was a reminder that hubris at the top of large and important organisations is a societal-scale risk which must be guarded against "at all costs".[19]

Hubris, *Hybris*, Mythology, and Nemesis

In the modern definition a hubristic leader is someone who systematically and repeatedly takes decisions that are over-confident and over-ambitious, and contemptuous of the advice and criticism of others and, in over-estimating the chances of what can go right and under-estimating what can go wrong, they create the conditions that make unintended negative consequences (i.e. 'nasty surprises') more likely.[20] It may come as no surprise to learn that the phenomenon of hubris isn't new; the origin of the term itself goes back well over 2,000 years. The modern word 'hubris' is derived from the Greek hybris, but as classics scholar Douglas Cairns from the University of Edinburgh has pointed out, its meaning for the ancient Greeks was somewhat different to the modern meaning.[21] For the ancient Greeks hybris was:

(1) a disposition or behaviour that was belittling and disrespectful of others and insulting to them;
(2) a tendency to self-aggrandisement and 'thinking big' which dishonoured and diminished the other (the victim) and risked provoking them into anger and thus bringing the hybrist into danger;[22]
(3) a characteristic of the young because of their recklessness and of the rich because of the power that their wealth brings;[23]
(4) an offence in Athenian law;
(5) a reflection ultimately of the perpetrator's dubious moral character.[24]

Hubris was evident in the leadership style of the great mythical Greek king of Thebes, Oedipus. In Sophocles' play from the fifth century BC *Oedipus Tyrannus* the chorus sing "Hubris breeds a tyrant, hubris, if it is over-filled in vain with many things that are not appropriate or helpful—climbing to the highest cornice, it tumbles into sheer necessity with no sure footing". In this translation by Douglas Cairns the verb 'breeds' literally means 'produces'; hubris breeds a tyranny as a plant produces fruit.[25] In Aristotle's *Rhetoric*, hybris (which is broadly equivalent to 'insolence') was a harmful act from which the person committing it gets pleasure:

> Doing and saying things that cause shame to the victim simply for the pleasure involved ... [the] cause of the pleasure thus enjoyed by the hybrist is that he thinks himself greatly superior to others when ill-treating them".[26]

Hybris in ancient Athens was fundamentally about having energy or power and using it self-indulgently. For the Athenians hybris was always bad.[27] The hybrists of Athens (who typically were youthful, often male, had plenty to eat and drink, and were wealthy) had a false idea of their own worth which gave them misplaced confidence in their successes and good fortune.[28] Classical hybris is a warning to leaders in the modern age for several reasons:

(1) it's an undesirable moral character trait;
(2) it dishonours and diminishes others unjustly;
(3) it takes the hybrist's good fortune and success for granted;
(4) it plays down the role that others, the situation, or sheer luck might have played in the hybrist's good fortune and successes;
(5) it's essentially self-aggrandising;
(6) its attributes of maleness and lack of moderation offer lessons for how we might avoid exposing modern organisations to the hubris hazard.[29]

The understanding of *hybris* as the perpetration of injustice by a person of dubious moral character (i.e. the hybrist) on a victim by dishonouring them contrasts with the view of *hybris* to be found in 'mythological' approaches in which hubris is paired with divine retribution in the form of nemesis (Nemesis was the goddess of retribution).[30] A principle of the mythological approach is that there's a divine or cosmic order in the universe in which humans are mortals and gods are immortals, and as such:

(1) mortals are expected to understand their position in the pecking order of the universe;
(2) any mortal who has the temerity to transgress the cosmic order by acting as though they were god-like will incur divine wrath;
(3) myths present us, as well as the ancient Greeks, with timeless, cautionary narratives.

This perspective, in which a presumptuous perpetrator meets divine retribution in the form of hubris-followed-by-nemesis, has entered popular discourse in the modern age, particularly in business and management.[31] Management researchers are especially fond of the myth of Daedalus and Icarus as a warning against CEOs 'flying too close to the sun'.[32]

> Daedalus, a master craftsman and his son, Icarus, had been incarcerated against their wishes by King Minos on the island of Crete. To escape from their captivity, Daedalus used his craftsmanship to fashion two pairs of wings made from feathers and wax. The wings gave Daedalus and Icarus the god-like power of flight which they were to use to flee the island. Before their escape Daedalus implored Icarus to exercise restraint and not fly too high; however, things did not go

exactly as Daedalus had hoped for or as Icarus had planned. Icarus, buoyed-up, to the extent of being intoxicated, with his new-found and god-like power of flight became overexuberant to the point of recklessness. Power and success went to his head, and against his father's advice, Icarus flew too close to the sun; the wax which held his wings together melted and he plunged to his self-inflicted doom in the sea below.

In the mythological view, hubris is the capital sin of not striking the right balance between excess and deficiency. As such it is the antithesis of two qualities greatly prized by the ancient Greeks, *aidos* (Αἰδώς, humble reverence for law, human, and divine) and *sophrosyne* (σωφροσύνη, self-restraint and a sense for proper limits).[33] Hubris is a disagreeable condition because it's a disturbance of an equilibrium between deficiency and excess and as such can lead to unintended negative consequences. This subtlety is sometimes crowded out by the 'don't fly too close to the sun' trope, but it's captured in the myth by Daedalus' exhortation to Icarus to avoid flying *neither* too high *nor* too low: "Let me warn you, Icarus, to take the middle way, in case the moisture weighs down your wings, if you fly too low, or if you go too high, the sun scorches them. Travel between the extremes [of deficiency and excess]."

The renowned Dutch leadership scholar and psychoanalyst Manfred Kets de Vries described this as an 'Icarus Syndrome' in which hubristic leaders, fuelled by power and success, are unable to rein in their reckless enthusiasm before it's too late.[34] According to Kets de Vries such individuals:

(1) place excessive confidence in their own judgement;
(2) harbour feelings of omnipotence;
(3) become reckless and restless;
(4) display contempt for the advice and criticism of others;
(5) ignore the practicalities, costs, or damaging consequences–albeit unintended–of their hubristic endeavours.

Management researchers Valérie Petit and Helen Bollaert believe that the myth of Daedalus and Icarus is of particular relevance to CEOs for two reasons. First, because onlookers ascribed god-like qualities to Daedalus and Icarus as they took flight in the same way that followers sometimes ascribe similar superhuman qualities to those 'celebrity CEOs' who become popular heroes, and by believing the hype that surrounds them they run the risk of hubris followed by nemesis. The myth is about hubrists getting what they deserve.[35] Second, the notion that Daedalus exhorted Icarus not to fly too high or too low, but to keep to a middle way, raises a fundamental tension for CEOs and other senior leaders. CEOs and prime ministers are by definition 'special' in that they're mandated to lead under the most taxing of circumstances and take risks. A consequence of their risk-taking mandate is that they may have to incline towards excess at times but also need the good judgement to be able to do so without falling prey to hubris and running the risk of unintentionally damaging themselves and their organisation.[36] Intrinsic to the myth is the idea of the razor's edge that divides deficiency from excess and success from failure.

The Paradox of Strengths into Weaknesses

Management researcher Danny Miller also used the Daedalus-Icarus myth in his book *The Icarus Paradox: How Exceptional Companies Bring about Their Own Downfall* (1991) as a metaphor for how once-successful companies can end up becoming derailed by hubris. It's a paradox because the qualities that drove the success of the outstanding companies studied by Miller when taken to excess became the root causes of their demise. For example, 'productive attention to detail' morphed into 'obsession with minutiae', 'rewarding innovation' escalated into 'gratuitous invention'; and 'measured growth' mutated into 'unbridled expansion'.

Miller offers the "glorious but ultimately tragic" history of the conglomerate ITT as a case study of a 'venturing' trajectory gone wrong. ITT was managed by a highly competent leader in Harold Geneen who built the business into a cohesive corporate entity out of a 'ragbag' of stale telecommunications operations. Under Geneen's leadership ITT bought over 100 companies and by 1977 his business-building strategy had made ITT into an entity that was more complex and diverse than many nation states with over a third of a million employees spread across 80 countries. But having consolidated and diversified by making sound acquisitions at bargain prices, Geneen and his senior team became over-confident in the levels of complexity that they were able to manage. They pursued ambitious

acquisitions that were far removed from the conglomerate's core competencies. Hubris had turned Geneen, in Miller's analysis, from a competent
'builder' into a grandiose 'imperialist'. As a result, the immense ITT business empire became too vast for those with their hands on the tiller to be
able to understand, let alone control its direction of travel. Even though
economics of scale are vital, and prudent growth is necessary, in complex markets it is possible to have too much of a good thing, and big isn't
always better.[37] What ITT failed to grasp or come to terms with was that
there's a fine line between prudent acquisition of value-adding businesses
and becoming a serial acquirer of value-diluting businesses. By the late
1970s, Geneen's successor as CEO, Rand Araskog, had to sell off vast chunks
of the company and shrink the workforce by more than 60 per cent.[38] The
same strengths that made ITT into a consummate 'builder' had morphed
into weaknesses which turned ITT into an imperialist. The company failed
to successfully tread the fine line that separates confidence and competence
from hubristic abandon and excess.

A leadership strength when over-amplified can become a leadership
weakness, this is the Icarus paradox, and it applies as much to individual leaders as it does to corporations.[39] It's an outcome of 'too-much-of-a-
good-thing' and has been referred to as the 'TMGT effect'.[40] For example,
commitment, dedication, and devotion to, plus identification with, an
organisation are undoubted strengths. But positive alignment can become
over-identification to the extent that the hubrist's own outlook and that of
the organisation as they see it are identical. Steve Jobs, judged by many to
be a hubrist as well as a genius, considered himself not only the leading
light in Silicon Valley, but he also identified with the business to the extent
that in his mind he *was* Apple and thus indispensable to the business. His
dismissal from the company in 1985 for him was catastrophic: "What had
been the focus of my entire adult life was gone, and it was devastating".[41]
The distinguished psychologist Adrian Furnham observed that there is a
paradox at work in the selection of leaders in that a person's dark-side profile (including hubris and narcissism) often explains in part how they managed to climb "the greasy pole of management life" but also explains why
so many of them slip back down it so dramatically and unpredictably.[42]
This is, in part, because dark-side traits have been found to be associated
with success in the recruitment and selection process for leaders who subsequently fail to deliver.

In the 'strengths-into-weaknesses paradox' of hubristic leadership, organisations, and individuals are impelled towards derailment and decline by the self-same forces that helped to make them great in the first place.[43] The rise and fall of 11 major companies (including once-famous names such as Ames Department Stores, Rubbermaid, and Motorola) was documented by management consultant Jim Collins in his book *How the Mighty Fall: And Why Some Companies Never Give In* (2009). In these stories of corporate demise, Collins identified five stages of corporate degeneration:

(1) hubris born of success: success is viewed as 'deserved' rather than hard-earned;
(2) undisciplined pursuit of more: hubristic leaders embark on an unsustainable quest for growth based on prior successes;
(3) denial of risk and peril: hubristic leaders accentuate the positive, wallow in praise and publicity, and discount or explain away the negative;
(4) grasping for salvation: leaders look for 'silver bullets' to catalyse much-needed salvation;
(5) capitulation to irrelevance or death: the organisation spirals out of control, options narrow, and hope fades.

Collins likens the process to those human diseases which are hard to detect and easier to cure in the initial stages but which become irreversible once the final stage is locked into. He concludes with the frank and harshly realistic observation that not all companies deserve to last; maybe the world is better off without some of them and it's better that they perish rather than continue to inflict their inadequacies on stakeholders, shareholders, and wider society.[44]

The Hubris Factor

In one of the earliest and most influential scientific studies of hubris in business management, Mathew Hayward and Donald Hambrick argued that there are three observable sources of CEO hubris: recent organisational successes; media praise and CEO celebrity status; and CEO self-importance. They grouped these three components together under the umbrella of a 'hubris factor'. They argued that the hubris factor has a detrimental effect on firm performance especially when it's combined with a lack of board vigilance, see Figure 1.1.

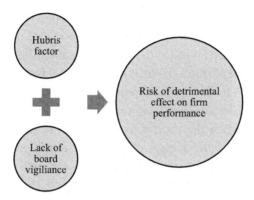

Figure 1.1 Hayward and Hambrick's 'Hubris Factor' in the Presence of Lack of Board
Vigilance Increases the Risk of Harm to Firm Financial Performance

According to Hayward and Hambrick recent successes will lead to hubris
because they:

(1) encourage CEOs to place too much faith in what worked well in the
past and trust that it will work well in the future;
(2) reinforces the CEO's stature in their own and other's eyes and boosts
their self-confidence;
(3) amplify substantially the CEO's beliefs and expectations about their
own abilities and what they're able to achieve.

Hayward and Hambrick reasoned that the greater the recent successes of an
organisation the more likely the CEO is to be "infected" with hubris.[45] Elon
Musk is a case in point: his record of successes with PayPal, SpaceX, and
Tesla may have boosted his confidence to the extent that he over-reached
himself in the controversial takeover of Twitter (see Chapter 9).

Heroic CEOs, such as Bezos, Musk, and Jobs, are favourites of the popular
and the business press. An article in *Harvard Business Review* offered an explanation for this seeming obsession with CEO celebrity: the world is volatile,
uncertain, complex, and ambiguous (VUCA) and events in an increasingly
VUCA world are easier to comprehend when we can put them down to the
actions of a single, all-powerful, charismatic, and successful individual rather
than by trying to make sense of them as a complex interplay of impersonal
social, economic, and situational forces. This tendency to under-estimate the

importance of external, situational factors in a business's internal and external environments whilst over-estimating the importance of a boss's internal motives and dispositions is called the 'fundamental attribution error'.

A classic example of this is the hiring and firing of managers and coaches of football clubs.[46] In the English Premier League, the world's top soccer league, there has been an increasing tendency in recent years to fire managers or coaches when the team doesn't perform to the owner's or fans' expectations. In 2022 the average tenure for a top-flight manager in the Premier League was two years and four days; a decade earlier managers lasted in their jobs for nearly four years on average.[47] This irrational behaviour by football club owners is based on the misguided assumption that football managers are more influential than they really are.[48]

The fundamental attribution error works both ways: in the owner's mind, if a coach or manager is responsible for a football club's failures then they're also responsible for its successes. Likewise with CEOs: as a result of the fundamental attribution error, superstar CEOs are given undue credit for their firm's performance which all too often goes to their heads.[49] This also helps to explain why charismatic leaders often emerge in times of crises as intended saviours after a 'failing' boss has been summarily dismissed for being unable to make the organisation successful. The praise that superstar CEOs receive from the media and their followers reinforces their confidence to the extent that they end up believing their own press and becoming susceptible to hubris.[50]

Amongst the hallmarks of a leader's hubris are "excessive confidence in their own judgement" and an "exaggerated self-belief, bordering on a sense of omnipotence, in what they personally can achieve".[51] A CEO's inflated view of their abilities and accomplishments, and hence their self-importance, is often reflected in their level of remuneration. Hayward and Hambrick reasoned that if CEOs receive usually between 30 and 50 per cent more remuneration that the next highest paid executive, then where this differential is much larger, say up to 100 per cent, this is likely to be a financial marker for a CEO who's infected with self-importance and hubris.

Heiner Langhein, who has almost six decades working in banking, trading, and corporate restructuring, comments that in his experience "it was most surprising to realise that many hubristic leaders—who were often brilliant and charismatic communicators and orators—could rely on an incredible amount of almost unquestioning loyalty of their immediate line management officers".[52] He cites the example of the 'publishing tycoon' Robert Maxwell (1923–1991), whose powerful leadership position within his empire which "had been achieved with the help of a large loyal group of key personnel". According to Langhein who worked on the restructuring of Maxwell's East Berlin publishing group, hubris caused Maxwell to believe that most of the success was down to him personally; as a result he stopped listening to reasoned argument, especially when he didn't like the critical message it contained: "Most staff who had direct access to Maxwell knew exactly what to say, and especially not to raise negative factual information". In the end Maxwell's decision-making abilities were "severely impaired", and his nemesis is well known.[53] In an article in the *New York Times* in 1991 it was remarked that Maxwell's "ballooning hubris" led him to see himself as a "global monarch of the information age." In 1989, Maxwell had to sell successful businesses, including the academic publisher Pergamon Press, to cover some of his debts. In 1991, his body was discovered floating in the Atlantic Ocean near to the Canary Islands, having apparently fallen overboard from his yacht 'The Lady Ghislaine'.[54] Langhein is also of the view that modern societies have so far failed just as much as the ancient world and societies during the recent past to avoid the "disastrous human affliction of hubris" which has caused "misery on a global scale" and that the search for mitigation and remission from hubris has never been more urgent.[55]

Self-importance is an aspect of personality which is captured in the concept of 'core self-evaluation' (CSE). Individuals who have a high CSE, score highly on self-esteem and self-efficacy; they have a strong belief that they're in control of events and they also benefit from low-anxiety/high-emotional stability. Like CEO remuneration, these traits are measurable. When exercised in moderation success, praise, and self-importance are healthy and productive. However, when they're present in excess, i.e. when CSE becomes hyper core self-evaluation (hCSE), more is not necessarily better. Such individuals, whether it's in business or politics, may hurtle headlong towards over-confident and over-ambitious behaviours. Their healthy CSE can turn easily into hCSE and lead to grandiosity and recklessness which creates the conditions for damaging outcomes.[56] The combination of recent organisational successes, media and follower praise for the leader, and the leader's self-importance comprise the Hayward and Hambrick 'hubris factor'.

Hayward and Hambrick tested whether the hubris factor and a lack of checks and balances had any impact on the financial bottom line in a study of mergers and acquisitions (M&As) in over 100 US firms. They found that hubristic CEOs paid higher premiums to acquire a firm which they had in their sights. The hubris factor was positively associated with acquisition premiums,[57] i.e., the excess paid for the shares over and above their market trading value. This meant that there were greater losses in shareholder wealth following acquisitions by those firms in which the CEO was "infected with hubris".[58] They also found that the relationship between hubris and over-paying was stronger when board vigilance was weaker. A weaker board is not able to prevent hubristic CEOs from paying higher premiums. Hubristic CEOs have a strong conviction that they can do no wrong and that their actions are in the best interests of shareholders even though they often turn out to be value destroying.[59] Hayward and Hambrick's research provides tangible and convincing evidence that CEO hubris can have detrimental consequences for an acquiring firm's financial performance. As far as M&As are concerned, hubris costs.

On the brighter side, Hayward and Hambrick also discovered that acquiring firms that have a proven track-record make better deals because they remove the CEO from the M&A process. In his book *Ego Check: Why Executive Hubris is Wrecking Companies* (2007), Hayward gives the example of General Electric (GE) as a firm which usually takes the CEO out of acquisition pricing. However, Hayward also cites the example of a GE acquisition that went badly wrong—its deal to acquire the investment bank Kidder Peabody which it bought in 1986 and, following heavy losses, sold on in 1994.[60] The then CEO, Jack Welch (a celebrity CEO if ever there was one), in his autobiography *Straight from the Gut* (2001) described the Kidder Peabody episode as: "my own worst nightmare. I had made a terrible mistake in buying Kidder in the first place. It had been nothing but a headache and an embarrassment from the start."[61] A colleague on the golf course remarked to him acerbically before the acquisition, "For crissakes Jack, what are you going to do next? Buy MacDonald's?" At least three GE board members weren't keen on it (including the Chairman of Citibank and the President of J.P. Morgan), but at a meeting in April 1986 Welch argued for it and won the board all over to his view. Subsequently he confessed to getting "too full" of himself both in terms of his commitment to the deal and how much he was willing to pay ($600 million). He himself described it as "a classic case of hubris".[62] Welch remarked pointedly that "there's only a razor's edge between self-confidence and hubris. This time, hubris won and taught me a lesson I'd never forget."[63] In so doing he demonstrated, on this occasion, a commodity that's all too often in short supply amongst hubristic politicians and business people: self-awareness.

By his own admission Welch failed to keep his ego in check, as a result his decisions were biased, irrational, and hubristic, and GE paid the price. According to a report in the *Washington Post* in 1994, "GE estimates that it has lost about $300million of the $1.4billion it had invested in Kidder since 1986 when it bought the firm".[64] Welch's behaviour is consistent with the 'hubris hypothesis' advanced by the eminent behavioural finance researcher Richard Roll in the 1980s: bidding firms infected by hubris simply pay too much for their targets because over-confident, over-exuberant executives in over-estimating the gains to be made think, with an "overbearing presumption", that their valuation is correct and that they know better than the market.[65]

Hubris and Pride

The epigraph for this chapter—"Pride goeth before destruction, and a haughty spirit before a fall"—sometimes shortened to 'pride goes before a fall', is from the Hebrew Bible and the Book of Proverbs of the Christian Old Testament (Chapter 16, Verse 18). The Book of Proverbs, along with the Book of Job and Ecclesiastes, is an example of 'biblical wisdom' literature which has been interpreted as one tributary in a "river of wisdom" that has "flowed from the earliest records of the human race to the present".[66] There are clear links to the Ancient Greek *hybris* which means 'pride, insolence, and arrogance' as well as to Confucianism ('Pride bringeth loss; humility increase. This is the way of heaven. He comes to ruin who says that others do not equal him', Book of Documents) and Hinduism ('Pride is the gateway to defeat'). For the Italian medieval poet Dante Alighieri, pride was the ultimate and deadliest of the Seven Deadly Sins ('love of self, perverted to hatred and contempt for one's neighbour').

Much of the Book of Proverbs consists of two-line aphorisms in the form of exhortations, observations, and paradoxes designed to aid in building character in the quest for the virtuous life passed on via an oral tradition in a pre-literal society, for example, "Better it is to be of a humble spirit with the lowly, than to divide the spoil with the proud" (Chapter 16, Verse 19). These have been interpreted as a manifestation of a hidden 'power' that rules the world that has been revealed to humankind and will ultimately be triumphant. This power picks witnesses in every age, as in the case of the ancient King Solomon and 'The Wisdom of Solomon'.[67]

The wisdom literature is relevant because, like Aristotle's moral philosophy (see Chapter 9), it deals with life directly (rather than 'salvation' per se), human beings' daily experiences, and the moral challenges that are part and parcel of being human. The knowledge contained within such books is always practical rather than theoretical and the "entire purpose is to walk the way of wisdom" ("how much better is it to get wisdom than gold", Chapter 16, Verse 16) as a general orientation to life, and as a way to "avoid the path of folly".[68] It's captured in the Judaeo-Christian tradition in the idea of 'falling from grace'. The moral dimension of pride is to be found in everyday language in colloquialisms such as 'comeuppance', 'just deserts', 'what goes around comes around', 'you sow as you reap', 'being taken down a peg or two', and 'karma'.[69] In Bertrand Russell's writings, hubris as a "certain kind of madness" and the "greatest danger of our times", happens when the "check upon pride" is removed.[70]

Hubris is often paired with divine retribution in the form of nemesis. The philosopher Mary Midgley argued that the pairing of hubris with nemesis can be interpreted as a "getting-what-we-asked-for".[71] In Midgley's view bad consequences are not just a matter of chance; doing things that are wrong in themselves can, in a just world, reasonably be expected to have adverse effects. As such, the bad outcome is a consequence of what was morally wrong with the act in the first place. Unanticipated negative consequences can be expected to follow hubristic acts "not because there is a direct, provable causal link between actions and outcomes, but because there are effects that someone who behaves hubristically invites and also, whether they like it or not, must therefore be committed to accepting".[72] As far as the consequences for a hubristic leader are concerned, their recklessness and pride combined with contempt, arrogance, and disrespect will put a strain on social relations and resources, this will cultivate disrespect, undermine trust, and promote resentment amongst followers and stakeholders, and in so doing create conditions for that are more likely to bring about negative outcomes. In other words, hubrists are likely to get nasty surprises which in retrospect are not accidental or unexpected.

Scholars of the biblical Book of Proverbs have argued that human beings have the capacity to direct their own life and that ignorance is not simply down to a lack of knowledge; it is an active aversion to knowledge which arises from pride. This gives wisdom a moral dimension. A wise person is a person of good moral character. The links to hubris are palpable: an active aversion to knowledge arises from the pride, superiority, haughtiness, and grandiosity which are the hallmarks of hubris. A corollary of this argument is that a hubristic person is therefore a person of dubious moral character. Humility, as a virtue, is a tempering influence on the corrupting effects of hubris on the moral character (see Chapter 10).[73]

Psychologists, Jessica Tracy and Richard Robins, have distinguished between two types of pride:

(1) *authentic pride*: this is a positive emotion felt upon recognising one's actual contribution to a desirable outcome;
(2) *hubristic (inauthentic) pride*: negative emotion associated with arrogance, conceit, and self-aggrandisement.[74]

They describe hubristic pride as being "sinful" and "defensive", more associated with narcissism, and contributing to aggression and hostility, interpersonal problems, relationship conflict, and a "host of maladaptive behaviours".[75] Leaders who show authentic pride are accomplished, triumphant, and humble and are likely to attribute their achievements to controllable causes such as 'I won because I am practised'. Leaders who show hubristic pride, on the other hand, are arrogant, cocky, and conceited and are more likely to attribute their successes to distortion and the self-aggrandised view that 'I won because I'm always great'.

In the case of the manufacturer of the self-balancing, two-wheeled, personal transporter, Segway, managers were accused of inauthentic pride in an article in *Industry Week* in 2007: "more driven by a need to feed their ego rather than by *true pride* in doing great work". Segway managers got ahead of themselves as well as too full of themselves: they built a 75,000 square foot facility with the aim of producing 40,000 units per month, based on wildly optimistic estimates that "the brand could capture 0.1% of all population of the world (6 billion people) and sell 6 million Segway scooters per year".[76] In 2020 the Chinese company Ninebot Inc, who bought the brand announced that they would cease production of the Segway. In the world of politics, Jessica Tracy, Professor of Psychology at the University of British Columbia, has suggested in a media commentary that Donald Trump typifies many of the attributes of hubristic pride: i.e. a grandiose and inflated sense of self, egotism, arrogance, conceitedness, problematic relationships; being disagreeable, anti-social, aggressive, and unempathetic.[77]

The Hubris of Donald Trump

Donald J. Trump doesn't figure as prominently in this book as might be expected, instead other examples of hubristic leaders are used. Rather than focusing on the specifics of the Trump 'phenomenon', his case illustrates two wider issues; first, the contentious issue of the diagnosis of personality disorders and mental illnesses in leaders who are in the public eye; second, structural matters around why there seems to be, in the words of neurologist and neuroscientist, Peter Gerrard, a "leadership hubris epidemic".[78]

At the time of his candidacy and during his presidency numerous commentators asked whether Trump might in fact be mentally ill and therefore be unsuited to being president.[79] For example, at the time of his inauguration it was said that he suffered from "malignant narcissism"[80] and that never has there been a president more at risk of hubris and who so lacked a "voice whispering in his ear, urging humility".[81] Early in Trump's term of office as the 45th president, the psychiatrist Thomas Singer commented that for many Trump has become the embodiment of everything that is bad about America: "self-promoting brand; an arrogant bully bursting with hubris; gross insensitivity to other's needs; possession by consumerism and greed; and entitlement".[82] He told Carol Leonnig and Philip Rucker in their second book about the Trump Whitehouse, *I Alone Can Fix* (2021), that "I think it would be hard if George Washington came back from the dead and he chose Abraham Lincoln as his vice-president, I think it would have been very hard for them to beat me".[83]

Lord David Owen, the co-originator of the concept of hubris syndrome, has argued that hubris is an acquired personality change as a result of, amongst other things, the intoxicating effects of power (see Chapter 2) and success in an environment in which checks and balances are absent or ineffectual (see Chapter 7). With regard to Trump, Owen is in no doubt that he "definitely exhibits many signs of hubris", but he asks the question, 'Has Trump's hubris been present for a long time?' Owen's view, having spoken to people who are close to the Trump phenomenon, is that there has been very little change in him over the years except that "Trump Tower [became] the White House". Owen also cautions against using pejoratives such as "unravelled", "paranoid", and "unhinged" to describe Trump.[84] Moreover, and, as noted elsewhere in this book, psychiatrists (most notably Allen Frances, originator of the criteria for narcissistic personality disorder) have made it clear that it would be unwise, as well as unethical (and contra the Goldwater Rule where by clinicians should not give a professional opinion about public figures whom they have not examined in person and named after the 1960s US Senator Barry Goldwater) to diagnose Trump as suffering from narcissistic personality disorder. Other psychiatrists have argued however that physicians should speak up against destructive governments.[85]

Readers will have their own views about whether Trump exhibits hubris syndrome (see Chapter 2 for a list of the syndrome's clinical features) or was suitable for high office. But rather than becoming embroiled in debates about Trump's personality and psyche, which can quickly become politically partisan, his case invites us to step back and consider broader and deeper structural issues in modern society which have created the conditions for a leader in extremis to be considered acceptable amongst voters as fit for the most powerful leadership position on the planet. Trump's election and the UK's decision to leave the European Union (EU) have been described as symptoms of a new nationalist populism in western Europe and the USA. In spite of some fundamental differences between the UK and the US variants of populism, the anthropologist Hugh Gusterson noted certain family resemblances, including: hostility towards immigrants and ethnic others; a claim to speak for working people; an insistence that established government institutions have become unresponsive to ordinary people; attacks on experts and transnational organisations such as the EU, North Atlantic Treaty Organisation (NATO), United Nations (UN), World Trade Organisation (WTO), etc.; and a call for a return to 'tradition' and its values.[86]

In Hubris: The Road to Donald Trump (2018) David Owen argues that Trump is an unashamed populist leader, where 'populism' is used to signify a belief in the wisdom not of elites but "of the common people".[87] In appealing to this mindset Trump by-passes conventional media to challenge 'fake news' and is able to land his own version of the truth on fertile ground, by intuitively playing on people's fears and anxieties, courting controversy, and thriving on chaos. Owen argues that Trump's supporters know that he is a loose cannon who is needy, unpredictable, and erratic but the perception that he is an outsider who 'tells it like it is' aligns with and appeals to their deep suspicion of mainstream politicians and gives voice to their concerns. Owen concludes that it is a "depressing fact" that in society more generally a rational, evidence-based, thoughtful leadership style seems to be less appealing than one which is "contemptuous, impetuous, narcissistic and hubristic".[88] For Owen, both in business and politics this mind set seems to reflect on the part of voters and shareholders a troubling neglect of leaders' temperament, character and trustworthiness. If Owen is right then it is incumbent upon those in positions of influence to be committed to recognising and raising awareness of hubris[89] and taking whatever steps are necessary to minimise society's exposure to the associated risks.

Risk and Hazard

The term 'hazard' refers to an inherent property of a situation, object, or substance that has the potential to cause an adverse or harmful effect. On the beaches of Australia sharks are a hazard; but sharks only become a risk when a swimmer is exposed to them by going into the water. If the swimmer stays on the beach, the shark hazard is no risk to them at all. The risk of a swimmer being killed by a shark is the combination of the hazard itself (a hungry shark) and exposure to it (by going into the sea where sharks live). Sunlight is a hazard for human beings because of the damage it can cause to the skin. Someone who lies on a beach in the summer under full sun without any protection runs the risk of getting skin cancer. The risk of getting skin cancer can be reduced by avoiding exposure to the hazard by lying in the shade, using sunscreen, covering the skin, or just staying indoors. The risk of getting skin cancer is the combination (the product) of the hazard itself (sunlight) and exposure to it (by not blocking it) as follows:

Risk (R) = Hazard (H) × Exposure (E)

If the exposure to the hazard is zero, the risk is zero. By way of example: in the case of GE, Jack Welch, and the Kidder Peabody acquisition, the hazard was Welch's self-admitted hubris, the GE board failed to stand in his way, and as a result GE was exposed to a high level of financial risk which in the end cost the business a lot of money. The risk of a financial loss in an M&A deal is the combination of the hazard itself (CEO hubris) and exposure to it (for example, because of a lack of checks and balances by the board, the CEO getting too involved in pricing decisions, etc.) as follows:

Risk of Financial Loss = CEO Hubris × Lack of Checks and Balances

As we shall see, the impact of the hubris hazard in business stretches far beyond financial losses in M&As. It also pervades senior leadership in politics where its effects are often magnified, impacting as they do at the social, economic, and geopolitical levels and with the potential to change the course of human history. Reducing exposure to hazards, as varied as sharks, sunlight, and hubristic senior leaders, reduces the chances of nasty surprises, i.e. it reduces the risk, see Figure 1.2.

Hubristic leadership is a hazard in politics and business. Hubris risk is the likelihood of harm taking place as a result of being exposed to the hubris hazard. Exposure to the hubris hazard can occur in a number of ways, for example, by appointing a hubristic leader in the first place, by a non-hubristic leader turning hubristic, by an absence of checks and balances on a hubristic leader, by complicit followers egging on a hubrist, by a conducive context enabling hubris to emerge, or any combination of these factors, see Figure 1.3. These are the hubris risk factors (HRFs, see below), and each of them is a subject of a particular chapter of this book (for example, 'intoxication of power' is the subject of Chapter 2). The risk for each

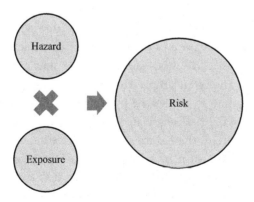

Figure 1.2 Hazard and Risk

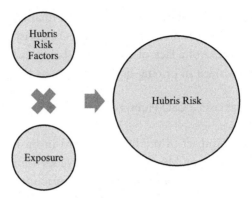

Figure 1.3 Hubris Hazards and Hubris Risk

of these factors is the product of the risk factor (HRF) and the organisation's or institution's exposure to it (E, see above). If there is no exposure to the risk factor there is no risk:

Hubris Risk (HR) = Hubris Risk Factor (HRF) × Exposure to HRF (E)

If exposure to the hubris hazard is eradicated or diminished, for example, by not appointing a hubrist in the first place, reining them in through checks and balances, moving them out of harm's way, or by firing them or removing them from office once they show the early signs of hubris, the hubris risk itself can be reduced or eliminated (by reducing the value of E). Each of the chapters concludes with a discussion of how exposure to each of the hubris risk factors might be reduced or eliminated.

In order to eliminate or reduce the risks associated with any hazard we need to understand the nature of the hazard (for example, 'Why do sharks attack swimmers?' or 'Why does sunlight cause skin cancer?') and then take the necessary, and often simple, steps to avoid being exposed to it (for example, by not going in the sea or by wearing sunscreen). Likewise, to eliminate or reduce the risks associated with the hubris hazard we need to understand the nature of the hazard (its characteristics, causes, and consequences) and then combat it by taking the necessary steps to avoid being exposed to it. This involves understanding what it is about leaders themselves that may predispose them to hubris and the circumstances they're operating in that enables hubristic behaviours, and what steps can be taken to reduce exposure to the hazard so as to eliminate or minimise the risk.

Hubris Risk Factors

Leadership, including hubristic leadership, is a process whereby an individual influences a group of individuals to achieve a common goal.[90] A leader's influence depends on their power. To paraphrase Bertrand Russell: 'what energy is to physics, so power is to leadership'.[91] However because power, by its very nature, can have detrimental effects on how humans behave, the misuse of power and its negative effects on leadership is a prime factor in hubris. Indeed, one of the hallmarks of hubris is a propensity to see the world as an arena within which to exercise power and seek glory.[92] This is why power is considered the lead risk factor in this book (see Chapter 2). Ian Robertson, an eminent neuroscientist at Trinity College Dublin, remarked that "absolute power changes the human brain" and with this comes "the delusional certainty in the rightness of one's own views and the consequent blindness to risk". Robertson's idea is prefigured in a letter written by the English politician, historian, and fierce opponent of state power, Lord Acton (1834–1902), to a Church of England bishop: "power tends to corrupt, and absolute power corrupts absolutely". By this Acton meant that even though many people enter fields such as politics or business with laudable aims to bring about positive change, when they get into a position of significant power their behaviours change all too frequently and they become self-serving and corrupt As noted earlier, this makes hubris an occupational hazard for leaders in all walks of life. But what is it that can cause leaders and managers to be so over-confident as to be blind to the risks and the potential consequences, unintended though they may be, of their actions? If a risk is 'hazard times exposure', then the risks associated with the hubris hazard can be avoided or managed by understanding the factors which cause hubris to be a risk and minimising exposure to the factors which cause hubris to be a risk.

This book is about the factors that cause hubristic leadership to be a risk and how to manage them: these are the hubris risk factors (HRFs). The prime mover in both leadership and hubris is power. But power, and more specifically its intoxication, is not the only factor that is at work. Inflated self-regard, over-confidence, self-deception, testosterone-fuelled irrational exuberance, unbridled intuition, and other excesses coupled with a lack of checks and balances and the support of complicit followers in a conducive context all have their roles to play. Exposure to these risk factors increases the likelihood of harm taking place; it creates the conditions which make unintended negative consequences more likely, see Figure 1.4. The total hubris risk (HR) to an organisation or an institution is the sum of all the individual hubris risk factors (n) as follows:

$$\text{Hubris Risk (HR)} = \{(HRF_1 \times E_1) + (HRF_2 \times E_2) + ... (HRF_n \times E_n)\}$$

If exposure (E) to the risk factors (HRFs) is high then the risk of unintended negative consequences is heightened; if exposure to the risk factors is absent or diminished then the risk of unintended negative consequences is removed or lessened. If there is exposure to more than one hubris risk factor then the hubris hazard is amplified.

Returning to 2008, many of the problems in the global financial crisis have been attributed to the over-reaching ambition and confidence of CEOs, such as RBS's Fred Goodwin in the UK and Richard Fuld at Lehman Brothers in the USA with their aspirations to become the 'biggest and the best'.[93] Hubris researcher Tim Wray draws parallels between Goodwin's leadership at RBS which contributed to the "enfeeblement" of RBS with that of Richard Fuld at Lehman Brothers in the USA which led to the "meltdown" of Lehman Brothers in September 2008.[94] The risk associated with

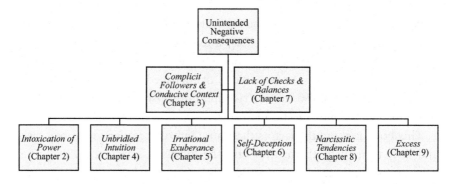

Figure 1.4 Hubris Risk Factors, Chapter Numbers in Brackets, and Consequences (Unintended and Generally Negative)

such "blinding overconfidence", to coin the phrase coined by Andrew Bailey the current governor of the Bank of England, and the executive over-reach which had infected the finance industry at the time of the global financial crisis could, according to him, have been reduced or avoided by:

(1) Restraint: ensuring that firms have robust governance controls in place including the opportunity to challenge from all levels within the organisation and separating out the roles of CEO and chair;
(2) Realism: an acceptance that not all news can be good and having a willingness to acknowledge and act upon unwelcome news;
(3) Remuneration: structuring senior managers' remuneration packages to ensure that they have 'skin in the game', for example, by retaining or deferring a meaningful amount of remuneration and putting senior managers remuneration at risk if problems emerge;
(4) Risk management: having in place internal audits and risk management systems that are effective in identifying and rooting out hubristic leader behaviours, weak controls, and poor incentives.

As Bailey noted in his 2016 speech, these elements are factors in the culture of an organisation that can either suppress or enable hubris, see Figure 1.5.

Restraint	Realism
Robust governance controls; opportunity to challenge CEO; non-duality of CEO/chair roles	Willingness to accept, acknowledge and act on bad news; self-reflection; humility
Remuneration	Risk Management
'Skin-in-the-game' executive remuneration packages; deferring / putting executive remuneration at risk	Risk management systems for rooting out executive hubris and weak controls

Figure 1.5 The Four Rs of a Hubris-resilient Organisational Culture
Source: Based on Bailey (2016).

Bailey is also at pains to point out that it's not for regulators to manage the culture of an organisation. Organisational culture is a matter, and a responsibility, for senior leaders themselves who create the climate in which hubris can either prosper or perish. Ultimately the choices that senior leaders make in this regard are matters both of moral character (i.e. the disposition to be able to think and feel in an ethical rather than unethical manner)[95] and practical wisdom (i.e. the capability to be able to figure out what is the right thing to do, and the will to do it at the right time, in the right place, and for the right reasons).[96]

Avoiding Exposure to the Hubris Hazard

Hubrists of recent times who have brought about negative, not to say calamitous, consequences for themselves, their organisations, institutions, and society did not, it would be logical and reasonable to assume, set out deliberately to be self-destructive. In the same way that Icarus didn't set out to bring about his own demise, the CEOs of the firms at the epicentre of the global financial crisis didn't set out to bring their businesses to the brink of a financial calamity nor did some of the recent occupants of 10 Downing Street actively seek to do the same. Nonetheless, severe and harmful unintended consequences ('nasty surprises') lie in wait when leaders and their organisations or institutions expose themselves to hubris risk factors.[97]

All of the modern-day hubrists discussed in this book ultimately succumbed to hubristic incompetence, which is the product of their intoxication with power, narcissistic propensities, unbridled intuitions, irrational exuberance, hyper core self-evaluations, over-confidence, and self-deception either singly or in combination. If these hubris risk factors are given free rein because of a lack of self-awareness or self-control on the part of a leader in the absence of the necessary institutional checks and balances, and are amplified by the complicity of followers, then hazard times exposure becomes a toxic and potentially lethal mix. Bailey's suggestions about hubris risk in the finance industry apply to leaders in other areas of business as well as in politics: the willingness to be challenged constructively, being realistically optimistic, having skin in the game, and being open to being found out and weeded out if one doesn't come up to scratch. These and other suggestions can help reduce the exposure of organisations and wider society to the potentially damaging effects of the hubris risk factors discussed in this book. Given the human and economic costs associated with hubris, business and society need to find ways in which exposure to the hubris hazard can be reduced and the risks from factors such as power, over-confidence, self-deception, etc. can be at least diminished if not eliminated entirely. Each of the chapters in this book deals with a specific hubris risk factor. Each hubris risk factor is illustrated with examples from business and politics. We begin with an analysis of the prime, and perhaps the most potent, of the hubris risk factors, power, and its intoxicating and ultimately destructive effects.

Notes

1 Bailey, A. (2016). *Culture in financial services–a regulator's perspective.* London: Bank of England. Available at: https://www.bankofengland.co.uk/-/media/boe/files/news/2016/may/culture-in-financial-services-a-regulators-perspective-speech-by-andrew-bailey.pdf

2 Warner, J. (2011). All were complicit in RBS's tale of hubris. *The Telegraph,* December 12. Available at: https://www.telegraph.co.uk/finance/comment/jeremy-warner/8952370/All-were-complicit-in-RBSs-tale-of-hubris.html

3 The Newsroom.(2012).RBS collapse down to Fred Goodwin's 'culture of fear'. *The Scotsman,* June 22. Available at: https://www.sundaypost.com/fp/alpha-male-culture-at-rbs-caused-collapse/;   https://www.scotsman.com/news/rbs-collapse-down-fred-goodwins-culture-fear-1620929

4 Robbins, M. (2009). Was ABN the worst takeover deal ever? *The Independent.* Available at: https://www.independent.co.uk/news/business/analysis-and-features/was-abn-the-worst-takeover-deal-ever-1451520.html

5 Sonnenfeld, J. A. (2011). BofA and the stuff of CEO hubris. *The Washington Post,* September 21. Available at: https://www.washingtonpost.com/national/on-leadership/bofa-and-the-stuff-of-ceo-hubris/2011/09/20/gIQApvsnjK_story.html

6 The House of Commons Treasury Committee. (2012). *The FSA's report into the failure of RBS.* London: House of Commons. Available at: https://publications.parliament.uk/pa/cm201213/cmselect/cmtreasy/640/640.pdf

7 Curtis, P. (2011). Reality check: how much did the banking crisis cost taxpayers? News Blog. *The Guardian,* Available at: https://www.theguardian.com/politics/reality-check-with-polly-curtis/2011/sep/12/reality-check-banking-bailout

8 BBC. (2012). Former RBS boss Fred Goodwin stripped of knighthood. *BBC News,* January 31. Available at: www.bbc.co.uk/news/uk-politics-16821650

9   Brummer, A. (2009). Hubris, overarching vanity and how one man's ego brought banking to the brink. *The Daily Mail*, January 20. Available at: https://www.dailymail.co.uk/debate/article-1123161/ALEX-BRUMMER-ANALYSIS-Hubris-overarching-vanity-mans-ego-brought-banking-brink.html

10 Donnelly, S. (2020). *A royal visit – Queen Elizabeth opens the NAB*. London School of Economics, November 5. Available at: https://blogs.lse.ac.uk/lsehistory/2020/11/05/a-royal-visit-queen-elizabeth-opens-the-nab

11 British Academician's letter to Her Majesty the Queen, July 22, 2009, emphasis added. Available at: https://www.ma.imperial.ac.uk/~bin06/M3A22/queen-lse.pdf

12 Mukunda, G. (2018). The social and political costs of the financial crisis, 10 years later. *Harvard Business Review*, September 25. Available at: https://hbr.org/2018/09/the-social-and-political-costs-of-the-financial-crisis-10-years-later

13 Santayana, G. (2011). *The life of reason*. Cambridge, MA: MIT Press, p.172.

14 Sadler-Smith, E., & Tourish, D. (2021). Hubris in management. In *Oxford research encyclopaedia of business and management*. Oxford: Oxford University Press. Available at: https://doi.org/10.1093/acrefore/9780190224851.013.334

15 Owen, D. (2008). Hubris syndrome. *Clinical Medicine*, 8(4), 428–432.

16 Owen, D. (2011). Psychiatry and politicians – afterword. *The Psychiatrist*, 35, 145–148.

17 Robinson, G. (2016). Making sense of hubris. In Garrard, P., & Robinson, G. (eds.). (2016). *The intoxication of power: Interdisciplinary insights*. Basingstoke: Palgrave Macmillan, pp.1–16.

18 Tourish, D. (2020). Towards an organisational theory of hubris: Symptoms, behaviours and social fields within finance and banking. *Organization*, 27(1), 88–109, p.103.

19 Bürkner, H-P. (2013). *Fighting corporate hubris: The four steps of the perpetuity principle*. Boston Consulting Group. Available at: https://web-assets.bcg.com/img-src/Fighting_Corporate_Hubris_June_2013_tcm9-97860.pdf

20 Sadler-Smith, E. (2019). *Hubristic leadership*. London: SAGE.

21 Cairns, D. 2023. Introduction. In Cairns, D., Bouras, N. and Sadler-Smith, E. (eds.) *Hubris, ancient and modern*. Cambridge: Cambridge University Press (in press).

22 Cairns, D. L. (1996). Hybris, dishonour, and thinking big. *The Journal of Hellenic Studies*, 116, 1–32.

23 MacDowell, D. M. (1976). Hybris in Athens. *Greece & Rome*, 23(1), 14–31.

24 Cairns, D. 2023. Introduction. In Cairns, D., Bouras, N. and Sadler-Smith, E. (eds.) *Hubris, ancient and modern*. Cambridge: Cambridge University Press (in press).

25 I am very grateful to Douglas Cairns of the University of Edinburgh for making this translation from Sophocles' *Oedipus Tyrannus* for me and for pointing out the plant metaphor as well.

26 Aristotle. *Rhetoric*, Book II, Chapter 2. Available at: https://kairos.technorhetoric.net/stasis/2017/honeycutt/aristotle/rhet2-2.html

27 MacDowell, D. M. (1976). Hybris in Athens1. *Greece & Rome*, 23(1), 14–31.

28 Cairns, D. L. (1996). Hybris, dishonour, and thinking big. *The Journal of Hellenic Studies*, 116, 1–32.

29 Nixon, M. (2016). *Pariahs: hubris, reputation and organizational crises.* Faringdon: Libri.

30 Cairns, D. (2023). Introduction. In Cairns, D., Bouras, N., & Sadler-Smith, E. (eds.). *Hubris, ancient and modern.* Cambridge: Cambridge University Press (in press).

31 Hansen, W. F. (2004). *Handbook of classical mythology.* Oxford: Oxford University Press.

32 Petit, V., & Bollaert, H. (2012). Flying too close to the sun? Hubris among CEOs and how to prevent it. *Journal of Business Ethics*, 108, 265–283.

33 Sadler-Smith, E. (2020). Don't fly too close to the sun: Using myth to understand the hazards of hubristic leadership. In Küpers, W. and Statler, M. (eds). *Leadership and wisdom: Narrating the future responsibly.* New York: Routledge, pp.44–61.

34 Kets de Vries, M. (2019). The Icarus syndrome: Execs who fly too close to the sun. *INSEAD Knowledge.* Available at: https://knowledge.insead.edu/leadership-organisations/icarus-syndrome-execs-who-fly-too-close-sun

35 Midgley, M. (2004). *The myths we live by.* Abingdon: Routledge.

36 Petit, V. & Bollaert, H. (2012). Flying too close to the sun? Hubris among CEOs and how to prevent it. *Journal of Business Ethics*, 108, 265–283.

37 Sonnenfeld, J. A. (2011). BofA and the stuff of CEO hubris. *The Washington Post,* September 21. Available at: https://www.washingtonpost.com/national/on-leadership/bofa-and-the-stuff-of-ceo-hubris/2011/09/20/glQApvsnjK_story.html

38 Miller, D. (1992). The Icarus paradox: How exceptional companies bring about their own downfall. *Business Horizons*, 35(1), 24–35.

39 Miller, D. (1992). The Icarus paradox: How exceptional companies bring about their own downfall. *Business Horizons*, 35(1), 24–35.

40 Pierce, J. R., & Aguinis, H. (2013). The too-much-of-a-good-thing effect in management. *Journal of Management*, 39(2), 313–338.

41 Hayward, M. (2007). *Ego check: Why executive hubris is wrecking companies and careers and how to avoid the trap.* Chicago: Kaplan Publishing, p.61.

42 Furnham, A. (2018). Management failure and derailment, pp.69–92. In Garrard, P. (ed.). *The leadership hubris epidemic*. Cham, Switzerland: Palgrave Macmillan, p.91.

43 Sadler-Smith, E. (2019). *Hubristic leadership*. London: SAGE.

44 Collins, J. (2009). *How the mighty fall, and why some companies never give in.* London: Random House.

45 Hayward, M., & Hambrick, D. (1997). Explaining the premiums paid for large acquisitions: Evidence of CEO hubris. *Administrative Science Quarterly*, 42, 103–27, p.108.

46 Arnulf, J. K., Mathisen, J. E., & Hærem, T. (2012). Heroic leadership illusions in football teams: Rationality, decision making and noise-signal ratio in the firing of football managers. *Leadership*, 8(2), 169–185.

47 Salley, E. (2022) How long does a Premier League manager's job last on average? *BBC Sport*, October 21. Available at: https://www.bbc.co.uk/sport/football/63341798#:~:text=Liverpool%20boss%20Jurgen%20Klopp%20and,one%20year%20and%20169%20days

48 Arnulf, J. K., Mathisen, J. E., & Hærem, T. (2012). Heroic leadership illusions in football teams: Rationality, decision making and noise-signal ratio in the firing of football managers. *Leadership*, 8(2), 169–185.

49 Malmendier, U., & Tate, G. (2009). Superstar CEOs. *Quarterly Journal of Economics*, 124, 1593–1638.

50 Hayward, M., & Hambrick, D. (1997). Explaining the premiums paid for large acquisitions: Evidence of CEO hubris. *Administrative Science Quarterly*, 42, 103–127, p.108.

51 Owen, D. & Davidson, J. (2009). Hubris syndrome: An acquired personality disorder? A study of US presidents and UK prime ministers over the last 100 years. *Brain*, 132(5), 1396–1406, 1398.

52 Langhein, H. (2023). Personal communication.

53 Langhein, H. (2023). Personal communication.

54 Cohen, R. (1991). Maxwell's Empire: how it grew, how it fell – A special report; Charming the big bankers out of billions. *New York Times*, December 20. Available at: https://www.nytimes.com/1991/12/20/business/maxwell-s-empire-it-grew-it-fell-special-report-charming-big-bankers-billions.html

55 Langhein, H. (2023). Personal communication.

56 Hiller, N. J., & Hambrick, D. C. (2005). Conceptualizing executive hubris: The role of (hyper) core self-evaluations in strategic decision-making. *Strategic Management Journal*, 26(4), 297–319.

57 The acquisition premium is the ratio of the ultimate price paid divided by the price prior to takeover news, for example, if the price paid for firm is $12 billion and the estimated value of the firm is $10 billion, the acquisition

premium is 20 per cent ($2 billion). It represents the increased cost of buy-ing a target company during an M&A. Premiums are indicators of acquiring CEO's expectations; substantial premiums of up to 100 per cent are not uncommon. See: Hayward & Hambrick, op cit.

58 Hayward, M., & Hambrick, D. (1997). Explaining the premiums paid for large acquisitions: Evidence of CEO hubris. *Administrative Science Quarterly*, 42, 103–127, p.106

59 Park, J. H., Kim, C., Chang, Y. K., Lee, D. H., & Sung, Y. D. (2018). CEO hubris and firm performance: Exploring the moderating roles of CEO power and board vigilance. *Journal of Business Ethics*, 147, 919–933.

60 Hayward, M. (2007). *Ego check: Why executive hubris is wrecking companies and careers and how to avoid the trap*. Chicago: Kaplan Publishing, p.81.

61 Welch, J. (2001). *Straight from the gut*. London: Hodder Headline, p.224.

62 Welch, J. (2001). *Straight from the gut*. London: Hodder Headline, p.217.

63 Welch, J. (2001). *Straight from the gut*. London: Hodder Headline, p.229.

64 Fromson, B. D. (1994). GE sells its loss-plagued Kidder unit. *The Washington Post*, October 18. Available at: https://www.washingtonpost.com/archive/business/1994/10/18/ge-sells-its-loss-plagued-kidder-unit/909638ed-23bd-48a0-a333-200da15e1012

65 Roll, R. (1986). The hubris hypothesis of corporate takeovers. *Journal of Business*, 59(2), 197–216, p.200.

66 Clifford, R. J. (1998). *The wisdom literature: Interpreting biblical texts*. Nashville, TN: Abingdon Press, p.19.

67 Clifford, R. J. (1998). *The wisdom literature: Interpreting biblical texts*. Nashville, TN: Abingdon Press.

68 Murphy, R. E. (1990). *The tree of life: An exploration of biblical wisdom litera-ture*. New York: Doubleday, p.232.

69 Sadler-Smith, E. (2019). *Hubristic leadership*. London: SAGE, p.20.

70 Russell cited in Sadler-Smith, E. (2019). *Hubristic leadership*. London: SAGE, p.55.

71 Midgley, M. (2004). *The myths we live by*. Abingdon: Routledge.

72 Sadler-Smith, E. (2019). *Hubristic leadership*. London: SAGE, p.35.

73 Clifford, R. J. (1998). *The wisdom literature: Interpreting biblical texts*. Nashville, TN: Abingdon Press

74 Tracy, J. L., & Robins, R. W. (2007). The psychological structure of pride: A tale of two facets. *Journal of Personality and Social Psychology*, 92(3), 506–525.

75 Tracy, J. L., & Robins, R. W. (2007). The nature of pride. In Tracy, J. L., Robins, R., & Tangney, J. P. (eds). *The self-conscious emotions: Theory and research*. New York: The Guilford Press, p.264.

76 Kim, M., Xiong, G., & Kim, K. H. (2018). Where does pride lead? Corporate managerial hubris and strategic emphasis. *Journal of the Academy of Marketing Science*, 46, 537–556, p.552.

77 www.cbc.ca/radio/tapestry/pride-and-compassion-1.3815584/donald-trump-a-case-study-for-hubristic-pride-1.3815587

78 Garrard, P. (ed.) *The leadership hubris epidemic*. Cham, Switzerland: Palgrave Macmillan.

79 Lozada, C. (2017). Is Trump mentally ill? *The Washington Post*, September 22. Available at: https://www.washingtonpost.com/news/book-party/wp/2017/9/22/is-trump-mentally-ill-or-is-america-psychiatrists-weigh-in

80 Hosie, R. (2017). 'Malignant narcissism': Donald Trump displays classic traits of mental illness, claim psychologists. *The Independent*, January 30. Available at: https://www.independent.co.uk/life-style/health-and-families/donald-trump-mental-illness-narcisissm-us-president-psychologists-inauguration-crowd-size-paranoia-delusion-reality-a7552661.html

81 Tierney, D. (2017). Can James Mattis protect Trump from hubris? *The Atlantic*, January 14. Available at: https://www.theatlantic.com/international/archive/2017/01/trump-mattis-hubris/513206

82 Singer, T. (2017). Trump and the collective American psyche. In Lee, B. (ed.). *The dangerous case of Donald Trump*. New York: St Martin's Press, pp.281–297, p.294.

83 Leonnig, C. & Rucker, P. (2021): *I alone can fix it*. London: Bloomsbury.

84 Owen, D. *Hubris: The road to Donald Trump*. York: Methuen, p.331.

85 Lewis, T. (2021). The shared psychosis of Trump and his loyalists. *Scientific American*, January 11. Available at: https://www.scientificamerican.com/article/the-shared-psychosis-of-donald-trump-and-his-loyalists

86 Gusterson, H. (2017). From Brexit to Trump: Anthropology and the rise of nationalist populism. *American Ethnologist*, 44(2), 209–214.

87 Owen, D. (2018). *Hubris: The road to Donald Trump*. York: Methuen, p.354.

88 Owen, D. (2018). *Hubris: The road to Donald Trump*. York: Methuen, p.361.

89 Owen established a charity in 2011, The Daedalus Trust, which was "committed to raising hubris awareness", see: /www.daedalustrust.com

90 Northouse, P. (2012). *Leadership*. London: SAGE, p.3.

91 In his 1938 book *Power: A new social analysis*, Bertrand Russell wrote "the fundamental concept in social science is Power, in the same sense in which Energy is the fundamental concept in physics" (p.4). Russell, B. (1938/2004). *Power: A new social analysis*. London: Routledge.

92 Owen, D., & Davidson, J. (2009). Hubris syndrome: An acquired personality disorder? A study of US presidents and UK prime ministers over the last 100 years. *Brain*, 132(5), 1396–1406.

93 Russo, C. A., Lastra, R. M., & Blair, W. (eds.). (2019). *Research handbook on law and ethics in banking and finance*. Cheltenham: Edward Elgar Publishing, p.288.

94 Wray, T. (2016). The role of leader hubris in the decline of RBS and Lehman Brothers. In Garrard, P., & Robinson, G. (eds). *The intoxication of power: Interdisciplinary insights*, Basingstoke: Palgrave Macmillan, pp.229–251.

95 Cohen, T. R., & Morse, L. (2014). Moral character: What it is and what it does. *Research in Organizational Behaviour*, 34, 43–61.

96 Schwartz, B. (2011). Practical wisdom and organizations. *Research in Organizational Behaviour*, 31, 3–23.

97 Sadler-Smith, E. (2020). Don't fly too close to the sun: Using myth to understand the hazards of hubristic leadership. In Küpers, W., & Statler, M. (eds). *Leadership and wisdom: Narrating the future responsibly*. New York: Routledge, pp.44–61.

2

INTOXICATION OF POWER

Intoxication of Power

The Nobel Prize-winning philosopher Bertrand Russell wrote in his book *Power: A New Social Analysis* (1938) that "the fundamental concept in social science is Power, in the same way in which Energy is the fundamental concept in physics". Russell also observed that whilst some leaders are in pursuit of great causes, others are driven by a love of power and the "multiplication of the ego" that can lead to a "distorted view of the world" and to a desire to find a "kind of mob that makes his success easy", a mob which is given more to "emotion than reflection" and filled with "fears and consequent hatreds".[1] Russell, writing shortly before the outbreak of the Second World War, commented portentously that:

> In excited times, a politician needs no power of reasoning, nor apprehension of impersonal facts, and no shred of wisdom. What he must

DOI: 10.4324/9781003128427-2

have is the capacity of persuading the multitude that what they passionately desire is attainable, and that he, through his ruthless determination, is the man to attain it.[2]

And that:

fear, rage, and all kinds of violent collective excitement, tend to make
men blindly follow a leader, who, in most cases, takes advantage of
their trust to establish himself as a tyrant.[3]

George Orwell's *Nineteen Eighty-Four* (published in 1949) is a dystopian vision
of power and tyranny. In this fictional future world the "intoxication of
power" is

constantly increasing and constantly growing subtler. Always, at every
moment, there will be the thrill of victory, the sensation of trampling
on an enemy who is helpless. If you want a picture of the future, imagine a boot stamping on a human face—for ever.[4]

Roughly contemporaneous with Orwell, in his *History of Western Philosophy*
(1946), Russell described the intoxication of power as a "certain kind of
madness" and "the greatest danger of our time" which increases "the danger of vast social disaster".[5]

Putin and the 'Hubris Syndrome'

One of the greatest dangers of our time has been the invasion of Ukraine
in February 2022 by Russia under the leadership of Vladimir Putin. Many
commentators have seen this as part of Putin's project to 'make Russia
great again' following the humiliation after the fall of the Soviet Union
in the 1990s.[6] As far as Putin's ambitions were concerned the writing
had been on the wall for a number of years. In 1999, as prime minister, he ordered military action in the North Caucasus region of Chechnya
to suppress the Chechens' aspirations for independence from Moscow. In
2008 Russia invaded Georgia to a muted international response. In 2011
Russia supported President Bashar Al Assad with direct military action in a

brutal Syrian civil war. In 2014 Russia invaded and subsequently annexed Crimea from Ukraine with minimal international condemnation or intervention which, in the eyes of Putinists, 'returned' Crimean to Russia. In February 2022 Russia invaded Ukraine itself in an attempt to bring Kyiv back under Moscow's direct control.

A number of commentators interpret Putin's behaviours as a manifestation of the intoxication of power. In 2014 shortly after the annexation of Crimea the clinical psychologist and neuroscientist Ian Robertson of Trinity College Dublin commented that "Putin's personality and thinking have become grossly distorted by the effects of enormous, largely unfettered power on his brain".[7] Robertson also acknowledged that interpreting a political leader's behaviour in purely psychological terms gives only a partial view and runs the risk of overlooking the role of context (for example, dismantling of the USSR, the power of Russian oil in the world economy, xenophobia, etc.) and followers (for example, the *siloviki* or 'strongmen' who are simultaneously Putin's echo chamber and his Praetorian Guard). Nonetheless, according to Robertson, after such a long time in office the effect of power on Putin's neuropsychological functioning has to be taken seriously.

Robertson based his assertion on the likelihood that the same reward network in the brain that gets 'switched on' whenever we are, for example, given a compliment, have sex, or take cocaine is also triggered whenever a person holds significant power and has a run of successes.[8] The problem with any intoxicant is that in consuming it, the brain needs more and more of it in order to achieve the same effects. In the pharmacological literature this phenomenon is known as 'tolerance' and is defined as "resulting from persistent use of a drug, characterized by a markedly diminished effect with regular use of the same dose of the drug or by a need to increase the dose markedly over time to achieve the same desired effect".[9] This insatiability provides a neuroscientific explanation for the intoxicating effects of power and the "multiplication of the ego" referred to by Bertrand Russell.

In Robertson's view there could be "little doubt" that Putin's brain had been changed both psychologically and neurologically by absolute power. The result, argued Robertson, was that Putin had become blind to risk and increasingly reckless and contemptuous of the views of all but a small inner circle. Moreover, his personal interests and purpose and those of the nation had become identical to the extent that he is Russia and its destiny. Robertson concluded his analysis with his view on how the West should respond to the 2014 annexation of Crimea:

Psychologically speaking, the very worst response would be appease-ment because this will simply fuel his contempt and strengthen the jus-tification for his position. Strong consequences have to follow from his contempt for international law and treaties. This will cost the West dearly, economically speaking, but the longer-term costs of appeasement will make the costs of strong, early action appear trivial in retrospect.[10]

This prescient warning, from an eminent clinical psychologist and neuro-scientist, was made eight years before the invasion of Ukraine.

According to a number of experts, Putin's behaviour is replete with the classic signs of the acquired personality change known as "hubris syn-drome".[11] Hubris syndrome is induced by power and success, and typically remits once power is lost (although there are exceptions to this rule).[12] This syndrome, and its 14 clinical features (see Table 2.1), was first proposed

Table 2.1 The 14 Clinical Features of Hubris Syndrome

Symptom	Description
Symptom 1	A narcissistic propensity to see their world primarily as an arena in which to exercise power and seek glory
Symptom 2	A predisposition to take actions which seem likely to cast the individual in a good light, i.e. in order to enhance image
Symptom 3	A disproportionate concern with image and presentation
Symptom 4	A messianic manner of talking about current activities and a tendency to exaltation
Symptom 5	An identification with the nation, or organisation to the extent that the individual regards his/her outlook and interests as identical
Symptom 6	A tendency to speak in the third person or use the royal 'we'
Symptom 7	Excessive confidence in the individual's own judgement and contempt for the advice or criticism of others
Symptom 8	Exaggerated self-belief, bordering on a sense of omnipotence, in what they personally can achieve
Symptom 9	A belief that rather than being accountable to the mundane court of colleagues or public opinion, the court to which they answer is history or God
Symptom 10	An unshakable belief that in that court they will be vindicated
Symptom 11	Loss of contact with reality; often associated with progressive isolation
Symptom 12	Restlessness, recklessness, and impulsiveness
Symptom 13	A tendency to allow their 'broad vision', about the moral rectitude of a proposed course, to obviate the need to consider practicality, cost, or outcomes
Symptom 14	Hubristic incompetence, where things go wrong because too much self-confidence has led the leader not to worry about the nuts and bolts of policy

Source: Reprinted from Garrard, P., Rentoumi, V., Lambert, C., & Owen, D. (2014). Linguistic biomark-ers of hubris syndrome. *Cortex*, 55, 167–181 with permission from Elsevier.

by the politician and neurologist Lord David Owen and the psychiatrist Jonathan Davidson in 2009. The hubrist's over-confidence results in them misinterpreting the reality of the situation in which they find themselves and this leads ultimately to hubristic incompetence, and catastrophic mis-judgement, see Table 2.1.

Rather than being a personality disorder as such (for example, narcis-sistic personality disorder), hubris syndrome is an acquired personality change associated with the possession of power and is therefore more of an illness of the position held by a person rather than of the person them-selves. Its potency is amplified by a run of successes over a number of years and its effects are intensified when there are minimal constraints on the leader's behaviour. As such it has the potential to affect any suc-cessful individual who has held considerable power for a period of time. Owen and Davidson argued that the experience of being in power can bring about negative changes in a leader's mental state which manifest in hubristic behaviours which typically occur together and collectively form hubris syndrome:

(1) the behavioural symptoms, of which there are 14, typically grow stronger the longer the individual holds significant power;
(2) 3–4 of the 14 symptoms should be present for a positive diagnosis;
(3) several of hubris syndrome's symptoms overlap with those of Narcissistic Personality Disorder (NPD), Anti-social Personality Disorder (APD) and Histrionic Personality Disorder (HPD);
(4) five of the symptoms are unique to hubris syndrome, for example 'rest-lessness, recklessness and impulsiveness' (Symptom 12);
(5) for a positive diagnosis at least one of the three or four of the identified symptoms must be one of the unique symptoms.

Unlike narcissism (which is a trait-like intoxication with the self), hubris is a state-like phenomenon which can manifest in leaders in any walk of life but only when in power for some time. As noted above, when power is lost the syndrome generally abates; in this sense hubris syndrome is, as noted above, an acquired personality change which arises as a conse-quence of the addictive and intoxicating effects of power. On the relation-ship between hubris and narcissism, the eminent psychiatrist Nick Bouras argued that it is a "common misconception" that hubris and narcissism are indistinguishable, but whilst "excessive narcissism might lead to or co-exist with hubris … the two are fundamentally distinct".[13] In the case of Putin some have argued that his hubris syndrome has led him to a state of paranoia which makes him impervious to any rational argument and makes him immovable in his beliefs that he is saving "holy Russia".[14]

Power and Leader-Follower Relationships

In understanding the hubris hazard it is necessary but not sufficient to understand the behaviour of individual hubristic leaders. Leadership, by definition, involves both leaders and followers, therefore in order to make sense of hubristic leadership (as opposed to simply making sense of a hubristic leader, which is only part of the picture) it is necessary also to examine the relationship between leaders and their followers.

Leadership is defined as "a process whereby an individual influences a group of individuals to pursue a common goal".[15] This straightforward definition of leadership has a number of implications:

> (1) leadership is 'relational' (i.e. it exists in the relationship between leaders and followers), and 'bidirectional' (i.e. it's a two-way phenomenon from leader to follower and vice versa), hence there can be no leaders without followers;
>
> (2) it's inevitable that followers are complicit in the processes of leadership and this includes the processes of destructive and hubristic leadership, for example, followers are complicit both when they are active participants in the leader's destructive behaviours or passive bystanders;
>
> (3) in the same way that leaders emerge into positions of power as a result of their relationship with their followers, so that same leader-follower relationship can lead to a leader's downfall.[16]

This dynamic, two-way relationship between a leader and their followers can be paradoxical in that it can create the conditions for a leader's rise as well as their fall. For example, a number of hubristic British political leaders including Prime Ministers Margaret Thatcher, Boris Johnson, and Liz Truss were brought to power by dedicated and devoted followers but also were brought down from power by their followers when the leader-follower relationship turned sour. For Thatcher it was following the highly controversial 'poll tax' riots in 1990, for Johnson it was after he admitted breaking his own Covid-19 lockdown restrictions in 2021 (see Chapter 8), and for Truss after her disastrous so-called 'mini-budget' in 2022 (see Chapter 6). In each of these cases the hallmarks of hubris were centre-stage and precipitated the leader's fall from power.

In the leader-follower relationship, social power, or simply 'power', is pivotal. Power is the ability of one individual in a relationship (the 'influencer') to exert an effect on another person (the 'influenced') in order that the influencer obtains the outcome they want from a given situation.[17] Power, and more specifically its intoxication, is focal to hubristic leadership because hubris is an "abuse of power by individuals who are overconfident and, on gaining positions of power, benefit themselves to the detriment of other members of the community".[18] In summary: power is a pivotal element in the leader-follower relationship and the context that gives rise to hubristic leadership.[19] It can have intoxicating and negative effects on leaders' behaviours and is therefore a risk factor which can lead to an increased possibility of harmful consequences arising.

Types of Power and Their Excesses

Hubristic leaders exercise influence over their followers. The influence that they, or any other type of leader, are able to exercise over others is a property of their power. Power is defined as the discretion, means, and resolve that one person has to exert their will over others.[20] One of the founding figures of sociology, Max Weber (1864–1920), defined power as "the possibility of imposing one's will upon the behaviour of other persons".[21] Power involves having the freedom to exercise one's will over others, for example, by occupying a particular position or role or by being in possession of certain knowledge or skill, and the means by which to exercise one's will over others.

Power comes from a number of sources, consequently the power that leaders exercise may take a number of different forms and have different effects. Over half a century ago social psychologists John French and Bertram Raven identified five sources (or bases) of power, each of which are associated with the use of different tactics by the influencer (for example, the leader) in order to produce a particular effect on the influenced (for example, the follower). The five sources of power identified by French and Raven are: legitimate power; reward power; coercive power; expert power; and referent power, as follows.

Legitimate power: the follower recognises that the leader is entitled to make demands, require compliance and respect based on the recognised authority designated to the holder of a particular position. When a manager asks an employee to work late they are exercising their legitimate power. When Putin ordered the Russian army to invade Ukraine he was exercising his legitimate power (even if, in the view of some critics, illegitimate means may have be used to gain or hold on to power).

Reward power: one party has the ability to recompense the other for their compliance with a reward; for example, when an employer pays employees to expend time and effort, or when a manager gives an employee a bonus they are exercising reward power. The strength of the reward power of the leader increases with the magnitude of the rewards which the follower perceives that the leader can make available to them. In allegedly granting favours and privileges to elites and oligarchs[22] Putin was exercising reward power.

Coercive power: this is the recognition by a follower that the leader has the ability to apply negative consequences for non-compliance, for example, when an employee complies with a manager's threats they are being subjected to coercive power. Coercive power stems from the expectation on the part of the follower that the leader will punish them if they fail to conform to the leader's attempts to influence them. When the Russian Parliament passed a law in March 2022 imposing a jail term of up to 15 years for spreading 'fake' news intentionally about the 'special military operation' in Ukraine, it was exercising coercive power.

Expert power: one party possesses superior skill and knowledge and the other party recognises that these skills and knowledge surpass their own. A patient deferring to a doctor's advice, a client accepting an attorney's legal advice, and a stranger accepting directions given by a native of an area are examples of expert power. When Putin instrumentalised his knowledge and interpretation of Russian history to pursue his personal goals he was exercising expert power, albeit based on an idiosyncratic view of history.

Referent power: one party recognises qualities in another that they admire, for example, when a consumer buys a product that is endorsed by an admired celebrity their behaviour is influenced by referent power. The basis of referent power is identification, a "feeling of oneness", with the person who is exerting the power and the desire for identity.[23] The referent power of attraction can be exerted by a group as well as an individual, and the person being influenced may not necessarily be aware that referent power is being exercised over them. Referent power exercised by a charismatic leader can be an especially potent form of influence both on individuals and groups. When Putin made use of his background, biography, martial arts expertise, and physical strength he promoted a charismatic image of himself and created a leadership brand that was designed to appeal to followers through the use of referent power.

Bertram Raven later distinguished informational power as a sixth type of power. Informational power is related to expert power in that the latter is driven by the power holder's "superior knowledge and information".[24] When informational power is being exercised the influencer has information that may be useful to the influenced, but the latter must cooperate with the former in order to get it. Putin, with his FSB secret service background, understands the value of information and is highly skilled in using it as a source of power.[25] In 2022 the Russian Yevgeny Prigozhin, a close confidante of Putin, former head of the Wagner mercenary group and latterly a mutineer who perished in a mysterious airplane crash in August 2023, admitted that "We have interfered (in U.S. elections), we are interfering and we will continue to interfere. Carefully, accurately, surgically and in our own way, as we know how to do."[26] In the social media age fake news has become a potent source of informational power in a "post-fact" society.[27]

The sources of power differ also in terms of their dynamics. For example, excessive coercion by a leader results in decreased attraction of the follower towards the leader and higher resistance which also may lead to resentment and ill-feelings. Reward power, on the other hand, results in increased attraction of the follower towards the leader, greater acceptance, and lower resistance.[28]

The original five sources of power are categorised as either: (1) 'positional', in that they emanate from a leader's position or role in the institution (such as government) or organisation (such as a business) in which the leader-follower relationship is embedded, or; (2) 'personal', in that they emanate from the personal qualities of the individual leader themselves and are independent of the institution or organisation. Coercive, legitimate, and reward power are positional sources of power; expert and referent power are personal sources of power, see Table 2.2.

Exercising these various sources of power with moderation and discretion can be bona fide use of power. For example, in the workplace reward power can exert a powerful influence over performance, and coercion can be a potent means of ensuring compliance in the short-term. However, power, in the hands of a hubristic leader who has been corrupted by its intoxicating effects, can lead to:

(1) oppression and tyranny by the leader and feelings of alienation and a desire for revenge amongst followers as a result of an excess of coercive power;
(2) conformity, minimal compliance, and submission as a result of an excess of legitimate power;
(3) dependency, manipulation, and exploitation as a result of an excess of reward power;

Table 2.2 Sources of Power

Source	Type	Description
Positional power	Coercive power	Based on follower's expectation that he or she will be punished for failing to obey or achieve the leader's goals.
	Legitimate power	Formal authority derived from the leader's position or followers' belief that the leader has a right to influence them and that they are obliged to accept leader's influence.
	Reward power	Based on the leader's ability to remunerate followers for obedience.
Personal power	Expert power	Derived from the task-relevant knowledge or abilities the leader possesses.
	Referent power.	Emanates from the admiration and attraction followers have toward the leader.

Source: French & Raven (1959).

Table 2.3 The Use and Abuse of the Different Forms of Power

Type	The appropriate use of this type of power	The abuse of this type of power can lead to
Coercive power	Is a potent means of ensuring compliance	Oppression and tyranny
Legitimate power	Reinforces institutions, structures, systems, and procedures	Conformity and submission
Reward power	Can exert a powerful leverage over performance	Manipulation and exploitation
Expert power	Is respected independent of position in the hierarchy	Vanity and conceit
Referent power	Can be a source of inspiration for others	Veneration and worship

(4) vanity and conceit on the part of the leader as a result of an excess of expert power;

(5) veneration and worship of the leader by followers as a result of an excess of referent power.

Table 2.3 shows the potential effects of the use and abuse of the different forms of power.

Most leaders exercise each of the five forms of power to varying degrees. In general, the personal sources of power (expert and referent) are more strongly related to positive outcomes (employee commitment, loyalty, and satisfaction) than are positional sources of power (coercive, legitimate, and reward).[29] Also, related to the concept of leader power is the concept of 'empowerment'. This is a process by which leaders or managers use their authority to downwardly distribute their power, for example, by delegating power to subordinates in order to enable them to take the initiative in solving problems and taking decisions.[30] Finally, it should be noted that the various sources of power can operate in parallel and interact. Expert power can amplify the traction that the leader's vision has; for example, when acolytes believe firmly that a leader who has legitimate power also holds superior expert power they are likely to be rewarded by benefitting personally and this is likely to enhance compliance.[31]

Extreme Manifestations of Leader Power

Excess as far as power is concerned is invariably a bad thing, and the two-way relationship between a leader and their followers can have an effect on how the various types of power manifest in leader-follower relations. For example, followers themselves who have excessive authoritarian tendencies are more likely to conform unconditionally with a leader's legitimate power because they accept unreservedly the leader's right to exert power over them.[32] If such conformers hold excessively strong internal values, for example, the social uniformity, prejudice towards different others, willingness to wield group authority to exercise coercive behaviour, cognitive rigidity, aggression and punitiveness towards perceived enemies, outsized concern for hierarchy, and moral absolutism associated with right- or left-wing authoritarianism, then obedience to leader authority and conformity to in-group norms is likely to take priority over reason, ethics, and acceptance of any negative consequences of the leader's behaviour.[33] Followers may obey a destructive leader's commands not necessarily because they seek approval or are worried about retribution from the leader, but simply because of the leader's institutional or organisational position (based on legitimate power) and their identification with the leader's core values (based on referent power). In extreme situations a conformer's mental rigidity allied to a deeply ingrained authoritarian ideology can lead to the 'crime of obedience'[34] and its negative consequences with which we are all too familiar.

Conformers become acolytes of a hubristic leader when they share the leader's core values, for example, in the Brexit debate the former UK Prime Minister Boris Johnson appealed to the core value of 'sovereignty' amongst potential supporters by using the three-word mantra 'Take back control [from Brussels]'. Charismatic leaders are capable of shaping a vision that resonates, sometimes unconsciously, with the core values of potential groups of acolytes. The aim is that acolytes identify themselves as 'true believers' in a shared mission, whether that be of 'making America great again' (MAGA) in the case of Trump, 'taking back control' in the case of Johnson, or Putin's vision of Russia's restoration by bringing Ukraine back into the fold.

The unconscious can be a potent influence on leaders' and followers' behaviours and relationships. The American anthropologist and psychotherapist, the late Michael Maccoby, argues that most male CEOs in traditional organisations unconsciously encourage "paternal transference".[35] He gives the example of Thomas J. Watson, a former CEO of IBM from 1914 to 1956, who discouraged team decision-making because he preferred direct links between employees and their bosses in order to create a paternalistic commitment between leader and followers. Maccoby cites this as an example of paternal transference. Moreover, people may follow leaders for both reasons that they themselves are aware of consciously (for example, because they explicitly recognise and acknowledge the authority that a leader possesses) and for reasons that they are not aware of (for example, because they may be being influenced subliminally by some aspect of the leader's personality or behaviour which resonates with their subconscious wants or needs). These motivations lie outside of followers' conscious awareness and are therefore beyond their ability to control and consequently can be a potent influence on how followers think, feel, and behave.

This phenomenon can be explained in terms of a follower relating to a leader because of their resemblance to some important person from their past, such as a parent. The phenomenon of transference comes from Freud and was based on his study of the relationship between a client and the therapist. Maccoby argued that Freudian transference is the missing link in leadership which acts as an emotional glue that binds followers to their leaders. Transference can work both ways, for example, followers in the grip of positive transference see their leader as better than they really are, whilst followers in the grip of negative transference are more likely to see a leader as someone they have to resist.[36] The negative effects of positive transference are palpable: followers are more likely to give a leader the benefit of the doubt and are more likely to acquiesce to a leader's requests or commands under the potent influence of transference. The phenomenon of transference might help to explain the power of Donald Trump's leadership and the nature of the relationship that he has with his followers. His followers seem prepared to give him the benefit of the doubt for even the most egregious acts, as he himself is all too well aware: "I [Trump] could stand in the middle of Fifth Avenue and shoot somebody and I wouldn't lose any voters".[37]

Positive transference is a powerful way in which leaders can exercise influence over followers. Charismatic leaders are skilled in leveraging positive transference. The most effective charismatic leaders are able to do so intuitively by appealing to the innate wants and needs of their followers. It's easy to dismiss Donald Trump; for example, a USA Today poll in 2015 found that many Americans described him as an 'idiot', 'jerk', 'stupid', and 'dumb'. But in his rallies for the 2016 election he was able to connect intuitively with the deep mistrust in politics and the gulf that had opened up between a great swathe of the American public and the political institutions and elites in Washington, hence the now famous three-word mantra 'Drain the [Washington]swamp'. This turned his clear and obvious weaknesses in lacking political experience into a strength in the eyes of potential followers. Trump, as a consummate performer, was not only able to articulate the views of those who felt, justifiably or not, disenfranchised but was also able to offer them a supposed solution (i.e. his presidency). His skilful and intuitive use of referent power and his undoubted charisma attracted and empowered potential followers.[38] This is one of the great populist paradoxes of Trump: a millionaire famed for displays of wealth and privilege who was able to relate directly to working-class followers and convince them that he was, in some ways, like them.[39]

Totalist Leaders and Cultic Leadership

Totalitarianism is an 'ism' that pretends, in the words of political philosopher and Holocaust survivor Hannah Arendt (1906–1969), to have found the key explanation for all the "mysteries of life and world".[40] In totalitarian groups led by 'totalist' leaders, alternative beliefs are blocked, critics and challengers are purged, and there are no checks and balances on the leader's unilateral power. Totalist leaders are consummate controllers and manipulators of the French and Raven dimensions of power.[41] For example, coercive power in the form of punishment is common; totalist leaders exercise control over rewards such as financial gain or sexual favours and their expert power is legitimised by them attaining a 'seer' or 'guru' status amongst spellbound followers. In such regimes, coercive power is enabled by surveillance, for example, through mass facial recognition technologies or the spying on citizens by a leader's acolytes and the institutions of the state. Totalist leaders are often charismatic and hence, by their nature, are admired deeply by their followers. Moreover, in totalitarian regimes, follower conformity is critical, and totalist leaders do not tolerate dissent.

Cultic leadership is an extreme manifestation of leader power; its consequences are often catastrophic both economically and in human terms. One of the most tragic examples of cultic leadership occurred in 1978 when more than 900 Americans who were members of a San Francisco-based religious cult called 'The Peoples Temple' were murdered by other members of the cult while some voluntarily committed suicide in a secluded jungle settlement, 'Jonestown', in Guyana. It became known as 'The Jonestown Massacre'. The Peoples Temple, which was led by the Reverend Jim Jones (hence Jonestown), is a notorious example of the way in which charismatic leaders can use control techniques to manipulate followers to perform the most extreme acts. In the words of Philip Zimbardo, the eminent psychologist who became famous for the renowned Stanford prison experiments in the 1970s, Jones "became the Devil incarnate, creating incredibly evil [and] destructive scenarios, but was still deeply loved by many of his followers as their Father and God on earth".[42] For Zimbardo, evil is the exercise of power to intentionally harm other people. Cults are places where evil can flourish, but they're also places where power can have other unintentionally negative consequences. In terms of the five sources of power, cultic leadership[43] is supported by hubristic leader behaviours in which:

(1) the leader, who followers believe has a vested interest in their welfare, is viewed in a semi-divine light (referent power);
(2) the leader is the main source of ideas and intellectual stimulation which is communicated from the top to the bottom of the organisation (expert power);
(3) power is concentrated in the leader's hands (legitimate power);
(4) dissent from the leader's vision is penalised (coercive power);
(5) members are rewarded for compliance (reward power);
(6) a common culture is promoted through the spread and control of (mis) information and deception (informational power).[44]

Leadership researchers Dennis Tourish and Naheed Vatcha argued that Enron was an example of a prototypical corporate cult in which leader behaviours led directly to catastrophic unintended negative consequences, not only for the leaders of Enron themselves but also for many victims of their fraudulent behaviours.[45]

At the helm of Enron, an energy, commodities, and services company based in Houston, Texas and famed as the most notorious scandal in corporate history, were two hubristic leaders Kenneth Lay and Jefferey Skilling. Lay, Enron's CEO and founder, has been described as the 'chief architect' of Enron's culture of arrogance, greed, and moral malfeasance; he masterminded Enron's 'creative accounting' behaviours in which the company's record $1.3 billion of income turned out to actually be $978 million in the audited reports. Lay and Skilling leveraged referent power by deliberately creating an aura of charisma around themselves. For example, according to Tourish and Vatcha, Skilling was known inside Enron as 'Darth Vader' the "master of the energy universe who has the ability to control people's minds".[46] Skilling was also known as "The Prince" after Machiavelli,[47] (Machiavellianism is one third of the 'Dark Triad' of leader personality, the others are narcissism and psychopathy).[48] The expert knowledge claimed by leaders at Enron regarding the off-balance-sheet 'Special Purpose Entities' (SPOs) and the complex financial transactions between Enron and these SPOs led followers to convince themselves that the conspirators knew more about the complex machinations behind the fraudulent transactions than they actually did.[49]

The end result was that Enron's leaders acquired great wealth and power at the expense of employees and shareholders many of whom lost their jobs, their retirements funds, and their life savings.[50] The unintended outcomes for Lay and Skilling were negative and consequential: Lay died of a heart attack while awaiting a prison sentence that could have lasted 45 years; Skilling was fined $45 million and served 12 years of a 14-year prison sentence. Unfortunately Lay and skilling were not the first and have been proven not to be the last leaders whose intoxication with power led to hubris which then had profound and unanticipated negative consequences for individuals, organisations, and society.

Effects of Power on Leaders

In order to be effective, leaders must be able to influence their followers. They achieve influence through power, and power can have a deeply transformative effect on the way in which people think, feel, and act[51] even to the extent of influencing brain function. The effects of power can be both positive and negative. Power has the potential to change leaders in three fundamental ways: how they think (cognitive changes); how they feel (affective changes); and how they act (behavioural changes). The changes in cognition, affect, and behaviour as a result of power's intoxicating effects on those who hold it can lead to undesirable outcomes, see Table 2.4 for a summary.

Power affects cognition, i.e. how people process information, in a number of ways. The possession of power induces a simplified approach to

Table 2.4 Processes by Which High Power Affects General Behaviours and Immoral
Behaviours

	General negative effects of power on behaviour	Negative effects of power on immoral behaviour
Disinhibition	Activating dopamine-driven pathways Increased pursuit of rewards Increased behaviours to satisfy current needs	More likely to betray More likely to engage in legal violations Disinhibited to cheat Better at lying because of reduced anxiety
Greater focus on self	Greater focus on the self and one's own wants/needs Perception of self as having greater value Sense of social distance from others Reduced ability to take other's perspective	Spend more resources on their own wants/needs than on others Decreased empathy and compassion Lowered concern for other's suffering Objectification and instrumentalisation of others Dehumanisation of others

processing information. As a result power seems to lead people to depend on single, rather than multiple, sources of information, and to a reliance on information that they find easy to retrieve.[52] We know from the heuristics and biases research pioneered by Nobel Prize-winning psychologist Daniel Kahneman and his colleague Amos Tversky that ease of retrieval leads to stereotyping which can lead to systematic errors in judgement and can ultimately have negative consequences for decision-making, for example, by precipitating unconscious biases. A reliance on stereotyping can be a default response because a brain that has evolved to be good at optimising the use of scarce cognitive resources is designed to respond automatically and effortlessly. However, high-power individuals may also deliberately use stereotypes, for example, gendered or racial stereotyping, as a way to legitimise power differentials and maintain control in order to serve their own interests.[53]

Researchers have also found that power makes people less individuating, i.e. they're less likely to take the views of others' into account and are more likely to impose strict moral standards on others whilst practising less strict moral behaviours themselves.[54] This moral slippage was witnessed during the Covid lockdown in the UK in 2020–2021. Prime Minister Boris Johnson espoused strict standards of behaviour and imposed stringent rules on social gatherings for the people of the UK whilst he and his colleagues in 10 Downing Street flagrantly broke their own rules by holding parties. This led to the so-called 'Partygate scandal' which contributed significantly to Johnson's downfall. Power also amplifies confidence. This can cause high-power individuals to over-estimate the accuracy of their own knowledge and to assign narrower confidence intervals to their own estimates compared to those of low-power individuals.[55] Power can also attenuate loss aversion, and hence boost confidence, by reducing the anticipated threat associated with a loss.[56]

Power can also affect the way leaders feel (i.e. their affective responses). For example, one of the effects of power on how leaders feel is that high-power individuals are more inclined to experience and express positive emotions such as desire, enthusiasm, and pride. They're also more inclined to be optimistic. Expressions of positive emotion, such as smiles are more likely to be displayed by high-power individuals, whilst expressions of sadness are more difficult to detect in power holders.[57] High-power individuals are also more likely to show decreased emotional reciprocity (i.e. they are less distressed in response to another person's distress) and reduced emotional complementarity, reduced compassion and empathy.[58]

Finally, power can also affect the way leaders act. The intoxicating effects of power lead to behavioural disinhibition, for example, power increases a person's action-orientation, and hence they're more likely to display initiating behaviours and interventions. In one lab study it was found that high-power individuals were more likely than low-power individuals to remove an annoying object such as a fan in an experiment, even though they weren't granted permission to do so. High-power individuals are also more likely to lavish greater spending on themselves than are low-power individuals, they're also more likely to use their power to violate social norms, engage in self-serving behaviours, express themselves more freely, resist social influences, engage in risk-seeking behaviours, engage in immoral behaviours (with reduced feelings of stress, anxiety, and guilt), and take more liberties in interpersonal behaviours such as touching.[59] At the time of writing the Confederation of British Industry (CBI), the UK's biggest business lobby group, is in the throes of a major scandal following a spate of sexual harassment accusations. One commentator has remarked that the CBI's "arrogance has become predictably hubristic"[60] and may yet prove to be its downfall.

Power also helps people to overcome inhibitions towards cheating, behaving selfishly, and committing immoral acts. It's thought that these behavioural disinhibitions occur as result of power triggering activation of dopamine-driven pathways in the brain (dopamine is a neurotransmitter associated with feelings of pleasure). This increases the pursuit of rewards and the immediate satisfaction of wants and needs.[61] Powerful people may even be better at covering up their misdemeanours because they don't experience the lying-induced cortisol rush that gives rise to the anxiety that can help to expose liars.[62]

These research findings may help to explain how power can have a corrupting effect on individuals: it encourages them to act more in accordance with their own desires, to engage in self-serving behaviours, and put their own interests ahead of those of others. The research seems to vindicate Lord Acton's maxim that "power tends to corrupt, and absolute power corrupts absolutely". However, the picture may not be as simple as it first seems or is suggested. The privilege of, or the intoxication with, power may have the reverse effect of producing benevolent and compassionate as well as manipulative and exploitative behaviours respectively.[63]

One reason for this is that a leader's underlying personality traits and predispositions may play a reinforcing role in how their power manifests. In this sense, power may be seen not as a cause of dysfunctional behaviours per se, but as a potent reinforcer of, or catalyst for, dysfunctional behaviours. For example, an individual's underlying predisposition towards moral behaviours may be activated and amplified in a positive way by the acquisition of power. For such individuals, the acquisition of power is an opportunity to act altruistically. Conversely, an immoral individual's predispositions may be similarly activated and amplified but in a negative way, giving rise to immoral behaviours. For these people, the acquisition of power is an opportunity to act in pursuit of unethical and immoral ends. Personality factors, such as narcissism also have a compounding effect: a narcissistic leader will be even more likely to engage in self-aggrandising behaviours once they've achieved a position of power which is then likely to fuel hubris.[64]

When seen as a catalyst or reinforcer, the acquisition of power makes it more likely that an individual will act on the basis of their innate preferences.[65] Because power reveals and amplifies innate tendencies, it can cause people to focus on their own needs rather than of those whom they lead, thereby neglecting the common good in favour of their own self-interests. In such circumstances and in the absence of the requisite checks and balances, power can create a vicious spiral of negative, self-centred, dysfunctional leader behaviours. Other research focusing on the context in which power is exercised has found that leaders tend to prioritise their own goals over the group's goals when the leader's power was threatened by instability within the group. It seems as though the selfish pursuit of personal goals may be more likely to happen when leaders feel that their power is threatened rather than when power was irrevocable.[66]

David Owen, one of the originators of the concept of hubris syndrome (see above), has commented that hubris could be an inevitable consequence of chronic, high-risk decision-making under stress where an excess of stress-inducing hormones such as serotonin depletes a leader's decision-making capabilities.[67] Owen has also speculated that one of the reasons for Vladimir Putin's hubristic excesses is that he felt threatened by the expansion of NATO. For example, before the Baltic states (Estonia, Latvia, and Lithuania) joined NATO St Petersburg was about 1,000 miles away from the nearest NATO forces in the West. Today St Petersburg is about 100 miles away from the nearest NATO forces.[68]

The trajectory of the hubristic leadership process is likely to depend both on the leader's personality and predispositions and on the business or political context in which they're operating. Because of power-induced dis-inhibition, the Victorian historian Lord Acton's maxim that 'power tends to corrupt' seems to apply most when we have the misfortune to be led by the wrong person (for example, a narcissist), at the wrong time, and in the wrong circumstances (for example, an unstable situation). Another example of this was the premiership of Boris Johnson in the UK: as a result of the political and constitutional challenges that the UK faced following the 2016 Brexit Referendum the country was, in the view of some commentators, more unstable than at any time since the Second World War. The situation was unstable because not only did events threaten the legitimacy of those in power at the time (for example, Prime Ministers David Cameron and then Theresa May) they also enhanced the legitimacy of the less powerful (for example, the substantial proportion of Brexit-voters who felt disenfranchised by the political system). In the end a lethal mixture of hubristic leader behaviours, a conducive context, and complicit followers led to Johnson's demise. This amalgam of destructive leader, conducive context, and susceptible followers is the 'toxic triangle' of leadership;[69] it is explored in more detail in Chapter 3.

Avoiding Exposure to the Intoxication of Power

One of the famous sayings inscribed on the Greek temple of Apollo at Delphi is 'nothing in excess' (see Chapter 9). This principle applies to leaders and power. For example, when the various sources of power are exercised to excess they can lead to abuses of power. Coercive power in the wrong hands can have negative side-effects on followers by creating anxiety, fear, and stress. Referent power is open to abuse when the power holder uses it for self-serving ends; the relationship between a leader and a follower is a fragile one and can be easily broken irreparably when trust in the leader is broken. Expert power in the wrong hands can be used for manipulative purposes, for example, when the power holder uses their expert knowledge to manipulate situations and people for their own ends. When expert power is taken to excess it can manifest as a 'know-it-all' and 'I-know-best' attitude and lead to so-called 'epistemic hubris' (i.e. being hubristic about the extent of one's knowledge).[70] When informational power is taken to excess it can be used against citizens and employees in order to control them and to serve the leader's interests.

Hubris is acquired through an intoxication with each of these sources of power. According to Ian Robertson and David Owen, whose work was discussed above, it's a "potent brain changer" which results in impaired judgement, diminished awareness of risk, over-confidence, recklessness, contempt for advice, and critics.[71] Power intoxicated leaders conflate their own interests with those of the institution or organisation which they have the privilege to lead. The outcomes for all involved can be catastrophic in human, economic, social, and geopolitical terms. The excesses and the abuse of power is a hazard that anyone who holds high office in government or a senior role in an organisation runs the risk of falling foul of. Ultimately when this happens leadership becomes exploitative,[72] rather than authentic, and there is an abusive use of power; it is a moral failing which reflects a dangerous flaw in a leader's character. Power by its nature is a challenging force to try to constrain. The constraint of a leader who is intoxicated by power and at risk therefore of hubris is doubly challenging.

Writing in his book *The Hubris Syndrome: Bush, Blair and the Intoxication of Power* (2007), David Owen commented that curbing hubristic presidents and prime ministers has to rely on the strengthening of checks and balances built up over the years in mature democracies. Fixed terms for heads of government and CEOs takes away the intoxicant at source, thus depleting its inebriating effect and nipping hubris in the bud or pruning it before it can do too much damage.

Owen thinks that for presidents and prime ministers, cabinet vigilance and scrutiny is perhaps the most important factor because cabinet members are the people who see the heads of government close up on a regular basis. Hence, they're well placed to spot the early warning signs of intoxication.[73] The same thoughts apply to the role of boards and top management teams in business organisations. In business the power of the CEO can be curbed by giving more discretion to other executives and managers, giving shareholders greater power to exercise control over CEO performance and reward, having tax policies that penalise firms for having excess worker to CEO pay ratios (which have been shown to be a reliable marker of hubris),[74] having worker representation on boards,[75] taking the views of activist investors seriously as they might be seeing things that are opaque to the board, having board members who aren't passive and are prepared to challenge a CEO who is showing signs of derailment, having the courage and honesty to face up to bad news, and avoiding delaying tactics in the hope that things will get better.[76] This requires engagement with, and the engagement of, the board, without this two-way relationship between the CEO and the rest of the top management team it's unlikely that a business can focus on the long term and deliver excellent results. For effective board engagement it's vital that the board has independence, which means wherever possible separating out the roles of CEO and chair, increasing the diversity of the board, and having a chair with whom the CEO can cooperate, on the other hand, a reliable warning sign of trouble ahead is when a CEO starts to see the board as a 'necessary evil'.[77]

It's perhaps ironic that exercising power can be draining on a CEO's energy to the extent that it can ultimately undermine their power and influence. The corollary of this is that to use power effectively and not become intoxicated by it CEOs need to accept the fact that they are not omnipotent, even though others may expect them to be or treat them as though they are.[78] Owen believes that we need more clues and more alerting information for if and when leaders might become intoxicated with power and develop hubris whilst in office. Such information gives those who are likely to be adversely affected by a leader's intoxication of power the power themselves to act and mitigate the unintended negative consequences of hubristic leadership.

Intoxication of Power: Signs to Look Out For

(1) Increased reliance on stereotyping by leader;
(2) Leader stops taking others' views into account;
(3) Decrease in leader's emotional reciprocity;
(4) Reduction in leader's compassion and empathy;
(5) Reduction in leader's behavioural inhibition;
(6) Increase in leader's violations of social norms;
(7) Increase in leader's self-serving behaviours;
(8) More lavish spending by leader.

Notes

1   Russell, B. (1938/1996). *Power: A new social analysis*. London: Routledge, p.18.
2   Russell, B. (1938/1996). *Power: A new social analysis*. London: Routledge, p.33.
3   Russell, B. (1938/1996). *Power: A new social analysis*. London: Routledge, p.308.
4   Orwell, G. (1949). *Nineteen eighty-four*. London: Penguin, p.280.
5   Russell, B. (1946//1996). *History of western philosophy*. London: Routledge, p.737.
6   Brzezinski, Z.(2008). Putin's choice. *Washington Quarterly*, 31(2), 95–116, p.98.
7   Robertson, I. (2014). The danger that lurks inside Vladimir Putin's brain. Psychology Today, March 17. Available at: https://www.psychologytoday.com/gb/blog/the-winner-effect/201403/the-danger-lurks-inside-vladimir-putins-brain

8   Daedalus Trust (no date). *Putin: The new tsar.* Available at: www.daedalus-trust.com/putin-the-new-tsar

9   American Psychological Association (no date). Tolerance. APA *dictionary of psychology.* Available at: https://dictionary.apa.org/tolerance

10 Robertson, I. (2014). The danger that lurks inside Vladimir Putin's brain. *Psychology Today,* March 17. Available at: https://www.psychologytoday.com/gb/blog/the-winner-effect/201403/the-danger-lurks-inside-vladimir-putins-brain

11 Owen, D., & Davidson, J. (2009). Hubris syndrome: An acquired personality disorder? A study of US presidents and UK prime ministers over the last 100 years. *Brain,* 132(5), 1396–1406.

12 Owen, D., & Davidson, J. (2009). Hubris syndrome: An acquired personality disorder? A study of US presidents and UK prime ministers over the last 100 years. *Brain,* 132(5), 1396–1406.

13 Bouras, N. (2018). Foreword. In Garrard, P. (ed.) The leadership hubris epidemic: Biological roots and strategies for prevention. Basingstoke: Palgrave Macmillan, p.x.

14 Mataillet, D. (2022) Hubris syndrome, a sickness of heads of state. *France-Amérique,* September 8. Available at: https://france-amerique.com/hubris-syndrome-a-sickness-of-heads-of-state

15 Northouse, P. (2012). *Leadership.* London: SAGE, p.3.

16 Reid, S. A., & Ng, S. H. (2003). Identity, power, and strategic social categorizations: Theorizing the language of leadership. In van Knippenberg, D., & Hogg, M. A. *Leadership and power: Identity processes in groups and organizations.* London: SAGE, pp.210–223.

17 Simpson, J. A., Farrell, A. K., Oriña, M. M., & Rothman, A. J. (2015). Power and social influence in relationships. In Mikulincer M., & Shaver and P. R. (eds.). *APA Handbook of personality and social psychology: Vol. 3. Interpersonal relations.* Washington, DC: American Psychological Association.

18 Berger, J., Osterloh, M., Rost, K., & Ehrmann, T. (2020). How to prevent leadership hubris? Comparing competitive selections, lotteries, and their combination. *Leadership Quarterly,* 31(5), 1–17, p.3.

19 Petit, V., & Bollaert, H. (2012). Flying too close to the sun? Hubris among CEOs and how to prevent it. *Journal of Business Ethics,* 108, 265–283.

20 Sturm, R. E., & Antonakis, J. (2015). Interpersonal power: A review, critique, and research agenda. *Journal of Management,* 41(1), 136–163.

21 Weber, 1954, p. 323 cited in Cormier, D., Lapointe-Antunes, P., & Magnan, M. (2016). CEO power and CEO hubris: A prelude to financial misreporting? *Management Decision,* 54(2), 522–554.

22 Frye, T. (2021). Russia's weak strongman: The perilous bargains that keep Putin in power. *Foreign Affairs*, 100, 116–127, p.122.

23 French, J. & Raven, B. (1959). The bases of social power. In Cartwright, D. (ed.) *Studies in social power*, pp. 150–167. Ann Arbor, MI: Institute for Social Research, p.154.

24 Elias, S. (2008). Fifty years of influence in the workplace: The evolution of the French and Raven power taxonomy. *Journal of Management History*, 14(3), 267–283, p.270.

25 Dougherty, J. (2015). How the media became one of Putin's most powerful weapons, *The Atlantic*, April 21. Available at: https://www.theatlantic.com/international/archive/2015/04/how-the-media-became-putins-most-powerful-weapon/391062

26 Reuters. (2022). Russia's Prigozhin admits interfering in U.S. elections. *Reuters*, November 7. Available at:
https://www.reuters.com/world/us/russias-prigozhin-admits-interfering-us-elections-2022-11-07

27 Mihailidis, P., & Viotty, S. (2017). Spreadable spectacle in digital culture: Civic expression, fake news, and the role of media literacies in "post-fact" society. *American Behavioral Scientist*, 61(4), 441–454.

28 French, J., & Raven, B. (1959). The bases of social power. In Cartwright, D. (ed.). *Studies in social power*, pp. 150–167. Ann Arbor, MI: Institute for Social Research.

29 Lunenburg, F. C. (2012). Power and leadership: An influence process. *International Journal of Management, Business, and Administration*, 15(1), 1–9.

30 Conger, J. A., & Kanungo, R. N. (1988). The empowerment process: Integrating theory and practice. *Academy of Management Review*, 13(3), 471–482.

31 Barbuto, J. E. (2000). Influence triggers: A framework for understanding follower compliance. *The Leadership Quarterly*, 11, 365–387.

32 Thoroughgood, C. N., Padilla, A., Hunter, S. T., & Tate, B. W. (2012). The susceptible circle: A taxonomy of followers associated with destructive leadership. *The Leadership Quarterly*, 23(5), 897–917.

33 Costello, T. H., Bowes, S. M., Stevens, S. T., Waldman, I. D., Tasimi, A., & Lilienfeld, S. O. (2022). Clarifying the structure and nature of left-wing authoritarianism. *Journal of Personality and Social Psychology*, 122(1), 135–170.

34 Thoroughgood, C. N., Padilla, A., Hunter, S. T., & Tate, B. W. (2012). The susceptible circle: A taxonomy of followers associated with destructive leadership. *The Leadership Quarterly*, 23(5), 897–917.

35 Maccoby, M. (2004). Why people follow the leader: The power of transference. *Harvard Business Review*, 82(9), 76–85, p.81.

36 Maccoby, M. (2004). Why people follow the leader: The power of transference. *Harvard Business Review*, 82(9), 76–85.

37 Reuters. (2016). Donald Trump: 'I could shoot somebody and I wouldn't lose any voters'. *The Guardian*, January 24. Available at: https://www.theguardian.com/us-news/2016/jan/24/donald-trump-says-he-could-shoot-somebody-and-still-not-lose-voters

38 Reicher, S. D., & Haslam, S. A. (2017). How Trump won. *Scientific American Mind*, 28(2), 42–51. Available online at: https://www.scientificamerican.com/article/trump-rsquo-s-appeal-what-psychology-tells-us   Accessed March 3, 2023.

39 Reicher, S. D., & Haslam, S. A. (2017). How Trump won. *Scientific American Mind*, 28(2), 42–51. Available online at: https://www.scientificamerican.com/article/trump-rsquo-s-appeal-what-psychology-tells-us

40 Arendt, H. (1948/1979). *The origins of totalitarianism*. New York: Harcourt Brace, p.365.

41 Baron, R. S., Crawley, K., & Paulina, D. (2003). Aberrations of power: Leadership in totalist groups. In Van Knippenberg, D., & Hogg, M. A. (eds.). *Leadership and power: Identity processes in groups and organizations*. London: SAGE, pp.169–183.

42 Zimbardo, P. G. (2020). How Orwell's 1984 has influenced Rev. Jim Jones to dominate and then destroy his followers: With extensions to current political leaders. Peace and Conflict: *Journal of Peace Psychology*, 26(1), 4–8, p.7.

43 Tourish, D., & Vatcha, N. (2005). Charismatic leadership and corporate cultism at Enron: The elimination of dissent, the promotion of conformity and organizational collapse. *Leadership*, 1(4), 455–480.

44 Tourish, D., & Vatcha, N. (2005). Charismatic leadership and corporate cultism at Enron: The elimination of dissent, the promotion of conformity and organizational collapse. *Leadership*, 1(4), 455–480.

45 Tourish, D., & Vatcha, N. (2005). Charismatic leadership and corporate cultism at Enron: The elimination of dissent, the promotion of conformity and organizational collapse. *Leadership*, 1(4), 455–480.

46 Tourish, D., & Vatcha, N. (2005). Charismatic leadership and corporate cultism at Enron: The elimination of dissent, the promotion of conformity and organizational collapse. Leadership, 1(4), 455–480, p.462.

47 Tourish, D., & Vatcha, N. (2005). Charismatic leadership and corporate cultism at Enron: The elimination of dissent, the promotion of conformity and organizational collapse. *Leadership*, 1(4), 455–480.

48 Paulhus, D. L., & Williams, K. M. (2002). The dark triad of personality: Narcissism, Machiavellianism, and psychopathy. *Journal of Research in Personality*, 36(6), 556–563.

49 Albrecht, C., Holland, D., Malagueño, R., Dolan, S., & Tzafrir, S. (2015). The role of power in financial statement fraud schemes. *Journal of Business Ethics*, 131, 803–813.

50 Goodwin, S. A. (2003). Power and Prejudice: A social–cognitive perspective on power and leadership. In Van Knippenberg, D., & Hogg, M. A. (eds.). *Leadership and power: Identity processes in groups and organizations.* London: SAGE, pp.138–152.

51 Lammers, J., Galinsky, A. D., Dubois, D., & Rucker, D. D. (2015). Power and morality. *Current Opinion in Psychology*, 6, 15–19.

52 Sturm, R. E., & Antonakis, J. (2015). Interpersonal power: A review, critique, and research agenda. *Journal of Management*, 41(1), 136–163.

53 Goodwin, S. A., Operario, D., & Fiske, S. T. (1998). Situational power and interpersonal dominance facilitate bias and inequality. *Journal of Social Issues*, 54, 677–698.

54 Lammers, J., Stapel, D. A., & Galinsky, A. D. (2010). Power increases hypocrisy: Moralizing in reasoning, immorality in behavior. *Psychological Science*, 21, 737–744.

55 Fast, N. J., Gruenfeld, D. H., Sivanathan, N., & Galinsky, A. D. (2009). Illusory control: A generative force behind power's far-reaching effects. *Psychological Science*, 20, 502–508; Fast, N. J., Sivanathan, N., Mayer, N. D., & Galinsky, A. D. (2012). Power and overconfident decision-making. *Organizational Behavior and Human Decision Processes*, 117, 249–260.

56 Inesi, M. E. (2010). Power and loss aversion. *Organizational Behavior and Human Decision Processes*, 112, 58–69.

57 Keltner, D., Young, R. C., Heerey, E. A., Oemig, C., & Monarch, N. D. (1998). Teasing in hierarchical and intimate relations. *Journal of Personality and Social Psychology*, 75, 1231–1247; Kemper, T. D. 1991. Predicting emotions from social relations. *Social Psychology Quarterly*, 54, 330–342.

58 van Kleef, G. A., Oveis, C., van der Löwe, I., LuoKogan, A., Goetz, J., & Keltner, D. (2008). Power, distress, and compassion: Turning a blind eye to the suffering of others. *Psychological Science*, 19, 1315–1322.

59 Sturm, R. E., & Antonakis, J. (2015). Interpersonal power: A review, critique, and research agenda. *Journal of Management*, 41(1), 136–163.

60 Kleimann, M. (2023). The CBI's arrogance has been breath taking. City AM, April 20. Available at: https://www.cityam.com/mark-kleinman-the-cbis-arrogance-has-been-breathtaking

61 Keltner, D., Gruenfeld, D. H., & Anderson, C. (2003). Power, approach, and inhibition. *Psychological Review*, 110, 265–284.

62 Carney et al., 2014 cited in Lammers, J., Stapel, D. A., & Galinsky, A. D. (2010). Power increases hypocrisy: Moralizing in reasoning, immorality in behavior. *Psychological Science*, 21, 737–744.

63 Kipnis, D. (1972). Does power corrupt? *Journal of Personality and Social Psychology*, 24(1), 33–41.

64 Lammers, J., Stapel, D. A., & Galinsky, A. D. (2010). Power increases hypocrisy: Moralizing in reasoning, immorality in behavior. *Psychological Science*, 21, 737–744.

65 Overbeck, J. R., & Droutman, V. (2013). One for all: Social power increases self-anchoring of traits, attitudes, and emotions. *Psychological Science*, 24: 1466–1476.

66 Manner, J. K., & Mead, N. L. (2010). The essential tension between leadership and power: When leaders sacrifice group goals for the sake of self-interest. *Journal of Personality and Social Psychology*, 99: 482–497.

67 Owen, L. D. (2018). Heads of government, 'toe-holders' and time limits. In P. Garrard (ed.). *The leadership hubris epidemic*. Basingstoke: Palgrave Macmillan, pp.165–178.

68 Owen, D. (2021). *Riddle, mystery, enigma*. London: Haus Publishing.

69 Padilla, A., Hogan, R., & Kaiser, R. B. (2007). The toxic triangle: Destructive leaders, susceptible followers, and conducive environments. *The Leadership Quarterly*, 18(3): 176–194.

70 Sadler-Smith, E., & Cojuharenco, I. (2021). Business schools and hubris: Cause or cure? *Academy of Management Learning & Education*, 20(2), 270–289.

71 Robertson, I., & Owen, D. (2022). Inside Putin's mind: How absolute power has blinded Russia's new tsar. *The Sunday Times*, February 26. Available at: https://www.thetimes.co.uk/article/inside-putins-mind-absolute-power-has-blinded-russias-new-tsar-q8gws3v5j

72 Bass, B. M., & Steidlmeier, P. (1999). Ethics, character, and authentic transformational leadership behavior. *The Leadership Quarterly*, 10(2), 181–217.

73 Owen, D. (2007). *The hubris syndrome: Bush, Blair and the intoxication of power*. London: Methuen, p.134.

74 Moosa, I. A. (2017). The hubris of excessive remuneration in the financial sector: The case for regulation. *Journal of Banking Regulation*, 18, 287–301.

75 Baker, D., Bivens, J., & Schieder, J. (2019). Reining in CEO compensation and curbing the rise of inequality. Economic Policy Institute, June 4. Available at: https://www.epi.org/publication/reining-in-ceo-compensation-and-curbing-the-rise-of-inequality

76 Charan, R. (2018). How to prevent a faltering CEO from damaging your company. *Strategy+Business*, April 5. Available at: https://www.strategy-business.com/article/How-to-Prevent-a-Faltering-CEO-from-Damaging-Your-Company

77 Dewar, C., Hirt, M., & Keller, S. (2019). The mindsets and practices of excellent CEOs. *McKinsey and Company*, October 25. Available at: https://www.mckinsey.com/capabilities/strategy-and-corporate-finance/our-insights/the-mindsets-and-practices-of-excellent-ceos

78 Porter, M.E., Lorsch, J. W., & Nohria, N. (2004). Seven surprises for new CEOs. *Harvard Business Review*, October. Available online at: https://hbr.org/2004/10/seven-surprises-for-new-ceos

3

THE TOXIC TRIANGLE

The Toxic Triangle of Hubristic Leadership

It's important to realise early on that the hubris hazard can't be understood and mitigated against by simply looking at the leader: hubristic leadership is a complex process that depends on the interactions between a leader's personality and predispositions, the support that they have from their followers, and the context in which they're operating.[1] A toxic mix of hubristic leader, conducive context, and complicit followers has led to the demise of numerous political and business leaders. Many, if not most, of the hubristic leaders discussed in this book have fallen foul of this 'toxic triangle'. For example, Fred Goodwin of RBS and Richard Fuld of Lehman Brothers (see Chapter 1) didn't intend to bring about their own demise in the global financial crisis of 2008: their downfall was a negative consequence, albeit unintended, of the interactions between leader behaviours (for example, over-confidence), a conducive context (for example, sub-prime mortgage

DOI: 10.4324/9781003128427-3

market in the USA) and the complicity of followers (for example, regulators, other executives, investors, etc.), see Figure 3.1.

Leadership researchers Art Padilla, Robert Hogan, and Robert Kaiser first proposed the idea that negative consequences are likely to emerge from interactions between leader, followers, and context in 2007.[2] Their 'toxic triangle of destructive leadership' model was based on the premise that many commentators, especially those in business education and the leadership development industry, have tended to take an overly positive view of leadership and focused mainly on its bright side when in actual fact there is a real need to acknowledge the dangerous, damaging, and destructive consequences of leadership's darker side. If leadership is a process whereby an individual attempts to influence a group of individuals to achieve a common goal[3] then it's unsurprising that damaging consequences can spring from the interplay between the behaviours of a hubristic leader and their complicit followers if circumstances allow this to happen.

A prime example of the potency of the interactions between the three elements of the toxic triangle is to be found in the tragic rise and fall of Elizabeth Holmes, the founder and CEO of the now defunct blood-testing company Theranos, and who at the time of writing is incarcerated in a Texas prison serving an 11-year sentence for fraud. Holmes' story is an epic tale

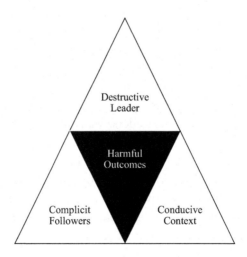

Figure 3.1 The Toxic Triangle

of a meteoric rise and fall of an entrepreneur who was lauded by the press and business and political luminaries in Silicon Valley's 'move fast and break things' (a Mark Zuckerberg motto) and 'fake it until you make it' culture. For Holmes the line between the ambition to change the world and overly grandiose claims became blurred and eventually transgressed. The Holmes/ Theranos case is not only one of the most extreme examples of a tech 'unicorn' (a privately held start-up with a value of over a billion dollars) overclaiming, over-promising, and under-delivering. It's also a striking example of the perfect storm that can be whipped up when a hubristic leader is enabled by investors, the press, and minimal constraints in a business culture that encourages and rewards excess. It's a classic case of a 'toxic triangle' of hubristic leadership[4] and a prime example of the fact that hubris costs.

Rise of Elizabeth Holmes

Elizabeth Ann Holmes was born on February 3, 1984 in Washington DC. Her father, Christian Rasmus Holmes IV, was for a time a vice president at Enron. In 2002 at the age of 18 Holmes became a chemical engineering first-year student at Stanford University in the heart of Northern California's Silicon Valley. While she was an undergraduate Holmes nailed her entrepreneurial colours to the mast by filing her first patent application for a wearable drug-delivery patch. After two years' study she was motivated by her experiences as an intern at the Genome Institute of Singapore in 2003 to drop out of Stanford to set up her own healthcare technology company.

While she was in Singapore, Holmes dreamt up her idea for a blood-testing device that could run up to 200 tests on a single drop of blood. This would not only eliminate the need for the use of needles to draw vials of blood it would also make testing easier, quicker, and cheaper. To realise this dream she founded the biotech company that derived its name from the combination of 'therapy' and 'diagnosis', Theranos.[5] The idea of doing blood tests using a single drop of blood analysed in a table-top minilab was, to the uninitiated at least, elegant and simple. Holmes claimed that her needle phobia was one of her main motivations in developing the needle-free technology. The company's mission was to "facilitate the early detection and prevention of disease and empower people everywhere to live their best possible lives".[6] Its marketing strap line was: "The blood test that needs just a drop".

The machine itself was a minilab about the size of a microwave oven that could fit comfortably onto a worksurface in a pharmacy or super-market (Figure 3.2). It was named the 'Edison' after Thomas Edison the famous inventor and entrepreneur who had over 1,000 patents to his name. The technology would enable tests to be done there and then and hence remove the need for drawing vials of blood and sending them off to be lab-tested in a more costly and time-consuming process. It was claimed that the Edison could do a wide range of blood tests almost instantaneously at 10 per cent of the cost of a centralised laboratory facility. In a speech to Theranos' employees Holmes described the minilab as "the most important thing humanity has ever built".[7] Her vision was for Theranos to become the Apple of healthcare and for the minilab to become the iPhone of medical devices. Admirers in the media championed her as "the new Steve Jobs".[8]

High-profile individuals and venture capitalists were convinced by Theranos' technological promises and its CEO's charisma, vision, and

Figure 3.2 Theranos Minilab Sampling Units

Source: Shutterstock Image 2037271856 reproduced under licence for editorial use.

rhetoric. But, worryingly, the scientific basis of Theranos' technology hadn't been scrutinised in peer-reviewed journals. Holmes obtained the backing of one of her Stanford professors, Channing Robertson, who became the first member of the Theranos board. The rest of the board consisted mainly of ex-political and ex-military luminaries, including Henry Kissinger and George Schultz, both former US Secretaries of State, William Perry former Secretary of Defense, Sam Nunn former US Senator, Gary Roughead former US Navy Admiral, and four-star General James 'Mad Dog' Mattis former US Secretary of Defence and commander in Afghanistan and Iraq. The board, whose average age was 80, had little if any medical or health care expertise and few of them knew a great deal about the technology.[9] One commentator remarked that the board seemed better suited to deciding on whether to wage war than oversee a blood-testing company.[10] The efficacy of the board in exercising the necessary checks and balances and its fitness for purpose was later called into question.

Investors in Theranos included the Australian business magnate and boss of News Corp Rupert Murdoch, who stumped-up $121 million, and the Walton family, who invested $150 million, as well as renowned venture capitalists Tim Draper and Steve Jurveston. Almost a billion dollars in funding from various sources flowed into Theranos. If the idea worked it would have upended the blood-testing industry that was worth $75 billion in 2014. As well as big-name, up-front investments, there were high-profile business partnerships between Theranos and the pharmacy Walgreens and the grocery retailer Walmart. Whist investors were keen to support the business, Theranos itself was somewhat reluctant to divulge to them how the minilab actually worked [11]

Holmes quickly became one of the biggest business celebrities in the USA.[12] She front-paged in the business press with headlines such as 'This CEO is Out for Blood' (Fortune, June 2014), 'Blood Simpler' (The New Yorker, December 2014), 'Holmes is Where the Heart Is' (The Economist, June 2015), and 'Why the Next Steve Jobs Will Be a Woman' (Inc., October 2015). Theranos became a tech unicorn in 2010. Its blood-testing system went live in 2013 with a roll-out into a small number of Walgreen pharmacies in California and then on to a bigger roll-out in Phoenix. At the time of the partnership deals and the roll-outs in 2014 Theranos was valued at more than $9 billion.[13]

Fall of Elizabeth Holmes

Although many in the business press and mass media, as well as its numerous high-profile investors, were persuaded by Holmes' vision, there were others who weren't so convinced. Google Ventures has a strong interest in medical technologies. In 2013 it weighed up whether or not to invest in Theranos. Google had someone from their life-sciences investment team go into a Walgreens store and take the finger-prick test. Alarm bells sounded immediately when several vials were drawn rather than the much-publicised 'one drop'.[14] This raised more questions than answers and Google decided to pass on the opportunity to invest. Holmes later claimed that Theranos turned down Google. Either way, Google's back-off was a portent of what was to come.[15]

In reality Theranos' minilab could only perform a small number of blood tests called 'immunoassays' (used to track different proteins, hormones, and antibodies). To do the 200 or so tests that Theranos claimed the Edison could perform (everything from testing cholesterol levels to testing for HIV and pancreatic cancer) it was claimed that they'd 'hacked' Siemens' machines and supplemented the minilab results with regular blood tests.[16] Also, they were able to sidestep the rules and regulations in the regulatory 'no man's land' between the Food and Drug Administration (FDA), which regulates and improves lab instruments as part of its mission to protect public health, and the Centres for Medicare and Medicaid Services (CMS), which is the regulator of clinical laboratories. Theranos' tests were in a third category developed and executed in labs using Theranos' own methods and machines (known as 'laboratory-developed tests' (LTDs)).[17] Having had little success in getting any of the big pharmaceutical companies to buy in to the use of its technology, Theranos decided to go directly to consumers.[18] As well as teaming up with Walgreens it also struck a deal with the supermarket chain Walmart.

The breakthrough in uncovering Theranos' claims came in a series of exposés in the *Wall Street Journal* in 2015 by Pulitzer Prize-winning investigative reporter, John Carreyrou. His book, *Bad Blood: Secrets and Lies in a Silicon Valley Start-Up* which documented the Holmes/Theranos story, was published in 2018. Carreyrou's suspicions were raised when he came across an analysis of Theranos' claims by the head of clinical biochemistry at Mount Sinai Hospital in Toronto, the Canadian-Cypriot biochemist Eleftherios

Diamandis. Diamandis wrote an opinion piece that was published in a scientific journal in 2018 which concluded that Theranos' claims for its technology were highly speculative and that many were likely to be grossly exaggerated. An interesting aside is that Diamandis, along with Professor of Psychiatry Nick Bouras from King's College London, commented in an article in 2018 on the relationship between hubris and fraud in scientific discovery:

> Jan Hendrik Schön rose to prominence after a series of breakthroughs in semiconductors, most of them published in *Nature* and *Science*, which were later discovered to be fraudulent. Hwang-Woo-Suk, until 2005, was considered one of the pioneering experts in the field of stem cells and was best known for two articles published in the journal *Science* in 2004 and 2005, where he reported that he had succeeded in creating human embryonic stem cells by cloning. He was called the 'Pride of Korea' in South Korea. These reports were later found to be fabricated. Another tragic example of possible hubris was the report in *Nature* of a new and simple way to produce inducible stem cells. The method was soon found to be irreproducible and was retracted, but in the meantime, one of the senior authors committed suicide.[19]

Whistle-blowers started to come forward. Tyler Shultz, the grandson of Theranos board member George Shultz (the US Secretary of State 1982–1989 under Ronald Reagan), was one of the first employees to voice his concerns. He first spoke to Carreyrou in 2013 in a risky and bold move given his family as well as professional connections. The 22-year-old Shultz went on record as saying that there was nothing that the minilab could do that he couldn't do with a pipette.[20] The dam broke with the publication of Carreyrou's article in October 2015 in the *Wall Street Journal* headlined 'Hot start-up Theranos has struggled with its blood-test technology'. In it Carreyrou revealed how the Silicon Valley lab wasn't using its own technology for all the tests it offered. He exposed both how Theranos' technology didn't actually work as was being claimed and how it tried to cover up its shortcomings. Once doubts surfaced and gained traction, Theranos was forced under pressure from regulators to stop using the one-drop, finger-prick blood samples for all but one of its tests and back away from its unique selling point 'one-drop' method. It was then that the commercial realities began to bite hard. Walgreens refused to open any new blood-testing centres until questions about the technology were answered satisfactorily.

In 2016 CMS investigators found serious irregularities at Theranos' laboratory in Northern California, including inadequate quality control checks, improper use of samples, incomplete documentation, running tests with unqualified personnel, and failing to notify patients when results were flawed.[21] Federal prosecutors launched a criminal investigation into whether Theranos had misled investors about the state of its technology and operations. In mid-2016 the laboratory regulators revoked Theranos' operating license and banned Holmes from the blood-testing business for two years. Walgreens terminated its partnership with Theranos. Holmes and her Chief Operating Officer, Sunny Balwani, were committed for trial in the US District Court of Northern California in San Jose. The charges were that she defrauded investors who'd put hundreds of millions of dollars into Theranos and patients who'd paid for tests and put their trust in the technology.[22]

The Securities and Exchange Commission (SEC) charged Holmes with numerous counts of fraud. In January 2022 after a nearly four-month trial the jury found Holmes guilty of three counts of committing fraud on individual investors and one count of conspiracy to commit fraud involving wire transfers of more than $140 million. Attorney Stephanie M. Hinds speaking on behalf of the US Attorney's Office, Northern District of California, summarised the case as one in which the defendant knew the analyser was not producing accurate and reliable results, could only perform a few basic tests, was slower than existing devices, and could not successfully compete with the established conventional machines, but also that the defendant lied about it unashamedly. The Attorney's Office also noted that alongside all of this, Holmes enjoyed a lavish lifestyle; she lived in a $15-million mansion and often travelled in $6.5-million Gulfstream 150 executive jet.[23] She is reported to have spent $100,000 on a single conference table.[24]

In November 2022 US District Judge Edward Davila sentenced Holmes, who was at the time 38 years old and pregnant with her second child, to 11 years and 3 months in prison for defrauding investors plus an additional 3 years of supervision following release from prison. No fine was assessed. Holmes began her prison sentence at a women's prison camp located in Bryan, Texas in May 2023. By the end of her sentence, barring release on parole, Elizabeth Holmes will be 50 years old. Judge Davila described the case as "troubling on so many levels", and questioned what could have motivated a "brilliant" entrepreneur to misrepresent her company and its claims to investors so egregiously. Judge Davila concluded that: "This is a fraud case where an exciting venture went forward with great expectations only to be dashed by untruths, misrepresentations, plain hubris and lies".[25]

Hubristic Leader: Charisma and Narcissism

The first element in the toxic triangle is the leader's behaviour. Padilla and his colleagues, who first came up with the model, identified leaders' charisma as one of the primary leader behaviour factors. The origins of the study of charismatic leadership can be traced back to the work of the German sociologist Max Weber (1864–1920) who used 'charisma' (from the Greek χάρισμα, khárisma, meaning 'gift of grace' or 'favour') to refer to the authority exercised by a leader over others emanating from their exceptional sanctity, heroism, or exemplary character.[26] According to leadership researchers Jay Conger and Rabindra Kanungo charismatic leaders: have an idealised vision that is discrepant from the status quo which they strive to change; are likeable and honourable 'heroes' who are worthy of identifying with and imitating; often use unconventional means to transcend the existing order and strongly articulate future vision and have strong motivation to lead; exercise power based on expertise, respect, and admiration and transform people so that they are able to share and participate in the radical change they advocate. On the downside, charisma can be manipulated by destructive leaders in the abuse of power for self-serving ends.[27] Theranos whistle-blower Tyler Shultz said in 2022 that

> Elizabeth is a very, very charismatic person, when she speaks to you, she makes you feel like you are the most important person in her world in that moment. She almost has this reality distortion field around her that people can just get sucked into.[28]

As well as having magnetic personalities, charismatic leaders may also be prone to exaggerating their achievements, taking unwarranted credit for positive outcomes, covering up their failings, blaming others for mistakes, and quashing criticism.[29] For example, Holmes is reported to have said to potential dissenters inside Theranos that "if you don't believe [that the minilab is] the most important thing humanity has ever built ... you should leave now".[30] Hubris (as a delusion of unassailability) has been described as being to the individual what groupthink (where a striving for unanimity overrides good decision-making) is to the group.[31]

Narcissism is also singled out by Padilla and colleagues as a factor in destructive leadership involving, as it does, dominance, grandiosity, arrogance, entitlement, over-reach, selfish pursuit of pleasure and the trappings of power, self-absorption, autocratic behaviours, low empathy and disregarding the viewpoints, needs, and well-being of others. Other leadership researchers have pointed out that transformational leaders can create and destroy organisations and institutions and that charismatic leaders who are narcissistic can embody a "dark side, mobilizing followers to pursue goals that are dangerous" citing the example of Holmes.[32] A psychiatrist, Richard Fuisz, who was familiar with Holmes from her childhood, speculated in *Forbes* in 2019 on aspects of her background (for example, the influence of her parents) that may have been contributory factors to the ways in which she led Theranos.[33] Others involved have claimed that she showed narcissistic tendencies.[34] However, a principle of the toxic triangle is that destructive leader behaviours such as narcissism, negative charisma,[35] and hubris are necessary but not sufficient conditions for destructive leadership to take hold. In most situations, destructive leaders are reliant on the support of their followers to achieve power and to exert their influence. Complicit followers have a pivotal role in enabling hubristic leaders to achieve and maintain power.

Complicit Followers: Conformers and Colluders

Leaders and followers are inseparable and indivisible; there can be no leaders without followers because leadership is fundamentally about the relationships between people moving forward together towards a common goal.[36] If hubristic leader behaviours, such as those exhibited by Holmes, are undesirable then why do followers not resist? Barbara Kellerman of Harvard University makes the point that followers can be every bit as important as leaders themselves: "You can't have bad leadership without ... bad followers".[37] She distinguishes between followers in terms of their level of engagement with the leader's project. Based on this, followers can range on a spectrum from those who feel and do "absolutely nothing" to those who are "passionately committed and deeply involved" as follows:[38]

(1) *Bystanders*: these are followers who seem to feel and do nothing; they simply allow bad leadership to happen. But by doing nothing they're passively condoning bad leadership and are susceptible by their own inaction to the influences of a destructive leader;

(2) *True believers*: these are followers who are actively involved and complicit in the process by actively colluding with the leader. They're likely to be both ambitious and share the leader's world view.[39] True believers are collusive with the leader in creating the conditions for negative consequences to arise by actively participating.

Leadership researcher Christian Thoroughgood and his colleagues distinguished between two different groups and sub-groups of followers in terms of French and Raven's five power bases (legitimate, reward, coercive, expert, and referent, and see Chapter 2). The two main groups of followers are 'conformers' and 'colluders'. Within the conformer group there are three sub-types:

(1) *Lost souls*: people who identify with the leader, are influenced mainly by the leader's referent power, and look to the leader to instil in them some sense of worth and direction;

(2) *Authoritarians*: people who conform because of the leader's legitimate role as the boss and accede rigidly and unconditionally to the leader's right to exercise control over them;

(3) *Bystanders*: people who are suppressed into conformity and submission in response to the leader's powers of coercion and are motivated by fear and a desire to minimise the costs of failing to conform. Bystanders may feel angry towards the leader but they're not motivated enough to take action.[40]

Within the colluder group there are two sub-types:

(1) *Acolytes*: people who collude as a result of identifying with the leader's goals in response and deference to the leader's supposed expert power.

Table 3.1 Groups and Sub-types of Followers

Type of follower	Sub-type of follower	Leader's power base
Conformers	Lost souls	Referent
	Authoritarians	Legitimate
	Bystanders	Coercive
Colluders	Acolytes	Expert
	Opportunists	Reward

They gain self-expression and self-worth via the leader's mission and therefore don't require strong inducements to lend the leader their support;

(2) *Opportunists*: people who anticipate a reward by engaging in a positive exchange with the leader and willingly follow the leader in anticipation of obtaining their share of financial, political, or professional advantage in exchange for their collusion,[41] see Table 3.1.

As far as collusion with Holmes' leadership at Theranos is concerned, in the eyes of many the firm's Chief Operating Officer (COO), Sunny Balwani, was an acolyte sub-type.[42] Some of the investors might be seen as opportunists, but in fairness the extent of Holmes' fraud did not become apparent until after they'd committed and eventually lost their money. Likewise, employees at Theranos who suspected that all was not as it ought to have been, might be criticised for being bystanders, but they probably chose not to quit and kept silent so as to preserve their livelihoods. Others, such as Theranos' chief scientist Ian Gibson (who committed suicide in 2013) and Tyler Shultz (see above), did choose to speak out but at significant cost to themselves.[43]

Complicit Followers: The Board and the Media

From a standing start in 2003 Theranos hit a peak valuation of $9 billion in 2014. It's perhaps not surprising therefore that the popular and business press became enthralled and captivated by the Holmes/Theranos project. At the time of Theranos' peak popularity Holmes:

(1) made the cover of *Forbes*, leading 'The Class of 2014' and was proclaimed as the youngest, self-made, female billionaire;

(2) spoke at *Vanity Fair's* 'New Establishment Summit' in 2015 and was named by *Time* as one of the '100 Most Influential People in the World';

(3) occupied the fringes of a rich and powerful American elite; for example, she participated in high-profile panels with former US President Bill Clinton and the Alibaba Group founder Jack Ma. Her 2014 TED talk chalked up millions of views.

Holmes gained an international profile as a business leader and an inspiration for up-and-coming female entrepreneurs; as well as *Time, Forbes,* and *Vanity Fair* she adorned the covers of *Fortune, Inc., Glamour,* and the *New York Times Style Magazine.* She dined at the White House. President Barack Obama recognised her as a US ambassador for global entrepreneurship. Senator Joe Biden praised her vision at the minilab's launch. At the height of her fame in 2015 no less an institution than Harvard University Medical School honoured the then 31-year-old Holmes as an inductee to its Board of Fellows.

A historian of Silicon Valley, Professor Margaret O'Mara of the University of Washington, commented that "here was a photogenic, telegenic young woman posing as the female Steve Jobs" which the media packaged into an "incredibly alluring narrative that everyone wanted to believe".[44] Holmes' youth and ambition made her the avatar of female entrepreneurialism and ambition. She was a favourite of Silicon Valley and investors. The media simultaneously helped to create and bought into the Holmes/Theranos project. Everyone wanted this young, charismatic, female entrepreneur, with her grand vision to up-end the world of blood testing, to succeed at all costs.[45]

Aside from the followers, what role did the Board play? The UK's Institute of Directors (IoD) describes the key purpose of a board of directors as ensuring "the company's prosperity by collectively directing the company's affairs, while meeting the appropriate interests of its shareholders and relevant stakeholders".[46] To be effective a board must operate as one element of a tripartite system of checks and balances in which, according to former US Secretary of Commerce Barbara Hackman Franklin, the shareholders own shares and elect the board of directors, the board sets policies and hires and fires the CEO, and the CEO and the management run the company.[47] One of the main functions of Theranos' board, which, as noted above, was packed with politicians and ex-military (with three former cabinet secretaries, two former senators, and retired military top brass, it was "a board like no other")[48] ought to have been setting company policy, constraining the CEO, and acting as a check and balance on the claims being made. After the firm's collapse one commentator described this as an "egregious failure".[49] A senior editor at Fortune writing in 2015, well before the company went bankrupt and Holmes ended up in court, put it like this:

> While it's probably useful to have a retired government official or two to teach and offer good leadership skills, when there are six with no medical or technology experience—with an average age, get this, of 80—one wonders just how plugged in they are to Theranos' day-to-day activities. Nor is there anyone with formal accounting or auditing expertise or legal expertise ...[50]

As well as being incapable of exercising effective oversight, it's also been claimed that the board could have been more active in challenging Theranos' climate of secrecy and the quashing of dissent.[51] It was reported that employee emails were strictly monitored, anyone who voiced suspicions or misgivings was reprimanded, and legal threats were made against naysayers both inside and outside the company.[52] As early as 2006 Theranos' Chief Financial Officer, Henry Mosely, cautioned Holmes and was fired for not being a team player.[53]

The Pulitzer Prize-nominated writer and digital strategist Aron Solomon summed up Theranos as a "really sad story of lives and ideas gone wrong".[54] Things might have been quite different, Solomon remarked, had the directors fulfilled their responsibilities by: first, having governance structures and controls in place to facilitate accurate financial reporting and marketing claims; second, being "engaged overseers" who understood how the technology was supposed to have worked; and finally, and perhaps most importantly, in guarding against hubris by fostering a strong culture of compliance to ensure that the business operated within the limits of what is possible and inside the requisite legal and ethical boundaries.[55]

Conducive Context: Fake It Until You Make It

The expression 'Fake it 'til you make it' (FITYMI) entered common parlance in the 1970s. It's a phrase that's been bandied around ever since, especially in sales and marketing. Its origins are traceable to a legal document from the US Court of Appeals in February 1973 reporting a case of "gigantic and successful fraud" in which a salesperson tried to sell the idea of a quick route to great riches and easy money. This document summed up the essence of the 'fake it 'til you make it' method of doing business:

> He [the salesperson] is told that to maximize his chances of success he should impart an aura of affluence, whether spurious or not to pretend that he has obtained wealth of no small proportions. He is to 'fake it 'til you make it,' or to give the impression of wealth even if it has not been attained. He is urged to go into debt if necessary to purchase a new and expensive automobile and flashy clothes, and to carry with him large sums of money, borrowing if necessary, so that it can be ostentatiously displayed. The purpose of all this is to put the [sales] prospect in a more receptive state of mind with respect to the inducements that he will be subject to at the meetings.[56]

When someone tries to 'Fake it 'til they make it' they attempt to project an image of themselves, for example, through self-confidence, charisma, ambition, and optimism, so as to convince others that they too can attain a goal that hasn't really been achieved. It involves consciously cultivating an attitude of competence that you don't currently have by pretending that you do. This is an act of deliberately deceiving others, and in case of self-deception, the vain hope is that it might eventually come true (see Chapter 6).

Faking it has acceptable and unacceptable sides. Faking, or feigning, behaviours such as smiling and nodding to appear interested in something or someone is a common practice. It helps to oil the wheels of polite social interaction and builds good social relationships. This could be seen as faking it for an acceptable and legitimate reason. Likewise consciously and forcibly making yourself appear to be confident by acting out a part even when you're tense or nervous, for example, when giving a presentation or being interviewed, can help a person lacking in confidence to achieve a legitimate goal. In the long run and if practised enough with coaching and feedback it may even help to build the skill that is deficient, and at the very least provide a coping strategy. The same can be true for a whole number of intra- and interpersonal skills. We identify what we need to achieve and then set ourselves stretch goals that are outside of our comfort zone, and hence to some extent we fake it, feign it, or act in order to conquer our inadequacies.

Problems set in when faking is used to excess and for the wrong reasons. The moral and practical challenge is knowing when it's acceptable to do so and when it's not. As already noted, as far as developing legitimate skills are concerned, faking it may not be ideal but it can help the process. An introvert adopting outgoing behaviours in a social context in order to cope, involves feigning confidence; arguably this is acceptable. On the other hand, faking competence is unacceptable. A person can either do something or they can't. It's definitely not acceptable to claim a skill, ability, or achievement that you don't have, or for a company to claim that its technology and products can do things that they patently cannot do. For example, faking crosses the Rubicon from being acceptable to unacceptable when a candidate tells a hiring panel that they have great team-working skills when they don't, or when a salesperson attempts to convince a customer that their product or service will meet their needs when it won't.[57]

The claims that were being made for Theranos' minilab were extravagant to say the least. When Theranos went 'live' the machine could only do a small class of blood tests.[58] For the rest of the over 200 tests on the menu (for example, a prostate specific antigen test at a cost of $12.52 and HIV at $16.39)[59] they used Siemens' machines modified to take small samples and carried out regular tests with commercial analysers using veinous draws of blood. Capillary blood drawn from a single finger prick, unlike veinous blood drawn from an arm, contains fluids from tissues and cells which make the test much less accurate. Moreover, blood taken from a finger counts as a bodily fluid and therefore FDA approval would have been needed for the tests. As noted earlier, Theranos avoided this requirement by falling between two distinct categories of test.[60].

Whether hubristic leaders lose their moral compass is an interesting question, but research shows that people can be more willing to lie and engage in unethical conduct when the gains are for what they see as a morally worthy cause.[61] Perhaps Holmes thought that her mission for "the early detection and prevention of disease and [to] empower people everywhere to live their best possible lives" justified her behaviours. Deception in pursuit of the common good can be a dangerous game to play because the person absolves themselves of the normal pangs of guilt that accompany unethical conduct.[62]

Theranos failed spectacularly. Failure is an inevitable and necessary part of doing business; through legitimate failures entrepreneurs make sense of and learn from their failed ventures, and many of them bounce back.[63] The culture and history of Silicon Valley is replete with examples of entrepreneurs who have raised hundreds of thousands of dollars based on ideas that may or may not come off or turn in any profits even if they do. One of the less edifying characteristics of the Silicon Valley culture is that entrepreneurs are often encouraged to act as if they and their business are successful before there's any solid proof of success. The reporter who broke the Theranos story, John Carreyrou, is of the view that Holmes is a "child of this culture" who "surfed on this myth of the genius founder who can see around corners".[64]

Hubris is enabled by cultures that are conducive to over-claiming and especially so in those places where hype is accepted. According to one of the first Theranos sceptics, John Ioannidis of Stanford, more than half of the Silicon Valley health-care unicorns have very few if any citations in the scientific literature for their work.[65] The *New York Times* attributed the Theranos project to the Silicon Valley culture of the 2000s and compared it to the excesses of Wall Street in the 1990s.[66]

Judge Davila, who sentenced Holmes in November 2022 to 135 months in prison, commented that "the industry that we know of here [Northern California] regrettably finds vectors with the financial and personal gain that clouds sometimes the good judgment of individuals". He noted:

> Ms. Holmes is brilliant. She had creative ideas. She is a big thinker. She was a woman moving into an industry that was dominated by, and let's face it, male ego. That young women entrepreneurs are regrettably denied access to, but she made that. She made that. She got into that world.

The judge also asked what was the cause: "Was it hubris? What caused that? Was it intoxication with the fame that comes with being a young entrepreneur?" He also commented that in this culture, with all its faults, that fraud is not okay, that fraud isn't part of failure, and that the culture for all its shortcomings, is not one that would ever condone fraud.[67]

Holmes was not the only Theranos executive to face the full force of the law. In December 2022 Theranos' COO and Holmes' ex-boyfriend, Suny Balwani, was sentenced by a judge to 13 years in prison after being convicted of all 12 charges brought against him for defrauding Theranos' investors and patients.[68]

Hubris all too often shines the spotlight on cultures where greed is seen to be good.[69] It seems that the lessons of the 2008 financial crisis still haven't been learned. Certain quarters of Silicon Valley culture seem to be especially vulnerable to hyperbole. Holmes isn't alone in falling foul of the hubris hazard. The bosses of WeWork, Uber, and Zenefits have been forced to resign for, amongst other things, exaggerating their successes. In line with the unwritten principle that "Silicon Valley starts companies and Hollywood makes movies about them"[70] in 2022 the streaming service Hulu premiered *The Dropout*, a TV mini-series based on the ABC Audio podcast of the same name about the rise and fall of Holmes and Theranos. It's perhaps a perverse twist of fate that a culture that helped to create failure also celebrated that failure.

The author of 'The Dropout' podcast, Peter Cohan, picked out five aspects of Silicon Valley's proclivity for 'hype narratives' that could add fuel to the fire of hubristic leadership:

(1) Silicon Valley loves a dropout, witness Bill Gates and Mark Zuckerberg (Harvard dropouts) and Steve Jobs (Reed College dropout);

(2) Silicon Valley thrives on disruption which can mean anything from a truly revolutionary product to targeting a big market with a lower-priced product. Theranos' minilab aspired to be both;

(3) Cohan also points out that lack of understanding of how Silicon Valley's products actually work might be fine for non-technically minded investors so long as there are people around them who do understand how they work, and when lives don't depend on it; but when patient well-being is at stake being able to prove the accuracy of one's claims matters a lot;

(4) hype created and stoked by the media is essential for any good Silicon valley start-up story especially if the central character is a misunderstood young genius;

(5) an 'eye-pooping' valuation; Theranos was worth $1.1 billion in 2014.

According to Cohan these five ingredients made Theranos a "made-for-Hollywood Silicon Valley scandal".[71] It was the conducive context needed to complete the toxic triangle of hubristic leadership.

It's ironic that the Theranos whistle-blower Tyler Shultz is now running his own biotech start-up and is having to pitch to potential investors. He inevitably finds himself in the position of having to make grand promises: "I'm under pressure to exaggerate technology claims, exaggerate revenue projection claims. Sometimes investors will straight-up tell you, you need to double, quadruple, or 10x any revenue projection you think is realistic". The parallels with his notorious former boss are palpable for Shultz and to the rest of us; he can "see how this environment could create an Elizabeth Holmes".[72] But faking it 'til you make it doesn't fly in a Federal court.

The Next Steve Jobs?

Steve Jobs is the Silicon Valley icon and the epitome of Silicon Valley culture. He was the embodiment of a strong entrepreneurial orientation; he gravitated towards bold, and sometimes extreme strategic choices through his innovativeness, proactiveness, and risk-taking behaviours. A downside of his entrepreneurialism was that he was inclined towards arrogance, over-confidence, over-ambition, undermining others, unpredictability, and even recklessness.[73] This made him difficult to work with but was Jobs a hubristic leader? Ben Laker and colleagues in their book *Too Proud to Lead* (2021) observed that Jobs' confidence, belief, boldness, and vision all mattered in the creation of the Macintosh computer, iMac, iTunes, iPod, iPhone, iPad, and Pixar, but what needs to be guarded against "is when it becomes all-encompassing, and a leader fails to see the blind spots to which s/he has become oblivious".[74] Mathew Hayward in his book *Ego Check: Why Executive Hubris is Wrecking Companies and Careers and How to Avoid the Trap* (2007), offered Jobs and Apple as a case study in executive hubris. Jobs relied too heavily on his own gut, he over-identified with the business. "Jobs was Apple", and crucially no-one "bought into the myth" of Steve Jobs more that Jobs did himself.[75]

Jobs is an influential background figure in the Theranos story. In her stream-of-consciousness diary Holmes wrote about "becoming Steve Jobs".[76] She was lauded by the press as "the next Steve Jobs". For example, Inc. said that "you'd have to look really hard not to see Steve Jobs in Elizabeth Holmes. Both Holmes and Jobs were loners as kids. As a teenager, Jobs discovered Plato; Holmes favoured Roman emperor-philosopher Marcus Aurelius".[77] Like Jobs, Holmes had huge ambitions and dropped out of university. It seems that she did so because the extra two years of study required to complete her chemical engineering degree would have held her back from realising her entrepreneurial dream. It's been commented that she comported herself in a 'Jobsian couture' and lifestyle by adopting a black turtleneck sweater uniform, working long hours, and eschewing vacations.[78] The ghost of being "the next Steve Jobs" has cast a long shadow over the Holmes-Theranos affair. But perhaps the comparison is unfair. Jobs was self-aware enough to know when he was in over his head and hired people to be around him, like Steve Wozniak, who had the experience and expertise to compensate for and complement his shortcomings.[79]

Avoiding Exposure by Managing Complicit Followers and Conducive Contexts

A 'fake it 'til you make it' and 'move fast and break things' culture can be a fertile breeding ground for hubris.[80] On the other hand, there are plenty of examples of tech unicorns who have worked with such cultures and didn't fake it, break things, or succumb to hubris. Airbnb's founder Brian Chesky didn't get investors on board with his venture until he was able to prove that renters were interested, the business could earn revenues, and the market had growth potential. The capital for setting up Google came from investors who were experts in the computer industry and could understand the potential behind the algorithm. Amazon started out with funding from Bezos and his family and other small investors and got venture capital from Silicon Valley only after he had proof of concept.[81]

In the case of Theranos, had they participated in scientific peer review to validate the science behind the technology the problems might have been spotted early on. This could have driven the business to be more open about what was possible and change course or cut its losses and get out before things went too far. Entrepreneurs need the freedom to dream, and it's easy with hindsight to deride Theranos' aim to disrupt biotech for the good of patients. But entrepreneurs also need checks and balances and a hubris-resilient corporate culture to keep their dreams on track, especially when they find themselves in a context that is conducive to hubris.[82]

In contexts that are conducive to hype and exaggeration and where complicit followers are easy to find entrepreneurs need to exercise the practical wisdom to be able to tread the fine line between positive thinking and unwarranted over-enthusiasm. This is a matter of balancing deficiencies and excesses, and as we shall see in Chapter 9, this is not something new (it will come as no surprise to learn that the Ancient Greeks warned against it with their aphorism 'nothing to excess') but it is nonetheless a vital part of CEO competence and of a company culture that is resilient to the potential effects of hubristic leadership.

The originators of the toxic triangle model, Art Padilla and colleagues, offered some suggestions for how to manage the relationships between leaders, followers, and context so that destructive outcomes are kept in abeyance:

(1) *Selection processes:* use effective procedures to identify potentially hubristic individuals in the recruitment and selection of leaders using proper psychometric assessments of dark-side personality traits such as narcissism and Machiavellianism, to which we can add hubris. That said, this is easier said than done because charismatic and narcissistic individuals are often highly skilled in convincing selection panels of their potential worth to the company. The same is true of some politicians and their electorate;

(2) *Identify the undesirable as well as the desirable:* expanding leader competencies beyond those which are desirable (which is where the focus lies currently) to dysfunctional behaviours which are deemed to be undesirable and using these as a filter in leader selection or for remediation in leader development. Stakeholders need to be alert to the darker and more destructive side of leadership;

(3) *Manage culture:* a culture of empowerment and a climate of psychological safety could enable stronger and less compliant followers and reward leaders who develop the leadership potential of their subordinates, for example, by making follower empowerment or development an explicit criterion for the job of leader and for leader's promotion;

(4) *Effective oversight:* because hubris emanates from the top of organisations, strong oversight by a committed, competent, strong, and independent board of directors is necessary with inputs into performance reviews and succession processes, and with the power to sanction the CEO;

(5) *Being extra-vigilant in turbulent times:* because hubris somehow seems to thrive in volatile, uncertain, complex, and ambiguous situations, extra vigilance is called for during such times on the part of boards (in the case of businesses) and cabinets (in the case of democratic governments)

since it is they who have the power to intervene and avoid exposing corporations and civil society to hubris hazard.[83]

A moral of most too-good-to-be-true tales is that if a proposition seems too good to be true it usually will be. Ambitious start-up entrepreneurs routinely promise 'moon-shots' and regularly fail; this is accepted in the world of business venturing. Investors, customers, and indeed voters need to be sceptical of exaggerated claims even if the business person or politician themselves appears to have bought into them. Whether self-delusion (see Chapter 6) played a role in the Theranos case may never be known, either way the Theranos toxic triangle was a tangled web that took on a life of its own. It ended up ensnaring all of its main players one way or another. In 2015 *Forbes* estimated Elizabeth Holmes' net worth to be $45 billion; in June 2016 *Forbes* re-estimated her Real Time Net Worth to be $0.[84] For Holmes, with the prospect of over 11 years in jail, the costs of hubris were much more than financial.

Complicit Followers: Signs to Look Out For

(1) Tacit support for the leader by conformers who are prepared to simply stand by;
(2) Explicit support for the leader by colluders who are prepared to connive actively;
(3) Leader has become a media celebrity;
(4) Leader is given free rein by an ineffective board or cabinet.

Conducive Context: Signs to Look Out For

(1) 'Fake it 'till you make it' attitude is acceptable;
(2) Grandeur of leader's vision over-rules ethical concerns;
(3) Leading a culture that's conducive to hype, over-claiming, and 'greed is good' mentality.

Notes

1   Sadler-Smith, E. (2019). *Hubristic leadership*. London: SAGE.
2   Padilla, A., Hogan, R., & Kaiser, R. B. (2007). The toxic triangle: Destructive leaders, susceptible followers, and conducive environments. *The Leadership Quarterly*, 18(3), 176–194.

3 Northouse, P. (2012). *Leadership*. London: SAGE.
4 The 'toxic triangle of destructive leadership' model was pioneered by Padilla et al. (2007) and later adapted with minor modifications as a 'toxic triangle of hubristic leadership' model by Sadler-Smith (2019), see: Padilla, A., Hogan, R., & Kaiser, R. B. (2007). The toxic triangle: Destructive leaders, susceptible followers, and conducive environments. *The Leadership Quarterly*, 18(3), 176–194; Sadler-Smith, E. (2019). *Hubristic leadership*. London: SAGE.
5 Auletta, K. (2014). Blood, simpler. *The New Yorker*, December 8. Available at: https://www.newyorker.com/magazine/2014/12/15/blood-simpler
6 Bulgarella, C. (2019). Mirage or vision? Four blind spots at the core of Theranos' failure. *Forbes*, April 22. Available at: https://www.forbes.com/sites/caterinabulgarella/2019/04/22/mirage-or-vision-four-blind-spots-at-the-core-of-theranos-failure/?sh=6c5b019a70bc
7 Torres, M. (2022). 4 ways Elizabeth Holmes manipulated her Theranos employees. *HuffPost*, November 18. Available at: https://www.huffingtonpost.co.uk/entry/elizabeth-holmes-office-employees_l_5c92abe3e4b01b14od351b6f
8 Stevenson, A. (2015). World's youngest female billionaire—next Steve Jobs? *CNBC Mad Money with Jim Cramer*, September 23. Available at: https://www.cnbc.com/2015/09/23/worlds-youngest-female-billionaire-next-steve-jobs.html
9 Cohan, P. (2015). Theranos Is Made-For-Hollywood Silicon Valley Scandal. *Forbes*, October 16. Available at: https://www.forbes.com/sites/petercohan/2015/10/16/theranos-is-made-for-hollywood-silicon-valley-scandal/?sh=1cc1df2f86ee
10 Bilton, N. (2016). Exclusive: How Elizabeth Holmes's house of cards came tumbling down. *Vanity Fair*, September 6. Available at: https://www.vanityfair.com/news/2016/09/elizabeth-holmes-theranos-exclusive
11 Bilton, N. 2016. How Elizabeth Holmes' house of cards came tumbling down. *Vanity Fair*, September 6, 2016.
12 Auletta, K. (2014). Blood, simpler. *The New Yorker*, December 8. Available at: https://www.newyorker.com/magazine/2014/12/15/blood-simpler
13 Chartr. (2021). Theranos: The rise and fall of a company that promised to change the world. *Chartr Newsletter*, September 1. Available at: https://www.chartr.co/stories/2021-09-01-1-rise-and-fall-of-theranos
14 D'Onfro, J.(2015). Bill Maris: Here's why Google Ventures didn't invest in Theranos. *Insider*, October 20. Available at: https://www.businessinsider.com/bill-maris-explains-why-gv-didnt-invest-in-theranos-2015-10?r=US&IR=T
15 Bergen, M. (2015). Theranos CEO Holmes: We turned down Google Ventures, not the other way around. *Vox*, October 21. Available at: https://www.vox.com/2015/10/21/11619842/theranos-ceo-holmes-we-turned-down-google-ventures-not-the-other-way

16 Carreyrou, J.(2018). A look inside Theranos' dysfunctional corporate culture. *Wired*, May 21. Available at: https://www.wired.com/story/a-new-look-inside-theranos-dysfunctional-corporate-culture

17 Business Insider. (2019). How Theranos pulled off its $9 billion scandal (video). Available at: https://www.youtube.com/watch?v=-kbja1El1kQ

18 Furlow, B. (2022). Theranos: The proof that public regulation matters. *The Lancet*, January 14. Available at: https://www.thelancet.com/pdfs/journals/lanonc/PIIS1470-2045(22)00024-9.pdf; Santos Rutschman, A. (2021). How Theranos' faulty blood tests got to market – and what that shows about gaps in FDA regulation. *The Conversation*, October 5. Available at: https://theconversation.com/how-theranos-faulty-blood-tests-got-to-market-and-what-that-shows-about-gaps-in-fda-regulation-168050

19 Diamandis, E. P., & Bouras, N. (2018). Hubris and sciences. National Institutes of Health (NIH). National Library of Medicine. *F1000Research*, 7. doi: 10.12688/f1000research.13848.1

20 Carreyrou, J. (2016) Theranos whistle-blower shook the company—and his family. *The Wall Street Journal*, November 16. Available at: https://www.wsj.com/articles/theranos-whistleblower-shook-the-companyand-his-family-1479335963

21 Gray, N. (2016). Federal inspection report reveals major problems at Theranos lab. *Biopharma Dive*, April 1. Available at: https://www.biopharmadive.com/news/federal-inspection-report-reveals-major-problems-at-theranos-lab/416680

22 *The Wall Street Journal*. (2021). Theranos and Elizabeth Holmes: History of the WSJ investigation. *The Wall Street Journal*, August 24. Available at: https://www.wsj.com/articles/theranos-and-elizabeth-holmes-history-of-the-wsj-investigation-11629815129

23 Bilton, N. (2016). Exclusive: How Elizabeth Holmes's house of cards came tumbling down. *Vanity Fair*, September 6. Available at: https://www.vanityfair.com/news/2016/09/elizabeth-holmes-theranos-exclusive

24 Bilton, N. (2019). In cold blood. *Vanity Fair*, April. Available at: https://archive.vanityfair.com/article/2019/4/in-cold-blood

25 Allyn, B. (2022). Read what a judge told Elizabeth Holmes before sending her to prison for 11 years. *National Public Radio (NPR)*, November 23. Available at: https://www.npr.org/2022/11/23/1138988456/read-what-a-judge-told-elizabeth-holmes-before-sending-her-to-prison-for-11-year

26 Sadler-Smith, E. (2019). *Hubristic leadership*. London: SAGE.

27 Conger, J. A., & Kanungo, R. N. (1987). Toward a behavioral theory of charismatic leadership in organizational settings. *Academy of Management Review*, 12(4): 637–647.

28 CBS. (2022). Theranos whistle-blower Tyler Shultz: Elizabeth Holmes 'a very, very charismatic person'. *CBS Bay Area*, January 4. Available at: https://www.cbsnews.com/sanfrancisco/news/theranos-whistleblower-tyler-schultz-elizabeth-holmes-is-a-very-very-charismatic-person

29 Mio, J. S., Riggio, R. E., Levin, S., & Reese, R. (2005). Presidential leadership and charisma: The effects of metaphor. *The Leadership Quarterly*, 16(2), 287–294.

30 A writer in *Forbes* magazine speculated that groupthink (where a group reaches an uncritical consensus which undermines effective decision making) had taken over at Theranos.

31 Karp, H. B., & Jackson, K. A. (2004). Hubris: A gestalt alternative to groupthink. *Gestalt Review*, 8(1), 18–34.

32 O'Reilly, C. A., & Chatman, J. A. (2020). Transformational leader or narcissist? How grandiose narcissists can create and destroy organizations and institutions. *California Management Review*, 62(3): 5–27.

33 Cohan, P. (2019). 4 startling insights into Elizabeth Holmes from psychiatrist who's known her since childhood. *Forbes*, February 17. Available at: https://www.forbes.com/sites/petercohan/2019/02/17/4-startling-insights-into-elizabeth-holmes-from-psychiatrist-whos-known-here-since-childhood/?sh=7b0b9c95366b

34 Leonard, T. (2022). How DID she fool them all? *The Daily Mail*, January 4. Available at: https://www.dailymail.co.uk/news/article-10369509/How-DID-Elizabeth-Holmes-fool-writes-TOM-LEONARD.html

35 Mio, J. S., Riggio, R. E., Levin, S., & Reese, R. (2005). Presidential leadership and charisma: The effects of metaphor. *The Leadership Quarterly*, 16(2), 287–294.

36 Graen, G. B., & Uhl-Bien, M. (1995). Relationship-based approach to leadership: Development of leader-member exchange (LMX) theory of leadership over 25 years: Applying a multi-level multi-domain perspective. *The Leadership Quarterly*, 6(2), 219–247.

37 Powell, A. (2004). Kellerman describes, descries 'bad leadership'. *The Harvard Gazette*, October 28. Available at: https://news.harvard.edu/gazette/story/2004/10/kellerman-describes-decries-bad-leadership/#:~:text=Without%20followers%2C%20after%20all%2C%20leaders,bad%20leaders%20and%20bad%20followers.%E2%80%9D

38 Kellerman, B. (2007). What every leader needs to know about followers. *Harvard Business Review*, December. Available at: https://hbr.org/2007/12/what-every-leader-needs-to-know-about-followers

39 Padilla, A., Hogan, R., & Kaiser, R. B. (2007). The toxic triangle: Destructive leaders, susceptible followers, and conducive environments. *The Leadership Quarterly*, 18(3), 176–194.

40 Thoroughgood, C. N., Padilla, A., Hunter, S. T., & Tate, B. W. (2012). The susceptible circle: A taxonomy of followers associated with destructive leadership. *The Leadership Quarterly*, 23(5), 897–917.

41 Thoroughgood, C. N., Padilla, A., Hunter, S. T., & Tate, B. W. (2012). The susceptible circle: A taxonomy of followers associated with destructive leadership. *The Leadership Quarterly*, 23(5), 897–917.

42 Carreyrou, J. (2018). *Bad blood: Secrets and lies in a silicon valley start-up.* New York: Alfred A. Knopf.

43 Templeton, A. (2022). How do destructive leaders attract followers? *Psychology Today*, March 24. Available at: https://www.psychologytoday.com/us/blog/the-leader-within/202203/how-do-destructive-leaders-attract-followers

44 Paul, K. (2021). Elizabeth Holmes: From Silicon Valley's female icon to disgraced CEO on trial. *The Guardian*, August 29. Available at: https://www.theguardian.com/technology/2021/aug/29/elizabeth-holmes-from-silicon-valleys-female-icon-to-disgraced-ceo-on-trial

45 Paul, K. (2021). Elizabeth Holmes: From Silicon Valley's female icon to disgraced CEO on trial. *The Guardian*, 29 August. Available at: https://www.theguardian.com/technology/2021/aug/29/elizabeth-holmes-from-silicon-valleys-female-icon-to-disgraced-ceo-on-trial

46 Institute of Directors. (2021). What is the role of the board? *Institute of Directors, Company Structure Factsheet.* London: IoD. Available at: https://www.iod.com/resources/factsheets/company-structure/what-is-the-role-of-the-board

47 Cliffe, S. (2017). The board view: Directors must balance all interests. *Harvard Business Review*, May–June. Available at: https://hbr.org/2017/05/the-board-view-directors-must-balance-all-interests

48 Reingold, J. (2015). Theranos' board: Plenty of political connections, little relevant expertise. *Fortune Magazine*, October 15. Available at: https://fortune.com/2015/10/15/theranos-board-leadership Accessed January 11, 2023.

49 Solomon, A. (2023). POV: Justice served for Elizabeth Holmes, but what about Theranos' board? *Fast Company*, June 1. Available at: https://www.fastcompany.com/90903580/pov-justice-served-for-elizabeth-holmes-but-what-about-theranos-board

50 Reingold, J. (2015). Theranos' board: Plenty of political connections, little relevant expertise. *Fortune Magazine*, October 15. Available at: https://fortune.com/2015/10/15/theranos-board-leadership Accessed January 11, 2023.

51 Wasley, P. (2016). The Theranos Crisis. Where was the Board? *Forbes Magazine*, April 27. Available at: https://www.forbes.com/sites/groupthink/

2016/04/27/the-theranos-crisis-where-was-the-board/?sh=237a3e03c58e. Accessed January 11, 2023.

52 Carreyrou, J. (2016). Theranos whistle-blower shook the company—and his family. *The Wall Street Journal*, November 16. Available at: https://www.wsj. com/articles/theranos-whistleblower-shook-the-companyand-his-family-1479335963

53 Jurkiewicz, N. (2022). What went wrong with Theranos. *ICDM Pulse*, July 28. Available at: https://pulse.icdm.com.my/article/what-went-wrong-with-theranos

54 Solomon, A. (2023). POV: Justice served for Elizabeth Holmes, but what about Theranos' board? *Fast Company*, June 1. Available at: https://www. fastcompany.com/90903580/pov-justice-served-for-elizabeth-holmes-but-what-about-theranos-board

55 Solomon, A. (2023). POV: Justice served for Elizabeth Holmes, but what about Theranos' board? *Fast Company*, June 1. Available at: https://www.fastcom pany.com/90903580/pov-justice-served-for-elizabeth-holmes-but-what-about-theranos-board

56 Justia US Law. (1973). *Federal Securities Legal Representative. P 93,748 Securities and Exchange Commission, Plaintiff-appellee, v. Glenn W. Turner Enterprises, Inc., et al., Defendants-appellants, 474 F.2d 476 (9th Cir. 1973)*. Available at: https://law.justia.com/cases/federal/appellate-courts/F2/474/476/124744/

57 O'Brien, S. (2019). The only time it's okay to 'fake it till you make it'. *Forbes*, February 21. Available at: https://www.forbes.com/sites/susan obrien/2019/02/21/the-only-time-its-ok-to-fake-it-till-you-make-it/? sh=604bb83f4f60

58 Carreyrou, J. (2018). *Bad blood: Secrets and lies in a silicon valley start-up*. New York: Alfred A. Knopf.

59 Way Back Machine. (2013). *Unparalleled transparency*. Available at: https:// web.archive.org/web/20160622193253/https://www.theranos.com/ test-menu

60 Jurkiewicz, N. (2022).What went wrong with Theranos? *ICDM Pulse*, July 28. Available at: https://pulse.icdm.com.my/article/what-went-wrong-with-theranos

61 Lewis, A. et al. 2012. Drawing the line somewhere: An experimental study of moral compromise. *Journal of Economic Psychology*, 33: 718–725.

62 Bulgarella, C. (2019). Mirage or vision? Four blind spots at the core of Theranos' failure. *Forbes*, April 22. Available at: https://www.forbes.com/ sites/caterinabulgarella/2019/04/22/mirage-or-vision-four-blind-spots-at-the-core-of-theranos-failure/?sh=6c5b019a70bc

63 Ucbasaran, D., Shepherd, D. A., Lockett, A., & Lyon, S. J. (2013). Life after business failure: The process and consequences of business failure for entrepreneurs. *Journal of Management*, 39(1), 163–202.

64 Lerman, R. (2021). Elizabeth Holmes court date puts Silicon Valley's 'fake it 'til you make it' culture on trial. *The Washington Post*, August 21. Available at: https://www.washingtonpost.com/technology/2021/08/31/theranos-elizabeth-holmes-trial-silicon-valley/

65 Lex. (2022). Five investor lessons from the downfall of Elizabeth Holmes. *Lex Opinion, The Financial Times*, January 4. Available at: https://www.ft.com/content/1da94cb8-4224-461e-baeb-de21d4af6e64

66 *The New York Times*. (2022). Five takeaways from the verdict in the Elizabeth Holmes trial. *The New York Times*, January 4. Available at: https://www.nytimes.com/2022/01/04/business/elizabeth-holmes-verdict-takeaways.html

67 Allyn, B. (2022). Read what a judge told Elizabeth Holmes before sending her to prison for 11 years. *National Public Radio (NPR) Technology*, November 23. Available at: https://www.npr.org/2022/11/23/1138988456/read-what-a-judge-told-elizabeth-holmes-before-sending-her-to-prison-for-11-year

68 Staff Reporter. (2022). Elizabeth Holmes' ex-boyfriend sentenced to nearly 13 years in prison for Theranos fraud. *The Daily Telegraph*, December 8. Available at: https://www.telegraph.co.uk/world-news/2022/12/08/elizabeth-holmes-ex-boyfriend-sentenced-nearly-13-years-prison

69 Alon-Beck, A. (2021). The rise and fall of startup darling Elizabeth Holmes. *Forbes*, September 21. Available at: https://www.forbes.com/sites/anatalonbeck/2021/09/02/the-rise-and-fall-of-startup-darling-elizabeth-holmes/?sh=293a2b9a357a

70 Cohan, P. (2015). Theranos is made-for-Hollywood Silicon Valley scandal. *Forbes*, October 16. Available at: https://www.forbes.com/sites/petercohan/2015/10/16/theranos-is-made-for-hollywood-silicon-valley-scandal/?sh=1cc1df2f86ee

71 Cohan, P. (2015). Theranos is made-for-Hollywood Silicon Valley scandal. *Forbes*, October 16. Available at: https://www.forbes.com/sites/petercohan/2015/10/16/theranos-is-made-for-hollywood-silicon-valley-scandal/?sh=1cc1df2f86ee

72 Allyn, B. (2022). Theranos whistle-blower celebrated Elizabeth Holmes verdict by 'popping champagne'. *NPR Technology*, January 5. Available at: https://www.npr.org/2022/01/05/1070474663/theranos-whistleblower-tyler-shultz-elizabeth-holmes-verdict-champagne

73 Chatterjee, A., & Hambrick, D. C. (2007). It's all about me: Narcissistic chief executive officers and their effects on company strategy and performance. *Administrative Science Quarterly*, 52(3), 351–386; Wales, W. J., Patel,

P. C., & Lumpkin, G. T. (2013). In pursuit of greatness: CEO narcissism, entrepreneurial orientation, and firm performance variance. *Journal of Management Studies*, 50(6), 1041–1069.

74 Laker, B., Cobb, D., & Trehan, R. (2021). *Too proud to lead*. London: Bloomsbury, p.67.

75 Hayward, M. (2007). *Ego check: Why executive hubris is wrecking companies and careers and how to avoid the trap*. Kaplan Publishing: Chicago, pp.61 & 69.

76 Khorram, Y. (2021). Elizabeth Holmes wrote personal notes to herself about 'becoming Steve Jobs' as Theranos collapse began. *CNBC Tech*, September 29. Available at: https://www.cnbc.com/2021/09/29/elizabeth-holmes-wrote-personal-notes-to-herself-about-becoming-steve-jobs.html

77 Weisul, K. (2015). How playing the long game made Elizabeth Holmes a billionaire. *Inc.*, October. Available at: https://www.inc.com/magazine/201510/kimberly-weisul/the-longest-game.html

78 Bilton, N. (2019). In cold blood. *Vanity Fair*, April. Available at: https://archive.vanityfair.com/article/2019/4/in-cold-blood

79 Jurkiewicz, N. (2022). What went wrong with Theranos? *ICDM Pulse*, 28 July. Available at: https://pulse.icdm.com.my/article/what-went-wrong-with-theranos

80 Simon, M. (2022). 5 Lessons cell cultured meat companies can learn from the Theranos verdict. *Forbes*, January 6. Available at: https://www.forbes.com/sites/michelesimon/2022/01/06/5-lessons-cell-cultured-meat-companies-can-learn-from-the-theranos-verdict/?sh=8873f6c19472

81 Rao, D. (2021). Fake it till you make it: is this one more lie from Silicon Valley . . . Like Theranos? *Forbes*, September 15. Available at: https://www.forbes.com/sites/dileeprao/2021/09/15/fake-it-till-you-make-it-is-this-one-more-lie-from-silicon-valley-like-theranos/?sh=767df898134e

82 Korman, J. (2021). Theranos is a cautionary tale that shouldn't dampen enthusiasm for entrepreneurs who dream big. *Forbes*, October 21. Available at: https://www.forbes.com/sites/forbescoachescouncil/2021/10/21/theranos-is-a-cautionary-tale-that-shouldnt-dampen-enthusiasm-for-entrepreneurs-who-dream-big/?sh=a7125cb1c65c

83 Padilla, A., Hogan, R., & Kaiser, R. B. (2007). The toxic triangle: Destructive leaders, susceptible followers, and conducive environments. *The Leadership Quarterly*, 18(3), 176–194.

84 Forbes. (2023). Elizabeth Holmes. *Forbes Profile*, May 8. Available at: https://www.forbes.com/profile/elizabeth-holmes/?sh=52d2d147a7b7

4

UNBRIDLED INTUITION

Intuition

Intuition is an important leadership skill. In situations that are fast-moving and where there simply isn't enough information available or the time to gather the necessary facts, intuition may be they only thing a leader has to rely on. The economist, banker, and former Governor of the Bank of England, Mark Carney, argued that effective leaders are uniquely able to instinctively assess the nuances of the context in which their organisation operates, and that they do so by "developing good intuitions about global developments and shifting technologies". Another economist, John Maynard Keynes, also held intuition in high regard. Keynes said of Isaac Newton that "his pre-eminence is due to his muscles of intuition being the strongest and most enduring with which a man has ever been gifted".[1] Clearly, intuition is a powerful tool for leaders and decision-makers, however it can, in the wrong hands and in a context of the intoxication of power, also be perilous. But the question of if and when to 'go with your gut' is one of the most challenging decisions any leader can face.

DOI: 10.4324/9781003128427-4

Intuition, sometimes referred to as 'gut feelings' or 'gut instincts', has proven to be a slippery concept.[2] It's been defined in several ways; for example, and most simply put, intuition is 'knowing without knowing how or why you know'. A more helpful definition was provided by the doyen of decision researchers and Nobel Laureate in Economics, Herbert Simon (1916–2001) of Carnegie Mellon University: intuitions are "analyses frozen into habit and the capacity for rapid response through recognition".[3] A more up-to-date and comprehensive definition (because it incorporate feelings or 'affect') is intuitions are "affectively charged judgements that arise through rapid, non-conscious, holistic associations".[4] In other words they involve gut feelings and hunches (this is their 'affective charge'), they're quick, we don't know where they come from (because they arise non-consciously) but they seem to involve pattern recognition and pattern matching processes ('holistic associations').

Simon's definition was based on simple but ingenious experiments he conducted in the 1970s on how grandmasters take decisions in the highly analytical game of chess. Surprisingly, for a game that seems to be the epitome of rational analysis, chess grandmasters often play by intuition.[5] Simon discovered that several seconds' glance by a grandmaster at the pattern of the chess pieces in a game will suggest automatically to their highly informed mind the best next move but without any conscious awareness of how this judgement was arrived at. Grandmasters are able to play chess intuitively because:

(1) their memory holds a vast collection of patterns that have been encountered as chess problems and thought-through (i.e. analysed) previously;
(2) each pattern of pieces on the board has information associated with it about its significance in terms of threats, opportunities, and likely outcomes which in the case of chess are, to some extent, predictable for experts.

This means that grandmasters have learned what's likely to work in a given situation without the need to unpack the reasons why. These patterns are the 'holistic associations' referred to above. Grandmasters' intuitions about the best next move are 'affectively charged' in that they're accompanied by 'gut feelings' or 'hunches' that are the product of an intuitive mind whose workings are fast and non-conscious.

Chess grandmasters are experts, and amongst experts in general intuitions are built up by previous analyses. As a result of learning and experience, with timely and accurate feedback about the consequences of their choices, experts become able to recognise patterns and decide effortlessly what action is likely to work in a given situation and what the likely outcome will be. This gives them the capacity to execute rapid responses with little cognitive effort. Experts' intuitions are, to paraphrase Simon, their prior analyses of complex situations that have become frozen into habit, which gives them the capacity to respond rapidly through recognition to achieve a particular outcome (for example, winning a game of chess). This process works well in chess when the player is an expert who knows what they want to achieve.

Simon extrapolated from chess to other areas of decision-making, such as management, and concluded that intuition and its converse, analysis, are in fact two complementary aspects of an information-processing system (the human brain) that evolved to be able to both sense (by intuition) and solve (by analysis).[6] Simon also remarked that decision-makers (in which we can include CEOs and political leaders) don't have the luxury of being able to choose between analytical and intuitive approaches to problems. Instead, being an effective decision-maker means being in command of both intuition *and* analysis and deploying them as and when it's appropriate to do so. Subsequent research has shown across multiple domains, from management to the military, that experienced decision-makers are well able to take effective, high-stakes decisions using intuition. However, things can start to go awry when either of them is used in the wrong circumstances or to excess.

Far from being a paranormal 'sixth sense', experts' intuitions are deep-rooted in many years of prior learning and experience. This gives us a clue as to why intuition can sometimes get it wrong in leadership and decision-making. In this chapter we'll explore the case of a leader who arguably put too much faith in his intuitions in a geopolitical decision and which resulted in unintended, negative consequences on a global scale. The leader in question is George W. Bush and the decision is the invasion of Iraq in 2003 which arguably ranks alongside other grave hubristic errors of judgement in the military and geopolitical arena, such as Napoleon's fatal March on Moscow in 1812, and provides us with yet another lesson in hubris where "all too often, successful leaders with many positive qualities become their own worst enemies" by allowing hubris, in this case fuelled by unbridled intuition, to cloud their decision-making.[7] One of the fundamental problems is that geopolitics isn't an area that's well suited to taking decisions on the basis of gut feelings and hunches.

The Invasion of Iraq

On March 19, 2003, the USA under the leadership of President George W. Bush launched an all-out simultaneous air and ground attack on the sovereign nation of Iraq. This 'shock and awe' campaign was the precursor to a full-scale invasion by the USA and its Coalition allies (principally the UK, led by Prime Minister Tony Blair). The invasion resulted in the removal from power of Iraq's President Saddam Hussein, leader of one of the countries in the so-called 'axis of evil' (along with Iran and North Korea). Proponents of the invasion claimed that Iraq already had, or was developing, weapons of mass destruction (WMD). The invasion itself was a brief affair. The Iraqi Government collapsed and its military capitulated within a few weeks. On May 1 Bush, clad theatrically in full flying gear, landed on the aircraft carrier USS Abraham Lincoln stationed off the San Diego coast to declare, in a televised address, that it was 'mission accomplished'.

Bush's pronouncement was premature to say the least. The ensuing campaign was a drawn-out affair as were its longer-term humanitarian, social, economic, and geopolitical consequences. The deposed President Saddam Hussein was captured on December 13, 2003 by US military forces. He was executed on December 30, 2006 after being convicted of crimes against humanity by an Iraqi Special Tribunal. After a long and bloody campaign, the Iraq war ended in 2011. Estimates of the casualties vary greatly. One study by a group of American and Canadian researchers put the total number of deaths from war-related causes at almost half a million people.[8] More than 60 per cent of these deaths were directly attributable to violence; the rest were associated with the collapse of infrastructure and other indirect, war-related causes such as health and sanitation. Civilians made up the majority of the total death count. According to the US Department of Defense, over 4,000 US military personnel lost their lives and almost 32,000 were wounded in action as a result of the war.

In 2010 Nobel Prize-winning economist Joseph Stiglitz of Columbia University and his Harvard Kennedy School colleague Linda Blimes put the total cost of the war and its broader impact on the US economy at $3 trillion.[9] Stiglitz and Blimes also point to 'what-might-have-beens' and other opportunity costs, for example, if there had not been a war in Iraq, would oil prices have risen so rapidly, would the federal debt be so high, and would the economic crisis of 2008 have been so severe? Their answer to these questions is 'probably not'. The 'three-trillion-dollar war' caused multiple humanitarian crises and had significant unintended, geopolitical consequences across the region that reverberate to this day. Critics have argued that America's standing in the world might have been higher, its economy stronger, and the reputations of Bush and Blair might have been less tarnished; some believe that it may even have strengthened America's enemies.[10]

Bush's principal foreign ally in the Coalition forces was the UK under the leadership of Prime Minister Tony Blair. Bush's decision to invade and Blair's involvement were highly controversial at the time and have been ever since. Historians have judged it to be one of the worst foreign policy decisions ever taken by a US president[11] or a British prime minister. The UK's 'Chilcot (Iraq) Inquiry' into the conduct of the war and the events leading up to the UK's involvement published in 2016 concluded that:

(1) the UK chose to join the invasion of Iraq before the peaceful options for disarmament had been exhausted;
(2) military action at that time was not a last resort;
(3) judgements about the severity of the threat posed by Iraq's WMDs were presented with a certainty that was not justified;
(4) despite explicit warnings, the consequences of the invasion were underestimated;
(5) the planning and preparations for Iraq after Saddam Hussein were wholly inadequate;
(6) the government failed to achieve its own stated objectives for the war.[12]

It's regrettable that the Iraq War still greatly tarnishes Blair's otherwise good reputation.

The decision to invade the sovereign nation of Iraq is recognised widely as one of the prime examples of hubristic political leadership. According to David Owen, author of *The Hubris Syndrome, Bush, Blair and the Intoxication of Power* (2007), Bush and Blair both had an "inner certainty that they are men of destiny".[13] Buoyed up by brashness, Bush and Blair broke free of the constraints on how leaders of nations ought to behave. Owen argues that they showed contempt for the international community and acted with disregard for the wider and longer-term consequences.[14] The US president was the driving force with the British prime minister as his principal supporter.

But why did Bush decide to invade Iraq? What was it about his character and psyche that drove him to it? There are many possible answers to these questions but in order to attempt to answer them we need to understand more about Bush and how his intuition, or more accurately his unbridled intuition, influenced his decision-making and what lessons can be learned.

George W. Bush

George W. Bush was born on July 6, 1946, in New Haven, Connecticut. He was the son of the 41st US President George H. W. Bush (1924–2018). He received a bachelor's degree in history from Yale University in 1968, served as an F-102 fighter pilot in the Texas Air National Guard, and received a Master of Business Administration from Harvard Business School in 1975. Following graduation, he began a career in the oil business, and worked on his father's successful 1988 presidential campaign. In 1994, George W. Bush was elected Governor of Texas. He became the 43rd President of the USA in 2001 and, following his re-election, was sworn in for a second and final term in 2005.

Bush became a 'wartime president' following the terrorist attacks on the Twin Towers in New York on September 11, 2001 in which nearly 3,000 Americans were killed. Bush's response was to form the Department of Homeland Security and send US forces into Afghanistan to break up the Taliban and capture its leader, Osama bin Laden, who had financed, trained, and exported the terrorist teams responsible for 9/11. The Taliban was successfully disrupted. Bin Laden escaped but was later killed by US Special Forces in an attack on his compound in Abbottabad, Pakistan in May 2012. According to the White House website George W. Bush's "most controversial act was the invasion of Iraq [based] on the belief that Iraqi President Saddam Hussein posed a grave threat to the United States".[15]

So much for Bush the politician; but what about the Bush personality? His autobiography was called Decision Points, he has referred to himself as "the decider",[16] and has, by his own admission, a "habitual personality".[17] Pulitzer Prize-winning journalist Ron Suskind captured the 'Bush style' succinctly in a New York Times article shortly after the Iraq invasion: "He truly believes he's on a mission from God. Absolute faith like that overwhelms a need for analysis. The whole thing about faith is to believe things for which there is no empirical evidence".[18] The Washington Post journalist Bob Woodward (author of three books about Bush and the Iraq War: Bush at War, Plan of Attack, and State of Denial) summed up Bush's instinctive style as "his second religion".[19] Bush's instinct for intuitive decision-making resonated with an emotionally charged, 'good-versus-evil', 'either/or' discourse, it was popular and best exemplified in his State of the Union Address on January 29, 2002:

> States like [Iran, Iran and North Korea], and their terrorist allies, constitute an axis of evil, arming to threaten the peace of the world and our responsibility to history is already clear: To answer these attacks and rid the world of evil.[20]

Bush has not only been criticised legitimately, but he's also been mocked unkindly. He is famed for his idiosyncratic statements including various semantic and linguistic errors, Freudian slips, and malapropisms (so-called 'Bushisms'), for example: "Rarely is the question asked: Is our children learning?", "I think we agree, the past is over", and "They misunderestimated me". In commenting on Putin's invasion of Ukraine in 2022, he said the "absence of checks and balances in Russia and the decision of one man to launch a wholly unjustified and brutal invasion of Iraq. I mean, of Ukraine".[21] In 2006 the Princeton University professor, and one of America's leading historians, Sean Wilentz, asked in an article in Rolling Stone magazine whether Bush was "the worst president in US history?".[22] In a poll of US presidents made one year after he left office Bush found himself in the bottom five at 39th, however more recently, Bush, the 43rd president, was literally 'trumped' by the 45th president.[23]

Scholars of political science have commented that Bush's "moral certainty" was combined with a tendency for visceral gut reaction over cognitive complexity and reflection[24] and this may have contributed to his hubris.[25] Bush's friend and ally, Tony Blair, maintained that the idea that Bush was stupid was itself a stupid misconception. He described Bush as being "straightforward and direct" and having "great intuition" about what he thought was the right thing to do.[26] Bush valued political instinct and intuition both in himself and in others, he remarked that: "People have either got instincts or they don't".[27] In this respect Bush and Blair were alike. For instance, Blair was described by his colleague and confidante Labour MP Peter Mandelson as having the "political gift" of intuition "in spades".[28] Instinct and intuition are often claimed to be "essential leadership tools" in business management[29] politics. As noted earlier, former Governor of the Bank of England, Mark Carney, thinks that effective leaders have to have an intuition for the bigger picture,[30] and former Prime Minister of New Zealand, Jacinda Ardern, has said that when she had to deal with terror attacks "very little of what I have done has been deliberate. It's intuitive".[31]

However, intuition has its downsides, which we will explore below, and following their instincts and intuitions seems to have led Bush (and Blair) into the decision to invade Iraq without:

(1) objectively establishing the facts about WMDs (instead of relying on dubious intelligence compiled into a so-called "dodgy dossier" in the case of the UK government)[32];
(2) any apparent foresight for the longer-term consequences of regime change (such as the insurrections by Isis fundamentalists across the region);
(3) any clear idea about what the end game in such a politically, socially, economically, and culturally complex situation would look like.

If instinct and intuition are such valuable leadership commodities why did they take Bush and Blair so seriously off course, and why should 'going-with-your-gut' be such a risk factor in managing the hubris hazard? The answer is because expertise is built up by learning and experience. Herbert Simon described intuition as analysis frozen into habit. This gives us some clue as to why intuition appears to have been an unreliable decision tool in the case of the Iraq invasion and prompts us to ask: how many prior experiences of invading sovereign nations with the aim of regime change did Bush have to go on? Furthermore, even though Bush had prior military experience as an air force pilot he hadn't served in any defence or foreign policy role in national government. All this points in the direction of Bush's decision to trust his gut as being questionable to say the least. He didn't have an established track-record in invading sovereign nations, changing incumbent regimes, and managing the longer-term consequences. That said this isn't something that any political leader is likely to have the requisite experience in, moreover the social, economic, political, and cultural complexity of the situation begs the question of whether in such a situation it was appropriate to make an intuitive judgement in the first place. It probably was not. The reasons why are explored below.

Why Intuition Gets It Right, and Wrong

From the point of view of the psychology of the individual, how can intuition be so right in some situations (such as chess) and so wrong in others (such as invasions)? One of the easiest ways to understand how intuition works, and its relationship to analysis, is to think of human beings as having two minds in one brain—an 'intuitive mind' and an 'analytical mind'. This 'two-minds model' has been around in psychology since at least the 1970s (psychologists refer to it as 'dual-process' or 'dual-systems' theory). Its ancestry can in fact be found in the work of one of the founders of psychology, William James (he referred to intuition as a 'secondary consciousness' that lies behind our primary consciousness) and goes back even further to the writings of ancient Greek philosophers (who distinguished between intellectual knowledge and intuitive knowledge).

Like many of the best ideas, dual-process theory is quite simple. The intuitive mind (which, by the way, isn't in the 'right brain') is a fast, parallel processor that operates using pattern recognition; its workings are nonconscious and context-dependent and it communicates to us via feelings. It's sometimes referred to as 'System 1'. The analytical mind (which isn't in the 'left brain') is a slow, serial processor that works by abstract reasoning; its operations are conscious and independent of the context, and it communicates to us via words or other symbols. It's sometimes referred to as 'System 2'.[33]

The intuitive mind is good at sensing, whereas the analytical mind is good at solving.[34] Each was designed by nature for these two general purposes. When intuition and analysis are used by the right person, in the right place, and at the right time they work well both individually and in combination. It's when intuition is used to excess or allowed to take over and crowd out analysis in situations that it's not well suited to or isn't held in check by analysis that decision-making can become biased, over-confident, and even reckless. When intuition is let off the leash at the wrong time, in the wrong place, and by the wrong person things can start go badly wrong. One of the reasons why the Iraq invasion went so wrong was that Bush's intuitions were both flawed and unbridled.[35]

Intuition is a conundrum and a paradox: it's both powerful and perilous, it can both help and hinder the decision-maker and be both their friend and foe. Exercised by the right person, at the right time, under the right circumstances intuition helps leaders to take quick and effective high-stakes decisions in time-pressured and information-poor situations. Exercised by the wrong person, at the wrong time, under the wrong circumstances it hinders decision-making, leads to biased decisions, and can end up derailing decision-makers. When that person is a powerful and previously successful leader in an unstable and uncertain situation unbridled intuition can hasten destructive, and sometimes disastrous, outcomes.

Heuristics and Biases

Intuition can get it wrong when it's used as a mental short cut (also known as a 'heuristic') in order to solve problems that it wasn't designed to solve in the first place. This can lead to biased decision-making. In the 1970s Daniel Kahneman (who was awarded the Nobel Prize in Economics for his work in this area in 2002) and Amos Tversky (1937–1996) discovered that the automatic and unconscious use of heuristics produces systematic errors of judgement (meaning that they occur consistently in different situations) which results in biased decisions. This phenomenon is the cornerstone of what's become known as the heuristics and biases research programme. In their original experiments they used what has become probably the most famous problem in psychology, the 'Linda Problem', to show how wrong our intuitive judgements can be. The Linda Problem goes like this:

> Linda is 31 years old, single, outspoken, and very bright. She majored in philosophy. As a student, she was deeply concerned with issues of discrimination and social justice, and also participated in anti-nuclear demonstrations.

The task is as follows: 'Based on this description, is Linda more likely to be: Option 1, a bank teller; or Option 2, a bank teller who is active in the feminist movement?' When asked to judge which is more likely, Option 1 or Option 2, most people, including students at America's most prestigious universities, choose the incorrect answer Option 2. The reason they do so is because they use similarity to a prototype to judge probability intuitively rather than analytically (i.e. by thinking through the logic and the maths). This is a mistake. Option 2 cannot be more likely than Option 1 because 'bank tellers who are active in the feminist movement' is a subset of 'bank tellers'. There must be less of them. This becomes clear if we imagine it as a Venn diagram. In terms of simple numbers, and hence probabilities, Option 1 must be more likely than Option 2.

Most people give the incorrect answer because in this simple but ingenious experiment the intuitive mind is being enticed to make a judgement about the relative probabilities of two options based on similarity. That's why most people judge Linda incorrectly. The intuitive mind didn't evolve to solve probabilities, its function is to simply sense similarities to prototypes and judge likelihoods imprecisely on the basis of concrete experiences rather than mathematical abstractions. In terms of how similar Linda is to the protype of a feminist bank teller, the intuitive mind arrives on the basis of experience at what it considers to be a reasonable judgement of the likelihood that Linda is a feminist bank teller. Even though Option 2 is plausible (and hence usable), it's not probable (and hence is incorrect in this instance). This is known as the representativeness heuristic (there are various other types of heuristics such as anchoring and adjustment, the affect heuristic, etc.). When offered this explanation many people are still unmoved and prefer to stick to their intuition that Linda is more likely to be *both* a banker teller *and* an active feminist.

Intuition gets it wrong in terms of probability because the intuitive mind substitutes an easy-to-answer question ('How similar is Linda to my prototype of a feminist bank teller?') for a harder-to-answer question ('What is the probability that Linda is a feminist bank teller?'). This is called 'attribute substitution'. We'll never know, but perhaps in Bush's mind Saddam Hussein fitted his prototype of an evil dictator who was highly likely to have been involved in the development of WMDs. To Bush's, and many other people's, intuitive mind this was entirely plausible and even probable. The easy-to-answer question was 'Is Saddam Hussein an evil dictator who's likely to have WMDs?'; the harder-to-answer question was 'Has Saddam Hussein actually developed WMDs?' This thinking process is shown in Figure 4.1 below.

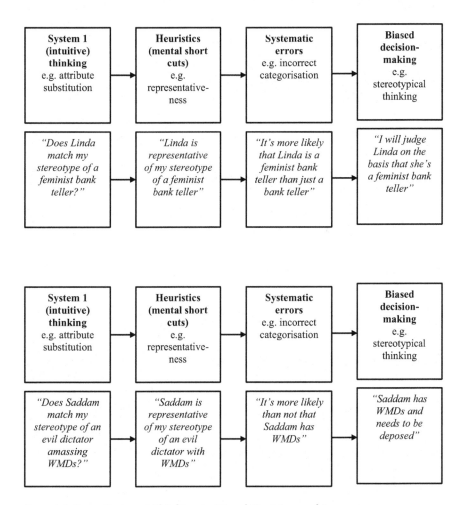

Figure 4.1 From System 1 Thinking to Biased Decision-making

Because the intuitive mind prefers to sense similarities to prototypes using a mental short cut, the easy-to-answer question ended up being the question that got answered: 'Saddam Hussein is evil and has developed WMDs'. This simple response then determined what was to be done: 'Saddam Hussein and his regime must be removed from power'. The heuristic, by definition, didn't take into account the political, religious, and ethnic complexities of the situation in Iraq and the wider region. The fact that the heuristic may also have been used as a convenient excuse for American neo-conservatives' long-held objective to change the regime is also part of the bigger picture.

This final point is pertinent: it's worth bearing in mind that the Iraq invasion is more complex than considering Bush's behaviour alone would suggest; a Republican neo-conservative ideology which had long-hankered for regime change in Iraq, together with complicit followers, and a conducive context also played important roles.[36] The Bush mindset, the complicit followers (i.e., Dick Cheney, Condoleezza Rice, and Donald Rumsfeld), and the conducive context (post 9/11) were the three elements of a toxic triangle of hubristic leadership (see Chapter 3).[37] As was noted in Chapter 1 and illustrated in Chapter 3 (the case of Elizabeth Holmes and Theranos), most case studies of hubristic leadership aren't strictly reducible to a single risk factor, instead a complex interplay of leader, followers, and situation are at work. The focus in this chapter is on the individual psychological factors involved in decision-making.

Over-confidence and Intuition

Using gut feelings as a short cut to answer complex questions in unstable and uncertain situations can lead to biased and inaccurate judgements. There can be an amplifying effect because even if intuitions are wrong they often feel right, and because of the power that they hold leaders have more authority to go with their gut than people lower down the political or corporate hierarchy.[38] This feeling of rightness boosts the leader's self-assurance which can lead to over-confident decision-making. Over-confidence is one of the defining attributes of hubristic leader behaviours, and intuition is linked to over-confidence for three reasons:

(1) the intuitive mind is quicker than the analytical mind—this gives it the advantage of speed;

(2) the intuitive mind tends to be sure about what it thinks—this gives it the advantage of conviction;

(3) the intuitive mind expresses itself through feelings—this gives it the advantage of potency.

Speed: the intuitive mind (System 1) is faster than the analytical mind (System 2). Metaphorically speaking, System 1 usually 'wins' in the 'race' with System 2, and as a result intuition gets its metaphorical foot in the decision door first. Analysis can then have a hard job over-turning an intuitive response. This is especially true in moral judgements, and moral intuitions are often not amenable to logic and hence become hard to shift.[39] Recent research in moral psychology has shown that when we make a moral judgement the intuitive response is immediate and instinctive. The intuitive moral response either resists being refuted by analysis, or analysis is co-opted *post hoc* to justify the intuition. Hence in moral judgements, intuition often ends up being in the driving seat. President Bush was convinced that he was morally right in invading Iraq, even to the extent that he was doing 'God's work'. He put together a case to support his instinctive moral reaction which was presented to the UN by his Secretary of State Colin Powell in an attempt to persuade the world of the rightness, as he saw it, of his moral intuition.[40]

Conviction: the intuitive mind can be self-assured to the extent that the judgements it arrives at tend to be hard to shift. Someone once said of intuition that it's "sometimes wrong but rarely in doubt".[41] The intuitive mind also typically only produces a single response, unlike the analytical mind which typically produces a number of responses that can be weighed against each other. This process is called 'singular evaluation'.[42] If the intuitive mind produces a solution that seems plausible that's the one which will be used. This contrasts with the analytical strategy of 'comparative evaluation' in which multiple options are considered.[43] Singular evaluation is analogous to driving through an unfamiliar neighbourhood and noticing that your vehicle is getting low on fuel. As decision researcher Gary Klein has pointed out, in this situation the sensible thing to do is to use singular venation and stop at the first 'reasonable' service station that you come across rather than doing a comparative evaluation and searching for the 'best service station in town'.[44] However, in some circumstances even when other options may be available, singular evaluation reinforces certainty and reduces cognitive complexity because competing options aren't considered. Bush's intuitions about Saddam Hussein were not in any doubt: when the then Senator for Delaware Joe Biden, asked President Bush shortly after the invasion "Mr President, how can you be so sure when you don't know the facts?" Bush stood up and put his hand on Biden's shoulder and said: "My instincts. My instincts". This wasn't the strongest of evidence, but it didn't prevent Bush holding on to his gut feelings and presenting the case for invasion emphatically and unequivocally to the world via Colin Powell at the UN. Bush's intuition led to a singular evaluation and, in his mind at least, obviated any need to engage in any kind of evaluation of alternative explanations and competing options.

Potency: intuitions involve feelings, and feelings by their nature are potent. The stronger the gut feeling the more compelling the intuition. The consequence is that gut feelings amplify confidence, over-confidence provokes recklessness, and recklessness is one of the hallmarks of hubris. Another thing about gut feelings is that they tend to be 'dumb' in the sense that they don't discriminate between good and bad intuitions: just because something feels right intuitively doesn't mean that it is right. Potent gut feelings narrow down the range of options, making decision-making easier, faster, and much less of a drain on the brain's scarce cognitive resources. This can be advantageous when speed is of the essence and is probably one of the reasons why intuition evolved in the human organism in the first place. Bush in his own words was "instinctive": "I'm not a textbook player. I'm a gut player".[45] He told Larry King in an interview on CNN "If you make decisions based upon what you believe in your heart of hearts, you stay resolved". When he was Governor of Texas he remarked that "I know there's no evidence that shows the death penalty has a deterrent effect, but I just feel in my gut it must be true". As already mentioned in an earlier chapter, after Bush had met Vladimir Putin he said: "I looked the man in the eye, [and] I was able to get a sense of his soul".[46] Subsequent events in Crimea and Ukraine have called Bush's intuitions about Putin into question.

Political and business leaders operate in extraordinarily complex and radically uncertain environments. These don't lend themselves to an indiscriminate reliance on unsubstantiated gut instincts. Over-reliance on intuition leads to increased tolerance for risk-taking and over-confident

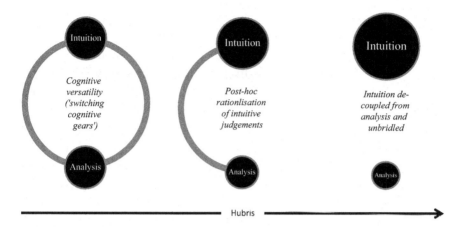

Figure 4.2 Unbridled Intuition Crowds Out Rationality (from Claxton et al., 2015)

decision-making. Taken to the extreme, recklessness takes hold and in the end intuition crowds out rationality (see Figure 4.2).

As hubris increases from left to right in the diagram (Figure 4.2) the balance shifts from a healthy balance between intuition and analysis (left-hand side), through using analysis to rationalise intuitive judgements post hoc (centre), to a situation in which intuition and analysis are decoupled (right-hand side). Intuition ends up crowding analysis, intuition becomes unbridled, decision-making is de-complexified, actions become over-confident and reckless, and the result is hubris and the "hubristic incompetence" which is Symptom 14 in the features of hubris syndrome.[47]

Right Person, Right Place, Right Time

As noted earlier, intuition works well when it's used by the right person, in the right place, and at the right time; it doesn't work well when it's used by the wrong person, in the wrong place, and at the wrong time.[48] But what constitutes 'right person, right place, and right time'? Was Bush the wrong leader, in the wrong place, at the wrong time? Researchers have discovered that the 'validity' of the environment (i.e. whether the situation lends itself to intuition) explains if, when, and why intuition is likely to work.[49]

The term validity is used in this context to describe the relationship between the cues in the environment (i.e. the signs and signals in the situation that an experienced decision-makers is able to notice and interpret) and relevant outcomes. For example, an experienced firefighter may have learned over many years' experience of fighting fires that certain cues about a burning building (e.g. the colour of the smoke or the sound of the fire) may indicate that the building is likely to collapse and therefore the firefighters should evacuate it immediately.[50] In this situation an experienced firefighter would be justified in trusting their intuition. This is because:

(1) the environment in which they're using their experience to make judgements has high validity for intuitive decision-making;
(2) it's a situation in which cue-outcome relationships are learnable;
(3) the person making the decision has learned those cue outcome relationships over many years of dealing with fires in burning buildings.

Another example of the power of intuition in high-validity environment was revealed by a study of the accuracy of cancer diagnoses by experienced physicians.[51] Doctors who had the experience to be able to 'go with their gut' were better at diagnosing cancer than those who mechanically went through a list of symptoms. Physicians sometimes struggled to put their gut feelings into words. A range of terms were used to describe the physicians' gut feelings including 'intuition', 'alarm bells', 'worry', 'suspicion', 'lurch of your stomach', and a 'sense of alarm' that occurred before the physician had a firm idea of what the diagnosis might be. When family doctors acted on these gut reactions the odds of an accurate cancer diagnosis were four times higher than when checklists of symptoms were followed.[52] Cancer diagnosis by experienced physicians is a high validity environment for intuitive judgement.

On the other hand, in the stock market there are unlikely to be cues in the form of publicly available information about a company that can be used to decide if its stock is likely to rise or fall on a day-by-day basis otherwise this would be reflected in the price being higher or lower in the first place. Betting on such a stock would be an easy way to make, or not lose, money. Hence, a day trader, especially one who's less experienced, wouldn't be justified in trusting their intuitions about the value of individual stocks. This is because the environment in which the day trader is operating has low validity for intuitive decision-making.

The same is true of the longer-term forecasting of political and geopolitical events. In 2005 the renowned political scientist Philip Tetlock published *Expert Political Judgement: How Good is It? How Can We Know?* Tetlock found that the ability of highly educated and experienced experts to make accurate, long-term forecasts of political events was no better than that of untrained readers of newspapers. In making long-term forecasts of political and geopolitical events novices appear to be no worse, or better, than experts, i.e. not particularly good.[53] The likely reason experts can't out do novices in such an environment is to do with the task itself rather than the person taking the decision. The task is so uncertain as to be impossible to make accurate predictions of long-term outcomes. As far as intuition is concerned making long-term forecasts of political and geopolitical events is a low validity environment; therefore it's probably not a clever idea to go with your gut in predicting the long-term outcomes of the invasion of a sovereign state.

Most political events are far too complex for anyone to be able to forecast accurately the long-term outcomes of a decision. But it's in exactly such situations that leaders often have to fall back on, or are tempted to rely on, their gut feelings. In December 2022 the *New York Times* Moscow Bureau chief, Anton Troianovski, reported that he had

> talked to many people who knew Putin personally, and they told me that the decision to go to war was based on his gut feeling. Putin didn't seem to think he needed advice on the wisdom of this invasion. Putin was convinced that he knew best.[54]

Putin was over-confident, so much so that he foresaw the rapid capitulation of Ukraine when he launched his 'special military operation' in January 2022. Subsequent events didn't match his expectations. Likewise, Bush's declaration of 'mission accomplished' in May 2003 just three months after the Iraq invasion proved to be wildly optimistic. Bush followed his gut instincts, but the social, economic, political, and cultural situation in Iraq and the wider region was a low validity environment for intuitive decision-making. Any gut feelings Bush had about Saddam Hussein and the outcome of wholescale invasion were difficult to place too much trust in because the decision was being taken in a low validity environment.

In mitigation for Bush's use of intuition, the Iraq invasion wasn't merely uncertain, it was radically uncertain. Situations are radically uncertain when it's neither possible to imagine all the possible outcomes nor to assign probabilities to future events. In such situations leaders may have little else to go on other than to gamble on their gut.[55] This was the situation that Barack Obama found himself in on May 2, 2011. He had to decide whether or not to attack the compound in Abbottabad, Pakistan where Osama bin Laden might have been hiding. The Central Intelligence Agency's (CIA's) team leader put the probability of bin Laden being in the compound at 95 per cent. Other advisers put it as low as 30 per cent. Averaged out, the decision was 50:50. The President had to make the tough judgement call on whether or not to storm the compound. Obama made his peace with 50:50 and called it right: bin Laden was killed by US Navy Seals and buried at sea later that day. Had bin Laden not been in the compound or if the raid had gone terribly wrong might Obama have been accused of over-confidence and hubris in what would perhaps have become an example of American over-reach for critics to seize upon?[56]

Avoiding Exposure to the Downsides of Gut Instinct

Intuition can be a problematic decision-making tool when it's used by the wrong person in the wrong situation and when it's used to excess. On the other hand, intuition can be a useful decision tool when it's used by the right person in the right situation and when it's used prudently. There are a number of ways in which leaders and other decision-makers can protect themselves against the risks of 'going-with-your-gut', these are: debiasing your decisions; challenging your intuitions; and building better intuitions.

Debiasing Your Decisions

One of the originators of the heuristics and biases research, Nobel Laureate Daniel Kahneman and author of *Thinking, Fast and Slow* (2011), has suggested that we can try our best to 'de-bug' the intuitive mind in at least two com-plementary ways: first, before it's committed its errors, i.e. by prevention; second, after it's arrived at a biased judgement, i.e. by correction.[57]

Prevention: intuitive judgements can be debiased beforehand by educating people in the fundamentals of probability and statistics in order to help them understand why and how they might fall into the trap of making intuitively biased decisions. For example, we intuitively prefer people who fit certain stereotypes, such as people who are like us, and recoil from people who fit other stereotypes of which we do not approve. This can lead to unconscious biases in a wide variety of social judgements, such as employee hiring decisions. The same applies to judgements of probabilities (as in the Linda problem). Educating decision-makers in how and why such biases work can help to debias their thinking processes. For example, in business 60 per cent of small business start-ups fail within the first three years. Therefore, educating aspiring entrepreneurs about the reality of new business failure rates and the perils of setting too much store by easy-to-remember, high-profile entrepreneurial successes can help them to arrive at a more realistic assessment of their chances of success. That said, debiasing the deeply held beliefs and ideologies that fuel intuitive decision-making, especially amongst political leaders, is likely to prove a more difficult challenge. As we've seen, George W. Bush's views on important matters, such as the death penalty and the need for regime change in Iraq, were held so deeply that they almost amounted to 'articles of faith'.

Correction: over-confident decision-makers are likely to make over-optimistic estimates of the accuracy and the success of their decisions. We witnessed this in Iraq when Bush declared mission accomplished in May 2003 only three months after the invasion had taken place. The Iraq War ended in December 2011. Decisions can be debiased by applying corrections to decision-makers' initial estimates based on informed, independent assessments by experts. For example, in the UK the check and balance which the Office for Budget Responsibility (OBR) is supposed to exercise over the longer-term viability of a prime minister's and chancellor's budget proposals was over-ridden by former Prime Minister Liz Truss (see Chapter 6). The consequences were significant and not as intended for Truss, her Chancellor Kwasi Kwarteng, and the UK economy.[58]

However, Kahneman is guarded about the chances of successfully deprogramming the human brain of its in-built tendencies to commit logical and statistical errors. This is because the human brain's intuitive mind was designed to make fast judgements based on similarities and frequencies rather than probabilities and likelihoods. A further reason for pessimism is that even informed judges who are able to apply statistical reasoning principles to judgements in one area of their expertise aren't immune from committing errors in other related areas. This variability is a product of what has been referred to as 'fractionated expertise', i.e. where an expert exhibits genuine expertise in some aspects of their activities but not in others. For example, auditors with outstanding levels of 'hard' expertise in financial accounting may perform less well in 'soft' areas such as detecting financial fraud.[59] This suggests that heterogenous teams with diverse expertise and a variety of opinions are less likely to fall foul of biased decisions than teams whose expertise is focused too narrowly. When hubristic leaders surround themselves with yes-people the opportunities for biased decision-making and groupthink are amplified. The good news and overall conclusion, as far as debiasing our decisions is concerned, is that two (or more) minds are better than one.

Challenging Your Intuitions

The term 'cognitive miser' has been used to describe human beings' natural tendency to rely on fast, automatic, and low-effort mental short cuts (i.e. heuristics) when making decisions and drawing inferences. As we know mental short cuts can work well under certain sets of conditions (for example, in the high-validity environments discussed above), however there are situations (for example, in low-validity environments) where, as we have seen, intuitive mental short cuts are likely to be biased and inaccurate and therefore need to be challenged. Even experts can place too much reliance on their intuitions. Challenging the intuitive mind requires significant cognitive effort. However, there are some techniques that decision-makers can use to manage this process.

One such method is 'devil's advocacy'. The term comes from the Catholic Church in the Middle Ages where the *advocatus diaboli* deliberately argued against a candidate for canonisation in order to expose any character flaws which might mitigate against sainthood. A devil's advocate deliberately adopts a sceptical stance in order to find holes in an argument. We can be a devil's advocate towards our own or someone else's intuitions in a number of different ways, for example: probing (asking penetrating questions about possible biases, prejudices, and wishful thinking); doubting (constructively casting doubts on the conclusions reached); countering (putting the case for an alternative approach). Devil's advocacy enables critical flaws to be spotted and failures anticipated before they happen, see Table 4.1.

Table 4.1 Devil's Advocacy Questions for Challenging Intuitions

Question	Purpose	Example
Probing	Asking penetrating questions about potential biases, personal prejudices, and wishful thinking	"Is this a genuine intuition or is it just wishful thinking for what I'd like to happen?"
Doubting	Constructively casting doubts on conclusions reached	"What are the other plausible reasons for the conclusion I've reached?"
Countering	Putting case for an alternative approach	"What alternative approaches are available to us to solve this problem?"

Devil's advocacy can function as a circuit breaker and is similar to the 'pre-mortem' technique advocated by decision researcher Gary Klein.[60] In pre-mortems, project teams describe their plan before it's been implemented. They then imagine that the plan has failed and the project has been a disaster. 'Prospective hindsight' is then used to identify weaknesses in the plan and any potential causes of failure before the fiasco has happened. Devil's advocacy and pre-mortems force decision-makers to be more honest and humble by reflecting on whether they actually know as much as they think they know. As such, devil's advocacy and pre-morteming can be antidotes to hubristic over-confidence. Their effectiveness is likely to be amplified by the fact that they're social processes: this means that they require decision-makers to engage in dialogue with colleagues some of whom may be, or consciously take on the role of, sceptics. One of the biggest self-inflicted risks can be if a leader creates an "echo chamber of their own making" as George W. Bush did in planning the Iraq invasion.[61]

Building Better Intuitions

The third way in which leaders can protect themselves against the going-with-your-gut risk is by simply getting better at intuition. They can do this by practising more and getting high-quality feedback on their decisions.

Practising

Intuition is acquired and honed through practice. Psychologists discovered that even the most accomplished performers in areas such as music and sport need approximately 10,000 hours (which equates to about ten years depending on the amount of daily practice) of intense training and deliberate practice in order to become an expert. Developing intuition is one area where an excess (of practice) is often condoned, and on the face of it exhortations to 'practise, practise, practise' suggest that 'more is better'. However, this isn't necessarily the best way for a leader to build intuitive expertise.[62] To build good intuitions, practice needs to be deliberate and stretching rather than simply repeating the same behaviours over and over again and staying inside your comfort zone. High-quality practice involves developing those things you can't do well currently.

One of the most surprising and disconcerting things about leadership, especially in areas such as business and politics, is that leaders spend more time performing in their role, often without any structured guidance, than practising deliberately under an expert. Business leaders and politicians often end up, in the words of the former head of group planning at Royal Dutch Shell and author of *The Living Company* (1997), Arie de Geus, 'experimenting with reality'.[63] This is potentially dangerous and the consequences can be dire. The UK's fiscal crisis of October 2022 was a product of a 'mini-budget' experiment by Prime Minister Liz Truss and her finance minister Kwasi Kwarteng. It demonstrated clearly how experimenting with reality can be very costly reputationally, financially, and politically. Business and politics stand in stark contrast with other fields, such as sport, chess, and the military, where people spend more time purposefully practising than actually playing or performing. Managers and leaders can develop better intuitions by putting in the necessary hours of high-quality practice and being given the opportunity to practise safely and without 'fear becoming the dominant emotion and everyone fearing the consequences'.[64]

Getting High Quality Feedback

One of the best ways for a leader to develop bad intuitions, and increase their hubris in the bargain, is to take decisions without getting feedback on the consequences of their actions. One counter to this is to deliberately seek out high-quality feedback and then act on it. For the intuition researcher and author of *Educating Intuition* (2001), Robin Hogarth, high-quality feedback is more than just comments and criticisms, to be high quality it should be:

(1) relevant: feedback needs to be specific rather than vague;
(2) accurate: accurate feedback is clear about the links between decisions and outcomes (whereas inaccurate feedback can lead to incorrect inferences about relationships between actions and outcomes);
(3) timely: decision-makers need to get feedback when it'll be most useful for improving their performance.

This is likely to involve both immediate feedback (feedback-in-action) to help decision-makers improve decision-making in-flight and delayed feedback (feedback-after-action) to help decision-makers reflect on what went well and how their decision-making could be improved. Overall, high-quality practice and high-quality feedback will help anyone who has to take decisions under conditions of volatility, uncertainty, ambiguity, and complexity to build better intuitions.

Intuitions are analyses frozen into habit and the capacity for rapid response through recognition. The main idea of this chapter is that trusting your intuition can be a good thing for experienced people to do in fast-moving, high-stakes situations where there are reliable relationships between cues and outcomes. Problems arise:

(1) in situations that aren't suited to intuition in the first place;
(2) when we don't have the requisite expertise;
(3) when we resort to unreliable mental short cuts;
(4) when we allow our intuitions to crowd out analysis.

An imbalance in favour of intuition at the expense of analysis can result in over-confident and reckless decision-making which leads to hubris. We can bring our unbridled intuitions under control by debiasing our decisions, challenging our intuitions, and building better intuitions.

The leadership psychologists Joyce and Robert Hogan have identified a number of leadership 'derailers', i.e. "counterproductive behavioral tendencies that emerge in times of stress and complacency".[65] Unbridled intuition is a counterproductive behavioral tendency that derailed G. W. Bush in his decision to invade Iraq. The decision was highly consequential. Consequential decisions tend to be decisions that have to be made in circumstances that don't often arise and where "I don't know" may not be an option, but before they go with their gut it's prudent for decision-makers to pause and reflect, call on others for their views, and ask what the consequences are likely to be if they make the wrong call.[66] Used by the right person, in the right way, in the right circumstances, and to the right amount, intuition can be an effective decision-making tool. When intuition is unbridled it crowds out rationality and can expose leaders and their organisations and institutions to the hubris hazard.

Unbridled Intuition: Signs to Look Out For

(1) Leader lacks curiosity;
(2) Leader is unwilling or unable to appreciate different sides to a problem;
(3) Leader's intuition is being used in situations to which it's not suited;
(4) Leader's intuition is beginning to crowd out rationality;
(5) Increased leader reliance on hard-to-justify gut feelings;
(6) Leader lacks requisite experience or expertise to take intuitive decisions.

Notes

1 Cited in Barnett, V. (2017). Keynes, animal spirits, and instinct: Reason plus intuition is better than rational. *Journal of the History of Economic Thought*, 39(3), 381–399.
2 Dane, E., & Pratt, M. G. (2009). Conceptualizing and measuring intuition: A review of recent trends. *International Review of Industrial and Organizational Psychology*, 40, 1–40, p.2.
3 Simon, H. A. (1987). Making management decisions: The role of intuition and emotion. *Academy of Management Executive*, 1(1), 57–64, p.63.
4 Dane, E. & Pratt, M. G. (2007). Exploring intuition and its role in managerial decision making. *Academy of Management Review*, 32(1), 33–54; Simon, H. A. (1987). Making management decisions: The role of intuition and emotion. *Academy of Management Perspectives*, 1(1), 57–64.
5 de Groot, A. D. (1965). *Thought and choice in chess*. The Hague: Mouton Publishers.
6 Sadler-Smith, E. (2023). *Intuition in business*. Oxford: Oxford University Press.
7 Kroll, M. J., Toombs, L. A., & Wright, P. (2000). Napoleon's tragic march home from Moscow: Lessons in hubris. *Academy of Management Perspectives*, 14(1), 117–128, p.126.

8   Hagopian, A., Flaxman, A. D., Takaro, T. K., Esa Al Shatari, S. A., Rajaratnam, J., Becker, S., . . . & Burnham, G. (2013). Mortality in Iraq associated with the 2003–2011 war and occupation: Findings from a national cluster sample survey by the university collaborative Iraq Mortality Study. *PLoS Medicine*, 10(10), e1001533.

9   Stiglitz, J., & Bilmes, L. J. (2010). The true cost of the Iraq war: $3 trillion and beyond. *The Washington Post*, September 5. Available at: https://www.washingtonpost.com/wp-dyn/content/article/2010/09/03/AR2010090302200.html

10 Galbraith, P. W. (2008). *Unintended consequences: How war in Iraq strengthened America's enemies*. New York: Simon & Schuster.

11 Smith, J. E. (2016). *Bush*. New York: Simon & Schuster.

12 The Iraq Inquiry. (2016). *Sir John Chilcot's public statement, 6 July*. London: The National Archives. Available at: http://www.iraqinquiry.org.uk/the-inquiry/sir-john-chilcots-public-statement

13 Owen, D. (2006). Hubris: the new Iraq War Syndrome. *The Guardian*, October 29. Available at: https://www.theguardian.com/commentisfree/2006/oct/29/comment.politics

14 Owen, D. (2007). *The hubris syndrome: Bush, Blair and the intoxication of power*. London: Politico's, p.46.

15 The White House (no date). *Presidents: George W. Bush*. Available at: https://www.whitehouse.gov/about-the-white-house/presidents/george-w-bush

16 Stolberg, S. G. (2006). The Decider. *The New York Times*, December 24. Available at: https://www.nytimes.com/2006/12/24/weekinreview/the-decider.html

17 Bush, G. W. (2010). *Decision points*. New York: Virgin Books, p.1.

18 Suskind, R. (2004). Faith, certainty and the presidency of George W Bush. New York Times Magazine, October 17. Available online at: https://www.nytimes.com/2004/10/17/magazine/faith-certainty-and-the-presidency-of-george-w-bush.html

19 Woodward, B. (2002). *Bush at war*. New York: Simon & Schuster, p.342.

20 Sadler-Smith, E. (2019). *Hubristic leadership*. London: SAGE, p.122.

21 *The Guardian*. (2022). Stephen Colbert on Bush's gaffe: 'A refreshingly light-hearted confession to war crimes'. *The Guardian*, 20 May. Available at: https://www.theguardian.com/culture/2022/may/20/stephen-colbert-george-w-bush-gaffe-late-night

22 The cover of *Rolling Stone* magazine of May 4, 2004 in which Wilentz's article appeared depicting Bush wearing a dunce's cap. Available at: https://www.rollingstone.com/politics/politics-news/george-w-bush-the-worst-president-in-history-192899

23 Adams, R. (2010). George Bush: Worst. president ever? *The Guardian*, July 1. Available at: https://www.theguardian.com/world/richard-adams-blog/2010/jul/01/george-bush-worst-us-president; Goldberg, N. (2022). Remember when we thought George W. Bush was the worst president ever? *Los Angeles Times*, August 29. Available at: https://www.latimes.com/opinion/story/2022-08-29/bush-trump-worst-president

24 Pfiffner, J. P. (2004). George W. Bush: Policy, politics, and personality. In Edwards, G. C. & Davies, P. J. (eds.). *New challenges for the American presidency*. New York: Pearson Education, pp.161–181, p.161.

25 Claxton, G., Owen, D., & Sadler-Smith, E. (2015). Hubris in leadership: A peril of unbridled intuition? *Leadership*, 11(1), 57–78.

26 Blair, T. (2010) *A journey*. London: Hutchison, p.5.

27 Smith, J. E. (2016). *Bush*. New York: Simon & Schuster.

28 Mandelson, P. (2010). *The third man: Life at the heart of New Labour*. London: Harper Press, p.10.

29 Marcus, B. (2015). Intuition is an essential leadership tool. *Forbes*, September 1. Available at: https://www.forbes.com/sites/bonniemarcus/2015/09/01/intuiton-is-an-essential-leadership-tool/?sh=7e0728621c18; Stupple, L. (2022). 4 reasons intuition is an essential leadership skill, *Entrepreneur*, May 30. Available at: https://www.entrepreneur.com/leadership/4-reasons-intuition-is-an-essential-leadership-skill/426726; Henley, D. (2019). Why intuitive leaders are the most successful. *Forbes*, June 14. Available at: https://www.forbes.com/sites/dedehenley/2019/06/14/why-intuitive-leaders-are-the-most-successful/?sh=2e280a727cfb

30 Carney, M. (2018). *Reflections on leadership in a disruptive age*. Bank of England. Available at: https://www.bankofengland.co.uk/-/media/boe/files/speech/2018/reflections-on-leadership-in-a-disruptive-age-speech-by-mark-carney.pdf

31 Manhire, T. (2019). Jacinda Ardern: 'Very little of what I have done has been deliberate. It's intuitive'. *he Guardian*, April 6. Available at: https://www.theguardian.com/world/2019/apr/06/jacinda-ardern-intuitive-courage-new-zealand

32 McSmith, A. (2016). Chilcot? Chaff? Dodgy dossier? Here's an Iraq War glossary. *The Independent*, July 5. Available at: https://www.independent.co.uk/news/uk/politics/chilcot-chaff-dodgy-dossier-here-s-an-iraq-war-glossary-a7119996.html

33 Kahneman, D. (2011). *Thinking, fast and slow*. London: Random House.

34 Sadler-Smith, E. (2023). *Intuition in business*. Oxford: Oxford University Press.

35 Claxton, G., Owen, D., & Sadler-Smith, E. (2015). Hubris in leadership: A peril of unbridled intuition? *Leadership*, 11(1), 57–78.

36 Sadler-Smith, E. (2019). *Hubristic leadership.* London: SAGE.

37 Sadler-Smith, E. (2019). *Hubristic leadership.* London: SAGE.

38 Hodgkinson, G. P., & Sadler-Smith, E. (2003). Complex or unitary? A critique and empirical re-assessment of the Allinson-Hayes Cognitive Style Index. *Journal of Occupational and Organizational Psychology,* 76(2), 243––268.

39 Haidt, J. (2001). The emotional dog and its rational tail: A social intuitionist approach to moral judgment. *Psychological Review,* 108(4), 814–834.

40 Sadler-Smith, E. (2019). *Hubristic leadership.* London: SAGE.

41 Sadler-Smith, E. (2008). *Inside intuition.* Abingdon: Routledge, p.28.

42 Klein, G. A. (1999). *Sources of power.* Cambridge, MA: MIT Press, p.20.

43 Klein, G. A. (1999). *Sources of power.* Cambridge, MA: MIT Press, p.20.

44 Klein, G. A. (1999). *Sources of power.* Cambridge, MA: MIT Press, p.20.

45 Woodward, B. (2002). *Bush at war.* New York: Simon & Schuster.

46 Myers, D. G. (2006). Intuition or intellect? Association for Psychological Science. October 1, 2006. Available at: http://www.psychologicalscience. org/observer/intuition-or-intellect

47 Owen, D., & Davidson, J. (2009). Hubris syndrome: An acquired personality disorder? A study of US presidents and UK prime ministers over the last 100 years. *Brain,* 132(5), 1396–1406, p.1398.

48 Sadler-Smith, E. (2023). *Intuition in business.* Oxford: Oxford University Press.

49 Kahneman, D., & Klein, G. (2009). Conditions for intuitive expertise: A failure to disagree. *American Psychologist,* 64(6), 515–526.

50 Klein, G. A. (2003). *Intuition at work.* New York: Doubleday.

51 Donnelly, L. (2020). Doctors' 'gut instincts' better at catching cancer than just a symptoms checklist. *The Daily Telegraph.* August 25. Available at: https://www.telegraph.co.uk/news/2020/08/25/doctors-gut-instincts-better-catching-cancer-just-symptoms-checklist

52 Smith, C. F., Drew, S., Ziebland, S., & Nicholson, B. D. (2020). Understanding the role of GPs' gut feelings in diagnosing cancer in primary care: A systematic review and meta-analysis of existing evidence. *British Journal of General Practice,* 70(698), e612-e621.

53 Tetlock, P. E. (2005). *Expert political judgment: How good is it? How can we know?* Princeton, NJ: Princeton University Press.

54 Moses, C. (2022). What Russia got wrong. *The New York Times,* December 18. https://www.nytimes.com/2022/12/18/briefing/russia-putin-ukraine-war.html

55 Kay, J., & King, M. (2020). *Radical uncertainty.* New York: W.W. Norton & Company.

56 Bergen, P. (2014). Obama says goodbye to American hubris. *CNN* May 28. Available at: https://edition.cnn.com/2014/05/28/opinion/bergen-obama-doctrine-smart-power/index.html

57 Kahneman, D., Sibony, O., & Thaler, R. (2021). *Noise: A flaw in human judgement*. London: William Collins.

58 BBC Reality Check Team. (2022). How much market chaos did the mini-budget cause? BBC, October 17. Available at: https://www.bbc.co.uk/news/63229204

59 Kahneman, D., & Klein, G. (2009).Conditions for intuitive expertise: A failure to disagree. *American Psychologist*, 64(6), 515–526.

60 Klein, G. (2007). Performing a project pre-mortem. *Harvard Business Review*, September. Available at: https://hbr.org/2007/09/performing-a-project-premortem

61 Sadler-Smith, E. (2019). *Hubristic leadership*. London: SAGE, p.126.

62 Sadler-Smith, E. (2023). *Intuition in business*. Oxford: Oxford University Press.

63 Arie de Geus quoted in Sadler-Smith, E. (2022). *Human resource development*. London: SAGE.

64 Arie de Geus quoted in Sadler-Smith, E. (2022). *Human resource development*. London: SAGE.

65 Hogan Development Survey. (no date). *Sub-scale interpretive guide*. Hogan Assessment Systems Inc., p.2. Available at: http://www.hoganassessments.com/sites/default/files/uploads/HDS_Subscale_Interp_Guide_10.2.14.pdf

66 Resnick, B. 2019. An expert on human blind spots gives advice on how to think. *Vox*. Available at: https://www.vox.com/science-and-health/2019/1/31/18200497/dunning-kruger-effect-explained-trump

5

IRRATIONAL EXUBERANCE

Sunfish and 'Tomato Cans'

In many animal species when a male wins a contest against another male of the same species it enhances his chances of victory in subsequent contests. For example, green sunfish (*Lepomis cyanellus*) are freshwater fishes which are popular with anglers and fish hobbyists alike. They've also been used by biologists in the study of male aggressive behaviour. If you put a small, male, green sunfish in the same tank as a large, male, green sunfish, the bigger fish's experience of dominating the smaller fish gives it a much better chance of winning in subsequent encounters. When the winning fish is put into a tank with an equal-sized opponent, having bullied the weaker fish in the previous combat, it has a statistically better chance of becoming dominant in the new encounter. The more the sunfish wins the greater the chance that it'll go on to win in subsequent contests. Winning a minor contest increases the chances of winning in the next contest and

DOI: 10.4324/9781003128427-5

so on up the sunfish hierarchy and ultimately the winning sunfish can end up dominating its social group.[1] Like hubrists, sunfish it seems can become intoxicated, not only with power, but also success. Is there some common biological mechanism at work?

In the fish tank 'success breeds success', and this applies to many other species in the animal kingdom including *Homo sapiens*. Eminent neuroscientist, Ian Robertson who studies the biology of hubris and whose work we met in Chapter 2, reminds us that US boxing promoters have known about this phenomenon for a long time. A 'tomato can' is a fighter who has poor or jaded boxing skills as a result of just not being very good or being past their prime. The tomato can (the exact meaning of which is obscure) is used deliberately to give his opponent a guaranteed win in order to improve their fight record or help with recovery from a setback. Tomato cans are picked because they have no chance of winning but they look okay in losing, at least in theory.

The controversial boxer Mike Tyson needed easy opposition after he came out of prison in 1995 having served three years of a six-year sentence for rape. The first opponent Tyson's promotor Don King put him in front of was Peter 'Hurricane' McNeely Jr. Before the fight McNeely said he would wrap Tyson in a "cocoon of horror".[2] To say that McNeely was getting ahead of himself is an understatement. Early in the first round Tyson knocked McNeely down twice. McNeely's manager stepped in after 89 seconds to stop him taking any more punishment. King then lined-up Buster Mathis as Tyson's second opponent. Mathis was admittedly undefeated, but also virtually unknown. Mathis fared slightly better than McNeely. He lasted three rounds before being beaten by a series of right uppercuts from Tyson which put him out for the count. Tyson went on to capture the World Boxing Council Heavyweight title in 1996.

In green sunfish contests, boxing matches and many other competitions besides, runs of successes are not uncommon. Psychologists working with human participants have observed this phenomenon in their experiments. In a laboratory study, a team of researchers from New York and London conferred early successes on 100 arbitrarily selected participants who were competing for donations to projects in technology, arts, and entertainment by randomly donating funding to their projects whilst arbitrarily withholding funding from a different group of 100 participants. The positive feedback from arbitrary endorsement produced significant improvements in subsequent success rates compared with the control group participants who didn't receive the early, but totally arbitrary, successes.[3] The researchers took this as hard evidence that success does indeed breed success: i.e. some people accumulate long strings of successes from "cascades of positive reinforcement" while others seem to fail repeatedly. This work is an important step forward in showing how initial success creates lasting disparities in success as a result of the psychological effects of feedback and reinforcement; however, it doesn't shed any light on any biological mechanisms that might be behind a run of successes.

The Winner Effect

In the cases of green sunfish and boxers, the mechanism that's at work is thought to be primarily biological: success breeds success through elevated post-encounter levels of steroid hormones, especially testosterone. Experimental biologists know that they can increase a male sunfish's chances of winning by giving it the opportunity to bully a smaller opponent; boxing promoters know that they can boost a rusty fighter's chances of success in subsequent encounters by deliberately putting them up against a 'tomato can'. Testosterone, it seems, boosts the successful combatants' levels of aggression, motivation, and confidence in subsequent contests. Little by little, minor contests against weaker members of one's group increase the chances of success in subsequent competitive encounters in a virtuous cycle, see Figure 5.1.

This virtuous cycle is called the 'Winner Effect'.[4] It works as follows. A winning male emerges from a contest with a higher level of testosterone (in rhesus monkeys, for example, the increase can be as much as ten-fold), the loser on the other hand experiences a drop to around 10 per cent in their baseline testosterone levels. This effect is based on the principle that success alters brain chemistry through the action of the steroid hormone testosterone. This leads to changes in temperament, feelings of greater potency, focus, and confidence, and heightened levels of aggressiveness. In athletic competitions levels of testosterone rise in athletes preparing for competition, they then rise further in the winning athlete and correspondingly fall in the loser. Testosterone priming of the winner increases their confidence and risk-taking behaviours and improves their chances of winning through a positive feedback loop (see Figure 5.1). Emboldened by

Figure 5.1 The Virtuous Cycle of the 'Winner Effect'
Source: Coates et al. (2018, p.38).

prior success a victor may unavoidably come to believe, and end up working on the inevitably false assumption, that they're invincible.

The fact that winners' altered testosterone levels persist for several weeks makes sense from an evolutionary point of view: the winner can prepare for the inevitable challenges that they're likely to experience at the peak of their social hierarchy; the loser can retreat to metaphorically, and perhaps literally as well, 'lick their wounds' thus avoiding any further damage to their physical and psychological well-being.[5] The combined effect of power and prior successes on the brain is likely to make winners, be that in the boxing ring, betting shop, or the boardroom, eager to try again. The release of the pleasure hormone amplifies this effect: the pleasure of victory predisposes a winner to want to approach similar situations again and again. The downside of this power/success/pleasure combination is that it can become physically addictive: an intoxication with success. The end result is that it can tip leaders over into the excesses of irrational exuberance, recklessness, and ultimately hubris; the inevitable, long-term result can be, and usually often is, a nasty surprise. The controversial British politician Enoch Powel (1912–1998) commented that "All political lives, unless they are cut off in midstream at a happy juncture, end in failure, because that is the nature of politics and of human affairs".[6]

Testosterone

Hubris, as well as being a product of an intoxication with power, can also be a product of a hormone-induced intoxication with prior successes. The word 'hormone' comes from the Greek *hormáō* (ὁρμάω), which means 'to excite', 'set in motion', or 'impel'. Hormones are chemical messengers that influence the brain and the body over both the long (i.e. 'developmental') term and short (i.e. 'activational') term. They include amines (for example, adrenaline which amongst other things increases heart rate and blood pressure, and decreases sensitivity to pain), peptides (for example, oxytocin which has effects on sexual arousal, empathy, and trust-building) and steroids (for example, testosterone and cortisol).[7] Steroids such as testosterone help to coordinate the brain and the body's responses in situations such as 'flight or fight', as well as in mating and status-seeking.

Testosterone has both a biological and a social function. It's the major sex hormone (androgen) in males; it's produced mainly in the testes and is also present in women but in much smaller quantities (about one eighth). Testosterone has the chemical formula $C_{19}H_{28}O_2$. It's released into the bloodstream in response to external stimuli such as the presence of an attractive potential mate or the motivation to win in a contest. It plays a number of pivotal roles in male physiology and physical development including the deepening of the voice during puberty, the development of the penis and testes, increased libido, appearance of facial and pubic hair starting at puberty, increases in muscle size, bone mass, body hair, and strength, enhanced sex drive, and increased sperm production.[8] Testosterone levels decrease with age; this results in decreased testicular size, lower libido, bone density, and muscle mass, and increased fat production.[9]

Amongst the behaviours associated with abnormally high levels of testosterone are elevated levels of aggression and libido, decreased risk aversion, and increased recklessness. For example, women who were injected with testosterone in an experimental gambling task switched from safer, low-risk/low-reward bets to higher-risk/higher-reward options.[10] High testosterone has also been linked to antisocial and egocentric behaviours, social dominance, heightened sensitivity to material rewards and acquisitiveness, and lower sensitivity to punishments. It's also been connected with lower levels of empathy and it appears to buffer individuals from the psychosocial costs that are incurred when a powerful person, such as a leader, has to take difficult, and sometimes unpopular, decisions. High testosterone individuals are worse at detecting the thoughts and feelings of others than low-testosterone individuals; they, in effect, are 'tuned out' from feeling the emotional impact that their decisions are likely to have, but they're also more 'tuned in' to maximising the benefits and payoffs to themselves.[11]

In species across the animal kingdom levels of testosterone fluctuate in accordance with changes in social status; for example, winning in a contest against an opponent leads to an increase in the levels of testosterone. As we saw in the winner effect, this mechanism is adaptive for competitive behaviours because it supports aggressive behaviour, competitive motivation, risk-taking, sensation-seeking, inhibited impulse control, and in-group affiliation. Losing tends to be associated with a decrease in circulating testosterone and this has resultant effects on the associated behaviours, for example, reduced competitiveness and risk-aversion.[12] Testosterone is powerful to the extent that its effects can also operate vicariously: levels of testosterone can be elevated in audience members who witness a victory of the team to which they have an affiliation. This is called the 'audience effect'. The audience effect on testosterone levels was observed during the 1994 football World Cup in which Brazil beat Italy in the final. Saliva samples from fans who were watching the game revealed that the testosterone levels of the supporters of Brazil went up whereas those of the supporters of Italy went down.[13]

Testosterone and Trading

Financial markets are arenas of intense competition. They're also both high risk and tend, even now, to be male-dominated. The fact that testosterone is implicated in risky competitive encounters in fish tanks and boxing rings might also be good reason to think that it might be associated with competitive economic behaviour and risk-taking in financial markets as well.[14] There have been several research studies that have shed light on the relationship between testosterone and risk-taking behaviours in financial markets. We'll look at two of them:

(1) the first is a field study conducted in the City of London in which traders' endogenous levels of testosterone (i.e. determined by an internal

cause rather than being artificially elevated) were measured and compared to their daily profit-and-loss (P&L) performance;

(2) the other is an experimental study conducted in a laboratory in which
testosterone levels were altered exogenously, i.e. where testosterone
was administered to participants by the experimenters to see what
effects it had on behaviours.

In the field study, John Coates (who previously traded derivatives for
Goldman Sachs and also ran a trading desk for Deutsche Bank) and the
Cambridge neuroscientist Joe Herbert studied the relationship between
daily testosterone levels amongst 17 male traders (mean age was 27.6 years)
in the City of London and their day-to-day profitability (profit and loss
(P&L) performance). Coates and Herbert took saliva samples from the traders at 11am and 4pm over an eight-day period. The nominal size of their
trades ranged from a modest £100,000 to an astonishing £500,000,000.
Coates and Herbert discovered that traders had significantly higher levels
of testosterone on the days when they made an above-average profit. From
their preliminary analysis it wasn't possible to say whether the traders'
profits were raising their testosterone levels or whether it was the other
way round.

In order to test the direction of the relationship between testosterone
and profitability, Coates and Herbert compared profits on the days when
each trader's 11am testosterone level was above their median ('high-
testosterone days') and below their median ('low-testosterone days'). They
found that on high-testosterone days the traders returned an afternoon
profit that was several times higher than on low-testosterone days. The
effect was amplified amongst more experienced traders. The researchers
concluded that "high morning testosterone predicts greater profitability for
the rest of that day".[15]

The researchers put this down to several potential mechanisms; for
example, perhaps testosterone increases the trader's search persistence, and
vigilance; perhaps it focuses their attention; and, maybe, it also elevates
their appetite for risk, and imbues them with fearlessness in the face of novelty. These behaviours are likely to be advantageous up to a point; however,
if testosterone levels continue to rise or became chronically (i.e. persistently) elevated this could lead to extreme and ultimately disadvantageous
behaviours including excessive confidence and risk-taking, impulsiveness,

recklessness, and sensation-seeking; it may even lead to mania and eupho-ria. In financial markets where contagion can be rife, even if these excesses were confined only to a relatively small number of traders it could none-theless spread like wildfire. As such, this testosterone-fuelled excitement could provide an explanation for the increasingly irrational exuberance and exaggerated risk-taking behaviours in bull markets (i.e. when asset prices have risen or are expected to rise). A classic example of a bull market was the so-called 'dot-com' bubble in the 1990s and early 2000s, driven by the rapid growth of internet and technology sectors. In the dot-com bubble the Standard & Poor's index of 500 of the largest stock market-listed companies in the USA (the S&P500 index) gained over 200 per cent.[16] The risk is that a testosterone-fuelled contagion effect could fuel a bubble and subsequent crash. The dot-com bubble burst in 2001 and equities entered a bear market with widespread pessimism and negative investor sentiment.[17]

Coates and Herbert speculate that the relationship between testoster-one levels and performance is an inverted U-shape: moderate levels of the androgen promote effective risk-taking whereas higher levels come with the cost of excessive risk-taking and lower levels carry the cost of risk aver-sion, see Figure 5.2. If this were to be correct, then testosterone amongst

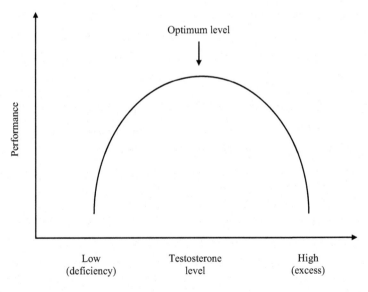

Figure 5.2 The Inverted U-shape Relationship Between Testosterone Levels and Performance

traders and the 'animal spirits' (to use J. M. Keynes' phrase) which it ignites becomes a risk factor when it's present to a deficiency or an excess.[18] It wouldn't be unreasonable to conclude that highly successful people in the world of investing might be particularly prone to becoming hubristic as a result of the actions of testosterone.[19] Testosterone could provide a biological explanation for the Keynesian animal spirits that all too often seem to drive stock markets and exert a potent influence on individuals' loss of self-control as well as contagion effects and 'herding' behaviours.[20]

Until comparatively recently the study of the effects of testosterone on human beings in social settings was quite limited, and much of what we knew and inferred about testosterone and human behaviour was extrapolated from animal studies. This changed with the advent of accurate, single-dose, testosterone administration studies in humans, for example, by applying patches containing testosterone gel to the skin. This exogenous approach to manipulating hormone levels is a powerful scientific tool because it can help to establish causalities rather than associations between testosterone levels and human social and economic behaviours.[21]

One such study was the laboratory research conducted by Amos Nadler of Ivey Business School in Ontario and colleagues. They set out to test the hypothesis that testosterone will cause traders to over-bid for financial assets and that this could fuel over-pricing and financial bubbles. Their project differed from Coates and Herbert's study of City of London traders in that it aimed to test the causal, rather than correlational, relationships between testosterone and trading behaviour. Nadler and colleagues did so by administering a gel containing either testosterone or a placebo to 140 male traders (average age was 23 years) in an experimental rather than field (i.e. real-world) setting. The experimenters chose the laboratory because doing this kind of research in a field setting could be problematical because of the potential real-market consequences. They found that the traders who'd received the testosterone displayed decreased risk-aversion which led them to pay more for riskier assets leading to larger bubbles. Moreover, the testosterone-treated traders attributed their performance more to their 'talent' and less to 'luck' than did placebo-treated traders. This fits with prior research on the effects of testosterone not only on behaviours but also on attributions of success. Brain and behaviour work together: testosterone affected the traders' beliefs about the markets by making them more bullish in their behaviours which caused them to expect higher prices than their counterparts who'd received the placebo. The fact that testosterone hampers cognitive reflection (see the cognitive reflection test (CRT) studies discussed below) but amplifies gut feel decision-making may have led the testosterone-treated traders to engage in quick, impulsive, and instinctive decisions.

Nadler and colleagues concluded that artificially elevating traders' levels of testosterone leads to increased bid prices and asset price bubbles as a result of over-pricing. Hormone-fuelled changes in patterns of buying and selling assets may also lead to subsequent crashes. Coates and Herbert in their City of London study found that traders' levels of cortisol (a primary stress hormone) rose in 38 per cent of their participants and increased by as much as 500 per cent between mornings and afternoons with variations of up to 4000 per cent between days. The researchers found that these variations in cortisol levels were associated with the levels of volatility in the Bund market (the German equivalent of US Treasury bonds) in which the traders were operating. Coates and Herbert concluded that whilst testosterone was likely to increase traders' appetite for risk, it may be that cortisol could affect work in the opposite direction giving rise to feelings of anxiety and a tendency to see threats and risks where none exist. Levels of cortisol would therefore be likely to intensify in a market crash giving rise to risk aversion and thereby amplify the market's down-ward movements. As a consequence of these feedback loops alternating over longer timescales, recklessness and alarm generated by testosterone and cortisol respectively could fuel 'boom-and-bust' cycles in which rational choice is crowded out by positive and negative swings in 'animal spirits'.

These field and laboratory studies provide compelling evidence that hormones can influence behaviours in financial markets, and that testosterone, in particular, can amplify capital risk. One recommendation that's been put forward for managing the testosterone risk in financial markets is to have a cooling-off period to interrupt exceptionally positive feedback cycles and help to calm down traders' animal spirits. However more systemically— given that female traders produce significantly smaller bubbles than males and outperform males in retail trading—the findings from the field and laboratory studies offer a compelling rationale for increasing female participation in financial trading. Coates and Herbert call for greater 'endocrine diversity' in the financial industry which can help to "dampen hormonal swings in the market".[22] In its report *Women in Finance: A Case for Closing*

Gaps (2018) the International Monetary Fund (IMF) recognised the risks of having a male-dominated financial system and concluded that "women as users, providers, and regulators of financial services would have benefits beyond addressing gender inequality. Narrowing the gender gap would foster greater stability in the banking system and support economic stability and growth."[23]

Testosterone and Decision-making

As well as affecting the male body and male behaviour, testosterone can also affect the ways in which the male brain works, and, in particular, it can have an effect on the prefrontal regions of the brain that are involved in decision-making and impulse control. This is likely to bias decision-making in favour of faster but more inaccurate intuitive processing rather than slower and more accurate responses to questions which require analysis, deliberation, reflection, and computation. Performance on such tasks can be measured using the Cognitive Reflection Test (CRT which consists of three seemingly simple questions, for example, including the well-known question "A bat and a ball cost $1.10 in total. The bat costs $1.00 more than the ball. How much does the ball cost?"[24] Researchers tested the effect of testosterone on reflective cognition by administering either testosterone or a placebo to a sample of 243 men (125 received testosterone and 118 received a placebo). The testosterone group performed significantly worse than the placebo group on the CRT: they gave approximately 20 per cent fewer correct answers.

The researchers, led by Gideon Nave, explained this clear and robust effect of testosterone on male cognition as follows. Although slow, deliberative (System 2) processing is advantageous in the CRT, in nature this would be disadvantageous in situations requiring fast, instinctive responses such as copulation or a physical contest. Testosterone reduces the likelihood of engaging in slow, effortful analytical processing but increases the likelihood of engaging in fast, automatic intuitive processing which is ill-suited to logical and computational tasks which require deliberation. However, outside of situations involving mating and physical combat the effect of testosterone will be to bias decision-making and problem-solving in favour of intuitive processing. At the neural level testosterone appears to reduce the levels of activation in those regions of the brain's prefrontal cortex that are involved in reflective (System 2) processes (and specifically the ventro-medial prefrontal cortex (VMPFC), see below). This gives free rein to the reflexive (i.e. 'instinctive') System 1 processes. In behavioural terms, situations that elevate levels of testosterone, such as winning over an opponent, will reduce cognitive reflection and therefore impair performance on tasks that require slow, deliberative, and reflective thinking.[25] As the researchers noted, "it works through confidence enhancement. If you're more confident, you'll feel like you're right and will not have enough self-doubt to correct mistakes".[26] The links to the winner effect, overconfidence, recklessness, and ultimately hubris are palpable.

As far as moral decision-making is concerned, high-testosterone individuals—even though they're under the influence of their emotions—are more likely, paradoxically, to approach moral decisions in a less affective (i.e. feelings-based) and more dispassionately utilitarian manner. Similar effects are found in patients who have incurred lesions to the frontal cortex of the brain, and specifically the ventro-medial prefrontal cortex VMPFC. For example, patients with VMPFC lesions are more likely than healthy controls to pursue outcomes that maximise aggregate welfare (such as the hypothetical scenario of suffocating their baby to prevent its crying from revealing the whereabouts of a group of villagers to enemy troops).[27] Such individuals have not suffered any diminishment of intelligence, and their knowledge of social norms and what constitutes moral behaviour is not diminished. The effect of testosterone on moral decision-making appears to be similar to that of having a brain lesion to the prefrontal cortex: it suppresses the sensitivity of the VMPFC to important intuitive and social signals of what is socially acceptable and morally right.[28] It also reduces empathy and negative social emotions such as guilt, embarrassment, and anxiety. Testosterone acts as a buffer that enables people to take what would otherwise be considered socially insensitive behaviours and to execute overly utilitarian moral actions without due regard for the human costs.[29]

The implications are worrisome: high-testosterone individuals are more likely to pursue intransigent utilitarian choices even when this involves aggression and the violation of established ethical norms.[30] David Owen, one of the originators of the theory of hubris syndrome, commented to Times Radio in the UK in February 2022 that Vladimir Putin's aggression could be a consequence of his taking anabolic steroids which are known to cause aggressiveness in body builders.[31] Putin is famed for cultivating a macho image having been pictured several times shirtless in Russian state media riding a horse, carrying a rifle, and going fishing.[32] Testosterone blunts social emotions, hence high testosterone individuals are more likely to pursue tough and morally dubious decisions even if the costs of doing so are high, provided it promotes what they see as the greater good and delivers on their 'mission'. This is consistent with a number of the features of hubris syndrome (HS), for example, a belief that "rather than being accountable to the mundane court of colleagues or public opinion, the court to which they answer is History or God" (HS Symptom 9), the "tendency to allow their 'broad vision', about the moral rectitude of a proposed course, to obviate the need to consider practicality, cost or outcomes" (HS Symptom 13), etc.[33]

Testosterone and Leader Behaviour

Testosterone has had a bad press so far in this chapter. It's been associated with aggression, high libido, decreased risk aversion, increased recklessness, antisocial and egocentric behaviours, social dominance, various deviant behaviours, greater sensitivity to material rewards and acquisitiveness, lower sensitivity to punishments, lower levels of empathy, and 'tuning out' from the impact that leaders have on others whilst 'tuning in' to maximising the benefits and payoffs to themselves. From an evolutionary perspective it would be unusual, not to say perverse and ultimately maladaptive, for a hormone to have exclusively negative effects in social situations. In financial markets it can fuel bubbles, but in other contexts such as policing, firefighting, and the military it likely motivates prosocial and desirable behaviours such as courage, bravery, gallantry, heroism, self-sacrifice, etc.

Testosterone is neither exclusively antisocial nor prosocial, nor does it operate in isolation from other endocrinal influences. A more nuanced position would seem to be that the effects of testosterone depend very much on the social situation in which testosterone-related behaviours are carried out, and on its interactions with other hormones. For a group-living primate such as Homo sapiens social hierarchies are the context in which testosterone-related behaviours play out and for which they are adaptive. Maintaining a high position in a social hierarchy is advantageous in many different respects, and testosterone appears to be able to influence this process in positive ways by conferring greater threat vigilance, higher motivational drive, lower fearfulness, and higher stress resilience; it does so both directly and via interactions with other hormones.[34] For example, higher levels of testosterone are associated with more heightened sensitivity to fearful and angry faces, suggesting greater threat vigilance.[35] This process operates via the amygdalae which are rich in androgen receptors and are part of the brain's limbic system which is responsible for processing responses to threats and fear.

Testosterone may also play a role in promoting status-seeking behaviour by reducing anxiety and fear and thereby helping to facilitate participation in competitive behaviours.[36] Participating in social hierarchies and competing for social status is stressful. Stress resilience helps individuals to cope with the demands of social competition. Testosterone is adaptive in this regard because it down regulates stress responses from the hypothalamic-pituitary-adrenal system (i.e. the complex system of endocrine pathways and feedback loops also known as the 'HPA axis').[37]

The mounting body of research evidence suggests that a simple view of testosterone needs to be refined.[38] Testosterone plays a significant role in creating and maintaining the social hierarchies which are an essential feature of group living. The peak of the social hierarchy in a business organisation is the CEO. To become a CEO takes the drive and ambition to compete and succeed, the energy to work extremely long hours, the resilience to withstand the stresses and strains of the top job along with the ability to listen, communicate, and connect.[39]

The picture is likely to be more complex than a simple linear relationship between hormones and hierarchy. Other endogenous factors (for example, other hormones) and exogenous factors (for example, power) must surely play a role. For example, as noted earlier in the context of the City of London research, cortisol is a steroid hormone that helps the body to respond to stress; it's part of the body's flight-or-fight response system and levels of cortisol spike during times of stress.[40] Research suggests that testosterone is only related to aggressive, antisocial, and status-related behaviours (such as competitiveness) when cortisol levels are low. Cortisol may act to constrain testosterone's influence by blocking androgen receptors. This is referred to as the 'dual-hormone hypothesis'.[41]

A team of researchers led by Gary Sherman of Harvard University studied the relationship between testosterone levels and status in terms of the number of subordinates the leader has authority over ('attained status'). They gathered saliva samples from 78 male executives enrolled in an executive education programme at Harvard along with data on the leaders' number of subordinates. They didn't find a simple relationship between attained status and testosterone. However, they did find a two-way relationship between cortisol and testosterone in their combined effect on attained status. High-testosterone/low-cortisol executives had higher attained status, whereas low-testosterone/high-cortisol individuals had lower attained status. It seems, therefore, at least for men, that a high-testosterone and low-cortisol hormone profile is a hallmark of powerful individuals.[42] However, the directionality of the relationship is not clear from this research.

This research may indicate that cortisol 'silences' testosterone-driven processes and makes it more difficult for high-cortisol individuals (perhaps because of uncontrollable chronic stressors, such as destructive leader behaviours) to attain status. On the other hand, individuals who are high on testosterone and low on cortisol are free of the restraining effects of cortisol; when they become pumped up by the amplifying effects of testosterone they may experience a hormonal regime that supports them in attaining significant power. The dual action of high levels of testosterone and low levels of cortisol may work in concert to promote attaining and sustaining power.[43] The mixture of high testosterone, low cortisol, and the intoxication of power is a potentially destructive cocktail which may open a hormonal door to hubris. When testosterone, unconstrained by cortisol, allied to an intoxication with power makes a leader feel that they're 'invincible,' hubris may take hold and entice executives into engaging in reckless and potentially destructive leader behaviours.[44]

Testosterone and Narcissism

The relationship between hubris and narcissism is one of the subjects of Chapter 8. In simple terms: hubris is intoxication with power and is a state-like (i.e. more temporary or transient) condition; narcissism is intoxication with self and is trait-like (i.e. more permanent). They are related in that narcissistic tendencies may predispose a leader to hubris. If this is the case then it might be important to understand whether or not narcissism itself has any links to biology, and, in particular, to testosterone, and hence if biology might predispose a leader to hubris.

Research has explored the relationships between basal testosterone levels in males and the three facets of the so-called 'Dark Triad' of personality.

The Dark Triad consists of three dysfunctional aspects of personality—narcissism, Machiavellianism and psychopathy—which are associated with various antisocial tendencies including disregard for the interests, preferences, and needs of others, derogating others, aggressiveness, and the manipulation of others to maximise one's own benefits.[45] Measures of basal testosterone levels from saliva samples from 129 healthy male volunteers at a German university (mean age, 22 years) were found to be corelated with narcissism but not with Machiavellianism or psychopathy.[46] Other research has substantiated this finding[47] and also found that high testosterone individuals may be inclined to misuse their power because having power over others makes them feel entitled to special treatment which feeds their narcissism.[48]

A conclusion from this and other research is that the Dark Triad trait of narcissism is "expressed in the endocrinology of individuals".[49] This is important because it suggests that there may be a biological basis for why some individuals are more narcissistic than others which could help to explain why people behave in ways that that are grandiose and ego-focused. These findings build on previous research that shows that basal testosterone is a biological marker of an interpersonal style that is cold, dominant, self-assertive, and antisocial.[50] The fact that narcissists have a propensity to leadership and dominance suggests that a study of the darker side of leadership, including narcissism and hubris, may be incomplete without considering their basal endocrinology.

As well as being linked to narcissism and behavioural traits such as aggression, risk tolerance, and sensation seeking,[51] testosterone is also linked to male physical appearance, for example, musculature, bone mass, hair, facial morphology, etc. [52] Facial morphology and bone structure are related to craniofacial bone growth as a result of exposure to testosterone during adolescence.[53] Facial morphology is a physical aspect of masculinity and facial masculinity, in particular the facial width to height ratio (fWHR), is readily accessible and measurable via secondary sources, such as photographs. The fWHR is defined as the width of the zygomatic bones (the pair of bones on each upper side of the face that forms the cheek and part of the eye socket) divided by the length of the upper face (i.e. from the upper lip to the upper eyelids). The fWHR is unrelated to body size, is higher on average in men than in women, and is thought to be related to testosterone levels in the prenatal stage and the pubertal stage (where it regulates facial bone growth).[54] Higher fWHR (i.e. faces that are wider rather than longer) is associated with masculinity. It has been suggested parameter can be used as a proxy, or 'biological marker', for masculinity and masculine behaviours. Researchers have discovered that compared to men with narrower faces, men with a high fWHR are more confident, optimistic, aggressive, and dominant; they've also been found to be less trustworthy in economic games, tend to cheat to serve their own interests, and to seek dominance in business decisions.[55]

Should we judge a book by its cover? Whether or not testosterone, and hence facial morphology, is related to hubris might be an interesting area for further research if facial structure is a valid and reliable 'honest signal'[56] which reliably transmits information about a leader and their likely destructive behaviours.[57] The advantage of this type of data for hubris and narcissism researchers through the analysis of leaders' facial appearance, which is impossible to conceal or alter, is that it's readily available in the public domain and can be accessed at a distance (i.e. from photographic images of leaders in the case of fWHR).[58] The use of computerised techniques for the analysis of parameters such as the fWHR increases the potency of such methods.[59] Facial morphology is a potentially useful type of real-life data for the study of hard-to-reach populations such as CEOs and heads of government. Such individuals are highly unlikely either to answer questions about negative aspects of their leadership behaviour (such as hubris and narcissism) or to provide samples for the analysis of basal testosterone. Proxy markers such as facial appearance might be a useful at-a-distance method to move such research forward. However, whilst this research is an interesting area for further investigation, drawing any firm conclusions or practical recommendations from it would be premature to say the least.

Avoiding Exposure to Irrational Exuberance

It is a biological fact that winning a contest, whether or not the opponent is artificially weakened, statistically increases the chances of winning the next contest, even if that's against a much stronger opponent. This effect is observed in settings that range from fish tanks to boxing rings. The mechanism is a biological one: testosterone. In the financial variant of the winner effect this can cause risk preferences to shift towards risk-seeking behaviours and spiral upwards until a point is reached at which exuberance becomes irrational and a bull market is pushed into a bubble.[60] Once the peak is reached the influence of another hormone kicks in: cortisol. This produces a stress response which itself becomes irrational and a bear market is pushed into a bust. As John Coates has noted steroid hormones such as testosterone may provide an important missing link in the study of human economic behaviour. Testosterone is especially important because of the amplifying effects that it has on confidence which leads to exaggerated self-belief bordering on a sense of omnipotence, restlessness, recklessness, and impulsiveness, coupled with contempt for the advice and criticism of others which are the hallmarks of hubris syndrome.

These effects are unlikely to be confined to the trading floor; they may be just as likely to occur in the boardroom as well as the cabinet room. From a biological perspective this risk is predominantly, though not exclusively, associated with men. If this is the case and it is a risk requiring mitigation then one clear and obvious solution is to reduce or dilute the levels of testosterone in circulation in these environments. As already noted, one way in which to do so is to increase the proportion of women, who are unlikely to suffer the debilitating effects of excessive testosterone on their decision-making be that on a trading floor, in the C-suite, or the cabinet room. Whilst questions about the effects of increased diversity on board and corporate performance continue to develop and be debated,[61] the risks associated with testosterone and its effects on decision-making is one situation in which having more women in leadership positions is likely to militate against unnecessary risk-taking. A testosterone-fuelled lack of self-control can not only fuel over-pricing on asset markets,[62] it can also help to create the conditions more generally, both in business and politics, for hubristic incompetence and make it more likely that unintended negative consequences will ensue.

In the final analysis, for J. M. Keynes, human economic behaviour (and behaviour more generally) is an amalgam of two fundamental sorts of mental processes that sometimes compete and sometimes collaborate. These two processes, which Keynes commented on insightfully over a century ago, may come as no surprise to us: they are an "amalgam of logic and intuition".[63] The dynamics of these two reflective and reflexive systems of thinking, deciding, and acting involves a delicate balance and a fine line to be trodden. Keynes believed firmly—and in common with the views expressed much more recently by many behavioural and brain scientists—that in some situations instinct should be over-ridden by reason, whilst in others it should be allowed to have its voice.[64] The key to harnessing Keynesian animals spirits productively in financial markets and beyond and hence to the taking of *necessary* risks is not to give our biologically fuelled instincts free rein but to become skilled in using them in the right amount, at the right time, and for the right purposes so that decision-makers may become capable ultimately of exercising prudence, self-control. and practical wisdom.

Irrational Exuberance: Signs to Look Out For

(1) A long run of uninterrupted successes by the leader;
(2) Leader over-confidence and over-ambition;
(3) Leader's increased bullishness, recklessness, and risk-seeking behaviours;
(4) Preponderance of high-testosterone individuals in senior leadership positions.

Notes

1 McDonald, A. L., Heimstra, N. W., & Damkot, D. K. (1968). Social modification of agonistic behaviour in fish. *Animal Behaviour*, 16(4), 437–441.
2 Byrne, K. (2020). TYSON'S FURY Peter McNeeley opens up on feeling Mike Tyson's fury in his 1995 comeback fight after serving three years in jail. *The Sun*, July 8. Available at: https://www.thesun.co.uk/sport/12067377/ peter-mcneeley-mike-tyson-comeback-prison
3 Van de Rijt, A., Kang, S. M., Restivo, M., & Patil, A. (2014). Field experiments of success-breeds-success dynamics. *Proceedings of the National Academy of Sciences*, 111(19), 6934–6939.
4 Robertson, I. H. (2018). The winner effect – the neuropsychology of power. In Garrard, P. (ed.) *The leadership hubris epidemic*. Cham, Switzerland: Palgrave Macmillan, pp.57–68, p.60.
5 Coates, J., Gurnell, M., & Sarnyai, Z. (2018). From molecule to market. In Garrard, P. (ed.) *The leadership hubris epidemic*. Cham, Switzerland: Palgrave Macmillan, pp.25–56.

6 *The Economist*. (1998). Obituary: Enoch Powell. The Economist, February 12. Available online at: https://www.economist.com/obituary/1998/02/12/enoch-powell

7 Nussey, S. & Whitehead, S. (2001). *Endocrinology: An integrated approach*. Oxford: BIOS Scientific Publishers. Available at: https://www.ncbi.nlm.nih.gov/books/NBK20. Accessed April 24, 2023.

8 Harvard Health Publishing. (2019). Testosterone – what it does and doesn't do. *Harvard Health Publishing Blog*. Available at: https://www.health.harvard.edu/medications/testosterone--what-it-does-and-doesn't-do

9 Nasser, G. N. & Leslie, S. W. (2023). Physiology, testosterone. *StatPearls*. Available at: https://www.ncbi.nlm.nih.gov/books/NBK526128

10 Van Honk, J., Schutter, D. J., Hermans, E. J., Putman, P., Tuiten, A., & Koppeschaar, H. (2004). Testosterone shifts the balance between sensitivity for punishment and reward in healthy young women. *Psychoneuroendocrinology*, 29(7), 937–943.

11 Bendahan, S., Zehnder, C., Pralong, F. P., & Antonakis, J. (2015). Leader corruption depends on power and testosterone. *The Leadership Quarterly*, 26(2), 101–122.

12 Zilioli, S., & Watson, N. V. (2014). Testosterone across successive competitions: Evidence for a 'winner effect' in humans? *Psychoneuroendocrinology*, 47, 1–9.

13 Bernhardt, P. C., Dabbs Jr, J. M., Fielden, J. A., & Lutter, C. D. (1998). Testosterone changes during vicarious experiences of winning and losing among fans at sporting events. *Physiology & Behavior*, 65(1), 59–62.

14 Apicella, C. L., Carré, J. M., & Dreber, A. (2015). Testosterone and economic risk taking: A review. *Adaptive Human Behavior and Physiology*, 1, 358–385.

15 Coates, J. M., & Herbert, J. (2008). Endogenous steroids and financial risk taking on a London trading floor. *Proceedings of the National Academy of Sciences*, 105(16), 6167–6172, p.6168.

16 Hayes, A. (2023). What is a bull market, and how can investors benefit from one? *Investopedia*. Available at: https://www.investopedia.com/terms/b/bullmarket.asp

17 Chen, J. (2022). Bear market. *Investopedia* Available at: https://www.investopedia.com/terms/b/bearmarket.asp

18 Coates, J., Gurnell, M., & Sarnyai, Z. (2018). From molecule to market. In Garrard, P. (ed.) *The leadership hubris epidemic*. Cham, Switzerland: Palgrave Macmillan, pp.25–56.

19 Langevoort, D. C. (2002). Taming the animal spirits of the stock markets: A behavioral approach to securities regulation. *Northwestern University Law Review*, 97, 135–188, p.147.

20 Baddeley, M. (2010). Herding, social influence and economic decision-making: socio-psychological and neuroscientific analyses. *Philosophical Transactions of the Royal Society B: Biological Sciences*, 365(1538), 281–290; Kocher, M. G., Lucks, K. E., & Schindler, D. (2019). Unleashing animal spirits: Self-control and overpricing in experimental asset markets. *The Review of Financial Studies*, 32(6), 2149–2178.

21 Eisenegger, C., Haushofer, J., & Fehr, E. (2011). The role of testosterone in social interaction. *Trends in Cognitive Sciences*, 15(6), 263–271.

22 Coates, J., Gurnell, M., & Sarnyai, Z. (2018). From molecule to market. In Garrard, P. (ed.) *The leadership hubris epidemic*. Cham, Switzerland: Palgrave Macmillan, pp.25–56, p.48.

23 Chiak, M. & Sahay, R. (2018). Women in finance: An economic case for gender equality. *International Monetary Fund Blog*, September 19. Available at: https://www.imf.org/en/Blogs/Articles/2018/09/19/blog-women-in-finance

24 Frederick, S. (2005). Cognitive reflection and decision making. *Journal of Economic Perspectives*, 19(4), 25–42.

25 Nave, G., Nadler, A., Zava, D., & Camerer, C. (2017). Single-dose testosterone administration impairs cognitive reflection in men. *Psychological Science*, 28(10), 1398–1407.

26 Velasco, E. (2017). Testosterone makes men less likely to question their impulses. *Caltech*, April 27. Available at: https://www.caltech.edu/about/news/testosterone-makes-men-less-likely-question-their-impulses-55864

27 Koenigs, M., Young, L., Adolphs, R., Tranel, D., Cushman, F., Hauser, M., & Damasio, A. (2007). Damage to the prefrontal cortex increases utilitarian moral judgements. *Nature*, 446(7138), 908–911.

28 Koenigs, M., Young, L., Adolphs, R., Tranel, D., Cushman, F., Hauser, M., & Damasio, A. (2007). Damage to the prefrontal cortex increases utilitarian moral judgements. *Nature*, 446(7138), 908–911.

29 Carney, D. R., & Mason, M. F. (2010). Decision making and testosterone: When the ends justify the means. *Journal of Experimental Social Psychology*, 46(4), 668–671.

30 Carney, D. R., & Mason, M. F. (2010). Decision making and testosterone: When the ends justify the means. *Journal of Experimental Social Psychology*, 46(4), 668–671.

31 *Mens Health*. (2022). Russian President Vladimir Putin accused of taking steroids that cause aggressiveness in bodybuilders. *Men's Health*, February 28. Available at: https://www.menshealth.com/uk/health/a39257659/russian-president-vladimir-putin-accused-of-taking-steroids

32 BBC. (2022). Vladimir Putin hits back at G7 leaders' topless photo jibes. *BBC News*, June 30. Available at: https://www.bbc.co.uk/news/uk-politics-61993157

33 Owen, D., & Davidson, J. (2009). Hubris syndrome: An acquired personality disorder? A study of US presidents and UK prime ministers over the last 100 years. *Brain*, 132(5), 1396–1406.

34 Eisenegger, C., Haushofer, J., & Fehr, E. (2011). The role of testosterone in social interaction. *Trends in Cognitive Sciences*, 15(6), 263–271.

35 Derntl, B., Windischberger, C., Robinson, S., Kryspin-Exner, I., Gur, R. C., Moser, E., & Habel, U. (2009). Amygdala activity to fear and anger in healthy young males is associated with testosterone. *Psychoneuroendocrinology*, 34(5), 687–693.

36 Eisenegger, C., Haushofer, J., & Fehr, E. (2011). The role of testosterone in social interaction. *Trends in Cognitive Sciences*, 15(6), 263–271.

37 Viau, V. (2002). Functional cross-talk between the hypothalamic-pituitary-gonadal and-adrenal axes. *Journal of Neuroendocrinology*, 14(6), 506–513.

38 Eisenegger, C., Haushofer, J., & Fehr, E. (2011). The role of testosterone in social interaction. *Trends in Cognitive Sciences*, 15(6), 263–271.

39 Stadler, C. (2015). How to become a CEO: These are the steps you should take. *Forbes*, March 12. Available at: https://www.forbes.com/sites/christianstadler/2015/03/12/how-to-become-a-ceo-these-are-the-steps-you-should-take/?sh=6ce0344a1217

40 Konkel, L. (2022). Cortisol: The stress hormone. *Everyday Health*, October 7. Available at: https://www.everydayhealth.com/cortisol/guide Accessed March 29, 2023.

41 Mehta, P. H., & Josephs, R. A. (2010). Testosterone and cortisol jointly regulate dominance: Evidence for a dual-hormone hypothesis. *Hormones and Behavior*, 58(5), 898–906.

42 Sherman, G. D., Lerner, J. S., Josephs, R. A., Renshon, J., & Gross, J. J. (2016). The interaction of testosterone and cortisol is associated with attained status in male executives. *Journal of Personality and Social Psychology*, 110(6), 921–929.

43 Sherman, G. D., Lerner, J. S., Josephs, R. A., Renshon, J., & Gross, J. J. (2016). The interaction of testosterone and cortisol is associated with attained status in male executives. *Journal of Personality and Social Psychology*, 110(6), 921–929.

44 Sarpong, D., Sajdakova, J., & Adams, K. (2019). The Mabey and Johnson bribery scandal: A case of executive hubris. *Thunderbird International Business Review*, 61(2), 387–396.

45 Paulhus, D. L., & Williams, K. M. (2002). The Dark Triad of personality: Narcissism, Machiavellianism, and psychopathy. *Journal of Research in Personality*, 36(6), 556–563.

46 Pfattheicher, S. (2016). Testosterone, cortisol and the Dark Triad: Narcissism (but not Machiavellianism or psychopathy) is positively related to basal testosterone and cortisol. *Personality and Individual Differences*, 97, 115–119.

47 Noser, E., Schoch, J., & Ehlert, U. (2018). The influence of income and testosterone on the validity of facial width-to-height ratio as a biomarker for dominance. *PloS One*, 13(11), e0207333.

48 Mead, N. L., Baumeister, R. F., Stuppy, A., & Vohs, K. D. (2018). Power increases the socially toxic component of narcissism among individuals with high baseline testosterone. *Journal of Experimental Psychology: General*, 147(4), 591–596.

49 Pfattheicher, S. (2016). Testosterone, cortisol and the Dark Triad: Narcissism (but not Machiavellianism or psychopathy) is positively related to basal testosterone and cortisol. *Personality and Individual Differences*, 97, 115–119, p.117.

50 Brown, R. P., & Zeigler-Hill, V. (2004). Narcissism and the non-equivalence of self-esteem measures: A matter of dominance? *Journal of Research in Personality*, 38(6), 585–592.

51 Apicella, C. L., Dreber, A., Campbell, B., Gray, P. B., Hoffman, M., & Little, A. C. (2008). Testosterone and financial risk preferences. *Evolution and Human Behavior*, 29(6), 384–390.

52 Ahmed, S., Sihvonen, J., & Vähämaa, S. (2019). CEO facial masculinity and bank risk-taking. *Personality and Individual Differences*, 138, 133–139.

53 Lindberg, M. K., Vandenput, L., Movèrare, S. S., Vanderschueren, D., Boonen, S., Bouillon, R., & Ohlsson, C. (2005). Androgens and the skeleton. *Minerva Endocrinologica*, 30(1), 15–25.

54 Lefevre, C. E., Lewis, G. J., Perrett, D. I., & Penke, L. (2013). Telling facial metrics: Facial width is associated with testosterone levels in men. *Evolution and Human Behavior*, 34(4), 273–279.

55 Zheng, Z., Li, D., Zhong, T., Wang, T., & He, L. (2023). CEO facial structure and stock price crash risk. *Accounting and Finance*, 63(S1), 873–905.

56 Pentland, A. (2010). *Honest signals: How they shape our world*. Cambridge, MA: MIT Press.

57 Jia, Y., Lent, L. V., & Zeng, Y. (2014). Masculinity, testosterone, and financial misreporting. *Journal of Accounting Research*, 52(5), 1195–1246.

58 Akstinaite, V., Robinson, G., & Sadler-Smith, E. (2020). Linguistic markers of CEO hubris. *Journal of Business Ethics*, 167, 687–705.

59 Kosinski, M. (2017). Facial width-to-height ratio does not predict self-reported behavioral tendencies. *Psychological Science*, 28(11), 1675–1682. This study, which used a large sample (N = 137,163), calls into question whether the "links between fWHR and behaviour generalize beyond the small samples and specific experimental settings that have been used in past fWHR research" (p.1675).

60 Gurnell, M. (2018). Stress in the world of finance. *Endocrinologist*, 130, Winter. Available at: https://www.endocrinology.org/endocrinologist/130-winter18/features/stress-in-the-world-of-finance

61 Eagly, A. H. (2016). When passionate advocates meet research on diversity, does the honest broker stand a chance? *Journal of Social Issues*, 72(1), 199–222.

62 Kocher, M. G., Lucks, K. E., & Schindler, D. (2019). Unleashing animal spirits: Self-control and overpricing in experimental asset markets. *The Review of Financial Studies*, 32(6), 2149–2178.

63 Barnett, V. (2017). Keynes, animal spirits, and instinct: Reason plus intuition is better than rational. *Journal of the History of Economic Thought*, 39(3), 381–399.

64 Barnett, V. (2017). Keynes, animal spirits, and instinct: Reason plus intuition is better than rational. *Journal of the History of Economic Thought*, 39(3), 381–399.

6

SELF-DECEPTION

The Better Than Average Effect

How good a driver are you? Are you better or worse than the average? When a sample of students were asked to compare their driving ability in terms of skill and safety to that of their fellow students in an experiment by the Swedish psychologist Ola Svenson in the 1980s over 80 per cent of them believed that they were safer and more skilful than their peers.[1] A moment's reflection reveals that it's mathematically impossible for more than 50 per cent to be better than average. This means that the overwhelming majority of students in the sample were over-confident to the extent that they were deluding themselves about their driving abilities. The scale of this kind of self-deception is even greater amongst academics. A study of university lecturers found that the vast majority (94 percent) thought that they were of above average teaching ability. Astonishingly, a significant majority (68 per cent) were confident enough to place their abilities in the top quartile.

DOI: 10.4324/9781003128427-6

The students' perceptions of themselves on the socially desirable skill of driving were upwardly distorted and self-enhancing. The same was true for the lecturers' upwardly biased assessments of their teaching abilities. The rule seems to be that most drivers think they're better than average at driving, most lecturers think they're better than average at lecturing; it's therefore likely that most managers think they're better than average at managing and most leaders think they're better than average at leading. People can even believe that they're less biased than others—they're biased about their biases (i.e. they're 'meta-biased').

The tendency to think we're higher on socially desirable traits and abilities is called the 'better-than-average effect' (BTAE). It's the tendency for people to perceive themselves as superior compared with their average peer. The finding that most people think they're better than average on socially valued dimensions, whether this be looks, intelligence, friendliness, honesty, sincerity, creativity, and so on has been observed across hundreds of studies.[2] The BTAE is a conundrum because mathematically speaking the average person in any given sample should rate themselves as average, but they don't. Our self-perceptions are skewed. The BTAE rule is as follows: substantially more than half the people in any given sample frequently rate themselves as better than average on abilities and traits that are perceived as desirable. For example, only about 5 per cent of people rate themselves as below average on intelligence.[3] This is both unintelligent and mathematically impossible.

Most people are to some extent 'self-enhancing',[4] however when self-enhancement is taken to excess it becomes self-aggrandisement, and it's then a short step to hubris. Whilst the research on self-enhancement and self-aggrandisement doesn't tell us directly whether self-enhancement and self-aggrandisement is self-deceptive or whether it aims to deceive others, it does offer strong "support [for] the idea that people believe their own self-enhancing stories".[5] As an aside: deceiving others ('other-deception') isn't something that'll be considered here, but needless to say, there are numerous high-profile examples of it in business and politics. The main idea of this chapter is that self-deception can be a significant source of bias in decision-making and self-deception can lead to incompetence.

Business Bosses Who Know Best

Self-deception can affect anybody, but when it afflicts CEOs and prime ministers its effects can be significant and potentially value-destroying and destructive. If, for whatever reason, a leader thinks they're good at something, even without any objective evidence to back this up, it's likely to boost their feelings of confidence, and how self-confident they are will affect how they think, take decisions, and behave. Ultimately when self-confidence becomes over-confidence it amounts to a form of self-deception.

One of the earliest studies of the extent to which CEOs are capable of deluding themselves was Richard Roll's pioneering work in the 1980s on the 'hubris hypothesis', or more accurately the 'hubris hypothesis of corporate takeovers'. Roll was interested in whether or not corporate takeovers actually result in an increase in a firm's market value. If there was no increase in market value of the combined firm post-merger this could be taken as reflecting the fact that CEOs were deluding themselves about their ability to estimate the value that could be created from an acquisition.

Roll argued that firms who are acquiring other businesses (the 'bidding firm') can pay too much for their targets (the 'target firm') if an over-confident CEO thinks that they, not the market, know best what the likely value of the acquisition to the combined business will be. Roll's prediction, on the basis that hubristically over-confident CEOs over-pay for their acquisitions, was that around the time of the takeover, the combined value of the target and bidding firms will fall because the value of the bidding firm decreases by more than the value of the target firm increases. Roll's own data confirmed his hypothesis that "bidding firms infected by hubris simply pay too much for their targets", and his results have been replicated many times in the intervening decades.[6]

The premium that bidding firm bosses are willing to pay for a potential acquisition reflects their over-confident, deluded, and ultimately hubristic beliefs about how much the target firm is worth and how much additional value they believe they can extract from the acquisition. This means that as well as being over-confident, bidding firm managers also appear to be under the 'illusion of control': they over-emphasise the extent to which their skills can improve performance whilst under-emphasising the role of chance and other factors in firm performance. Hubristic bidding firm CEOs believe that they, rather than the market, know the true value of the target firm, and they think they can run the target firm better than the target firm managers.[7]

Over-confidence in Political Leadership

The better-than-average effect can be amplified by power and entice business and political leaders to believe they're more likely to succeed, making them more prone to over-estimating what can go right and under-estimating what can go wrong with their grand ambitions. Politics is a turbulent environment in which "a week is a long time"[8] and when political leaders become prone to over-confidence events can end up taking on a life of their own and have negative impacts well beyond the individuals concerned.

In UK politics the former Prime Minister Liz Truss holds the record for the shortest tenure of any British prime minister, having held the office for 49 days (from September 6 to October 25, 2022). Her demise, and that of her finance minister the Chancellor of the Exchequer Kwasi Kwarteng, has been directly linked to their ambitious 'Growth Plan 2022' which they announced on September 23, 2022. The plan was fatal to Truss' premiership. The BBC's economics editor, Faisal Islam, remarked in October 2022 that "Liz Truss would still be prime minister had she not pushed ahead with the mini-budget".[9] The Truss/Kwarteng mini-budget was as controversial as it was ambitious from the moment it was announced. By cutting the top rate of income tax from 45 per cent to 40 per cent Truss and Kwarteng promised big tax cuts that would benefit the wealthiest in British society. Their big idea was this would spur growth and the benefits would 'trickle down' to the masses in the second-ever biggest tax giveaway. Unfortunately the plan, had it been implemented, would also have left the poorest in British society less well off in real terms and there was nothing in the plan to say how the tax giveaway would be paid for. An added complication was that Truss and Kwarteng chose not to follow the accepted practice of inviting the independent Office for Budget Responsibility (OBR) to give its view on the financial probity of the Chancellor's proposals and provide a a check and balance on government plans.

The scale of the planned tax cuts and the lack of any OBR assessment surprised everyone, not least the financial markets who reacted instantaneously and adversely. The pound plunged to an all-time low of $1.03 against the US dollar in Asian markets. The cost of government borrowing—the 30-year gilt price—skyrocketed to over 5 per cent. To save the British financial system from a serious meltdown, the Bank of England was forced to intervene on September 28 with a £65-billion UK gilt-buying programme aimed at reducing the damage and protecting a pension system which was in serious danger of collapse. There were wider systemic effects. Mortgage rates rocketed which added an average of several hundred pounds per month in repayments to the typical borrower.

From this point forward events took on a life of their own. Truss and Kwarteng reversed the cut in the higher rate of income tax on October 3 in a series of turnarounds. Truss recalled Kwarteng from a meeting of finance ministers at the International Monetary Fund (IMF) in Washington on October 14 and fired him the next day. Her new chancellor, Jeremy Hunt, overturned almost all of the measures in a new mini-budget on October 17. By this time many of Truss's own Conservative Party colleagues were clamouring for her resignation. On October 21, she resigned as prime minister. George Osborne who was Conservative Chancellor of the Exchequer between 2010 and 2016, blamed the Truss government for a "self-induced financial crisis".[10]

The political commentator John Rentoul cited the Truss premiership as a warning about the dangers of over-confidence and ambition in politics.[11] One of the problems with politics is that when a predisposition to over-confidence is combined with significant power, the negative effects reverberate beyond the individual concerned. For example, economists at the independent Resolution Foundation estimated that in Liz Truss's seven-week premiership "£20bn was blown on unfunded cuts to national insurance and stamp duty, with a further £10bn added by higher interest rates and government borrowing costs as the markets reacted with dismay to the former prime minister's dash for growth".[12] Liz Truss herself attributed her downfall to the efforts of the "left-wing economic establishment".[13]

The Dunning-Kruger Effect and Meta-ignorance

Hubristic incompetence is amplified when a leader not only over-estimates their capabilities but also lacks the self-awareness to recognise and acknowledge the shortcomings in their capabilities and performance. This latter point adds a further (i.e. second-order or 'meta') dimension to the notion of hubristic incompetence, the liability of labouring under a double burden:

(1) the burden of one's incompetence itself and;
(2) the burden of one's lack of awareness of one's incompetence.

In the words of Charles Darwin: "ignorance more frequently begets confidence than does knowledge",[14] in other words 'ignorance of ignorance' breeds over-confidence.

Arguably, one of the biggest errors of judgement that a leader can make is to be 'meta-ignorant', i.e. ignorant of their own ignorance. First-order ignorance involves mistaken beliefs or lack of beliefs. Second order ignorance, meta-ignorance, is an attitude of mind that limits a person's ability to identify and correct their first-order ignorance.[15] In this situation the subject's epistemic limits (i.e. the limits of their knowledge) are occluded by their own arrogance, conceit, and pride. Ignorance is especially intractable and dangerous when it operates at the meta-level.[16] Leaders who find themselves in the unfortunate and unenviable position of being both unskilled and unaware end up deceiving themselves.

The BTAE is one of a number of 'self-evaluation biases'.[17] These biases are one of the root causes of over-confidence and self-deception/delusion. Another self-evaluation bias is the 'Dunning-Kruger effect(DKE).[18] It's named after the two psychologists, David Dunning and Justin Kruger, who first discovered this phenomenon in the 1990s.[19] The DKE is where someone with low ability, expertise, or experience in a specific task or an area of knowledge tends to over-estimate what they can actually do or how much they actually know in that area.

In Dunning and Kruger's original study students who scored in the lowest percentiles on grammar, humour, and reasoning dramatically over-estimated how well they had performed. You can see this on the graph from Dunning and Kruger's work in Figure 6.1 where the gap between actual and perceived performance narrows from left to right. The more capable people assessed their capabilities more accurately than did the less capable people. For example, people who were exceptionally poor at judging how funny people would find different jokes also described themselves as excellent judges of humour. Such people have the double drawback of

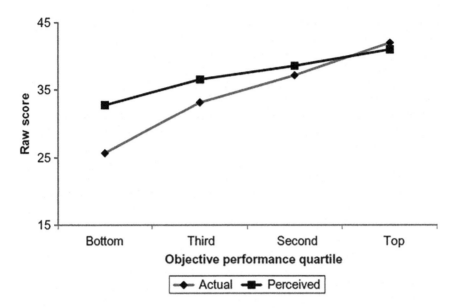

Figure 6.1 Relationship Between Actual Performance and Perceived Performance

Source: Reprinted from Dunning, D. (2011). The Dunning–Kruger effect: On being ignorant of one's own ignorance. *Advances in Experimental Social Psychology*, 44, 247–296 with permission from Elsevier.

being both unskilled (i.e. ignorant) and unaware of how unskilled they are (i.e. meta-ignorant).

The DKE has been observed in a wide variety of settings in the lab and in the real world including mathematical skill, emotional intelligence, debating, firearm use and safety, laboratory procedures, chess, driving, pharmacy, and medicine.[20] A leader who takes overly confident and ambitious decisions without sufficient expertise or experience might exhibit an upwardly biased estimate in their own abilities to make predictions and control events. This would be consistent with the DKE. In the words of one of the originators of the DKE, David Dunning, human beings are "destined not to know where the solid land of their knowledge ends and the slippery shores of their ignorance begin".[21] This is because:

(1) poor performers tend to greatly over-estimate their ability, whereas top performers make more accurate self-assessments;
(2) incompetent people lack the metacognitive[22] ability to recognise their shortcomings and have trouble evaluating their own performance;

(3) being unskilled and unaware leads to misplaced confidence;

(4) incompetent people tend to be buoyed up by the feeling that they know best, because for them their 'ignorance is bliss'.

A politician who does not suffer from any lack of confidence or ambition and whom some experts think personifies the DKE is Donald Trump.[23] The coronavirus pandemic provided the ideal stage for Trump to display this aspect of his psyche. For example, he suggested that people should wear scarves instead of masks as face protection against the virus, and that bleach could be used to kill the coronavirus inside the human body:

> And then I see the disinfectant where it knocks it out in a minute. One minute. And [in an aside to a doctor] is there a way we can do something like that, by injection inside or almost a cleaning?

At a visit to the Centers for Disease Control and Prevention in March 2020, he remarked:

> You know, my uncle was a great person. He was at MIT. He taught at MIT for, I think, like a record number of years. He was a great super genius. Dr John Trump. I like this stuff. I really get it. People are surprised that I understand it. Every one of these doctors said, "How do you know so much about this?" Maybe I have a natural ability. Maybe I should have done that instead of running for president.[24]

Being meta-ignorant as a result of the DKE is a form of self-deception, it leads to over-confidence, over-confidence creates the conditions for incompetent decisions, and incompetent decisions can bring about significant, unintended, negative consequences in the hands of those who control the levers of power. The DKE makes sense logically because for poor performers to recognise their ineptitude they'd need to possess the very expertise they lack. For example, to know how skilled or unskilled you are at using the rules of grammar requires that you know the rules of grammar. Likewise, for a CEO or prime minister to know how competent or incompetent they are requires self-reflection, self-awareness, and expertise. It's a Catch-22.

Self-deception and Obfuscation

The phrase 'Catch 22' was made famous in the novel of the same name by Joseph Heller published in 1961. In the story—which is about US pilots in the Second World War— military psychiatrist, Doc Daneeka, invokes Catch-22 to explain why any pilot requesting a psychiatric diagnosis of insanity so that he could be declared unfit to fly (and therefore escape life-threatening missions) in the very act of asking to be declared insane demonstrated his sanity and therefore was fit to fly. The term Catch-22 has come to be used to describe a situation from which there is no escape because of mutually conflicting or mutually dependent conditions.

Self-deception is a potential Catch-22 for leaders who are incompetent and unaware. There is no escape from it for incompetent leaders because they are unaware of their own incompetence. Plus, if leaders lack the humility to admit their mistakes and learn from them this compounds the problem. Arguably, if they were competent—and all things being equal—they would realise their ineptness and therefore wouldn't behave incompetently in the first place and seek to manage their deficiencies rather than continue to deceive themselves.

In some psychological accounts of self-deception the self-deceiver has two separate representations of reality, one in the unconscious mind (the truth) and one in the conscious mind (falsehood). Self-deception is an unconscious tendency to see oneself in a positive light while denying information that threatens the self. It involves holding two conflicting, i.e. positive and negative, self-beliefs; the more negative self-belief is outside conscious awareness, the more positive belief is within conscious awareness.[25] This situation is also referred to as "motivated unawareness" and "motivated lying to oneself".[26] Self-deceivers maintain a positive self-view by ignoring criticisms, discounting failures, blaming others, and generally avoiding negative thoughts.[27] Self-deceivers are fully taken in by their own act and do so in order to defend, maintain, and promote self-esteem.[28] It may be possible that a self-deceiver has actually convinced themselves that a lie is true, but this is hard to prove. For example, did Trump really believe that bleach could be used to kill coronavirus? A bigger question is why are humans prone to self-deception and why do they engage in it?

A convincing view of how self-deception works is to be found in the evolutionary psychology and anthropology literatures. William von Hippel and Robert Trivers made the common-sense observation that in social situations lying directly is one way in which to deceive other people. A less direct, more subtle approach is to avoid, obfuscate, exaggerate, or cast doubt on the truth, for example, by avoiding or down-playing critical assumptions. In both cases self-deception may prove to be adaptive, even if it's unethical. The 16th-century Florentine diplomat, philosopher, and master of manipulation, Niccolò Machiavelli, author of The Prince, recommended that "Occasionally words must serve to veil the facts. But let this happen in such a way that no one become aware of it; or, if it should be noticed, excuses must be at hand to be produced immediately."[29]

However, Von Hippel and Trivers also noted that this method of deception can be applied to the self in a process of avoidance and obfuscation whereby favourable information, i.e. information that's congruent with one's motivations and goals, is welcomed whilst unfavourable information is made unwelcome. This is tantamount to not telling oneself the whole truth; it is the active misrepresentation of reality to the conscious mind.[30] They argued that self-deception by obfuscation falls into three categories: biased information search, biased interpretation of information, and biased (mis)misremembering, see Table 6.1.[31]

In 'biased information search' people can avoid the whole truth by: adopting information searches that stop when they find the information

Table 6.1 Obfuscation of Reality by Self-deception

Method of self-deception	Description
Biased information search	Adopting information searches that stop when they find the information they hoped to find; selectively searching for information that suits their goals; selectively attending to information
Biased interpretation of information	'Selective scepticism' and convincing themselves that the data support their preformed view point; people mobilise their scepticism selectively when they encounter information which they find uncongenial to their motivations and intentions
Biased remembering	Tendency to forget information that's inconsistent with their preferences in order to maintain or enhance a positive self-view

they hoped to find, for example, avoid searching for alternative products once a purchase that can't be undone has been made; selectively searching for information that suits their goals, for example, by inhabiting a Twittersphere or reading a newspaper that acts as an echo chamber for their own preformed views; selectively attending to information, analogous to the well-known 'cocktail party phenomenon'—the ability to focus one's attention on certain personally relevant information whilst filtering out non-relevant information.

When people engage in 'biased interpretation of information' they practise 'selective scepticism' and convince themselves that the data support their preformed view point. A positive self-view or self-evaluation can be healthy and helpful, but only up to a point. In a classic study of biased interpretation, psychologists discovered that when people who are in favour of capital punishment are presented with the pros and cons of capital punishment as a deterrent they tended to accept the information that supported capital punishment and rejected the information that opposed it. The reverse was true for people who were against capital punishment. People mobilise their scepticism selectively when they encounter information which they find uncongenial to their motivations and intentions.[32] In the Iraq invasion of 2003 the faulty intelligence about Saddam Hussein's WMDs was a convenient bolster for neo-conservatives who had long-held ambitions for regime change in Iraq.

In 'biased remembering' people have a tendency to forget information that's inconsistent with their preferences; they do so in order to maintain or enhance a positive self-view. For example, in recollecting daily experiences, people are better able to recall their own good behaviours than their bad behaviours, but they don't show this bias in their recall of the good and bad behaviours of others.[33] Bad deeds can be rationalised and explained away by reinterpreting one's motives so as to make them more acceptable, for example, eating a second helping of a dessert whilst on a diet in order to 'avoid wasting it'.

Robert Trivers is of little doubt that self-deception makes a substantial contribution to human disasters and miseries be that in the waging of war, or in making political misjudgements or incompetent business decisions. In the case of warfare Trivers makes the point that this usually involves intergroup rather than intragroup conflict, and as we know only too well, can be very costly and damaging. Intragroup conflicts on the other hand are likely to be inhibited by overlaps in self-interest between individuals within the group and within group interactions providing a corrective and restraining function, whereas in intergroup conflicts these check and balances are likely to be diminished. The situation can be made worse in groups because members' motivations are likely to be aligned; hence they reinforce each other and countervailing opinions are suppressed, as in the case of 'groupthink'. Trivers concludes that self-deception is a "universal human trait" and that we should be "especially vigilant" in guarding against it, particularly when the stakes are high.[34]

Overclaiming and Over-confidence

Some people are prone to over-estimating their knowledge even to the extent of claiming knowledge of things that do not actually exist or are clearly false. This phenomenon is known as 'overclaiming'. In one study participants were tested on their knowledge of biology, literature, and philosophy. They were presented with real items and completely made-up items and asked to rate how much they knew about them, for example, in knowledge of biology, the real items included 'mammal', 'adrenal gland', and 'sciatica' and the fake items, which sounded plausibly real such as 'meta-toxins', 'bio-sexual', and 'retroplex'. Rather worryingly the majority of participants (87 per cent) claimed some knowledge of at least one fake item.[35] But the main finding from this research was that the extent to which people over-claimed knowledge was related to their self-perceived knowledge of the subject. People who thought they knew a lot about biology, literature, and philosophy claimed as much knowledge about the fake items as they did about the real items. A little, or a lack of, knowledge can be a very dangerous thing, especially when we think we know more than we do.

The more people think they know about a topic, the more likely they are to claim knowledge about it that they cannot possibly possess. Rather than accessing a mental index of their actual knowledge, people who think they know a lot draw on their pre-existing self-perception of how knowledgeable they feel they are. They then use this personal construct, rather than their actual knowledge about the topic, to make an inference about how much they know. This can have real-world consequences in politics and business. For example, someone who thinks of themselves as an expert on a topic may exude confidence such that other people are likely to believe what that person is saying. When this is allied to a leader's charisma and positional power, this can be a very convincing method by which to influence and persuade people to follow them in a shared cause, as we saw in the case of cults and gurus in Chapter 1. The problem of over-claiming can also be made worse as a result of:

(1) epistemic hubris: someone thinking they know a lot about a topic, or who once knew a lot about a topic but whose knowledge is out-of-date and who is unwilling to educate or update themselves because of their 'epistemic hubris'[36] (where 'epistemic' refers to knowledge);
(2) gut instincts: where a leader relies too much on their gut feelings, hunches, and intuitions in the absence of the requisite expertise and experience and is unwilling to engage in slower, more deliberative thinking.

To make matters worse, intuitive thinkers who lack the necessary knowledge or expertise tend to not only over-estimate their performance, but they also think they're being more rational than they actually are.[37] As was the case in the better-than-average and Dunning-Kruger effects, a predisposition to over-claim may be especially dangerous when an individual holds significant power. Senior leaders, whose views are the ones that need to be challenged and corrected most because of the consequences of their hubristic incompetence, are less likely to recognise their over-confidence or to be challenged by followers. The Catch-22 of over-claiming is that those people who are most likely to be biased are also those who are the least likely to recognise their bias.[38] The result is over-confidence bias, and when over-confidence is exercised from a position of significant power the decision-maker is much less likely to be challenged.

Over-confidence can be a double-edged sword, and the effects of misplaced confidence are likely to vary depending on the context. For example, over-confidence can be beneficial in the execution stages of a political project or business venture when followers need to be encouraged and energised to overcome obstacles and rallied and driven towards achieving a challenging goal. In certain circumstances an excess of confidence might be permissible, prudent, and sometimes desirable (see Chapter 9). On the other hand, being both unskilled and unaware of being unskilled, especially in the planning stages of a project, can be problematic because it can lead to under-estimating the viability of the project, the resources required, and the obstacles that are likely to be encountered, for example, timescales, resources, regulations, etc.[39] In the case of Liz Truss, most commentators agreed that an ambitious target of a 2.5 per cent GDP increase in itself was commendable, however the way in which she sought to achieve this was based on "misguided faith";[40] she herself admitted later that "mistakes were made" and that she "should've laid the ground better".[41]

The Pros and Cons of Over-confidence

In an area of business such as entrepreneurship, above average levels of confidence are necessary given the high rates of business start-up failures. Ambitious and aspiring business entrepreneurs need to believe that they are the ones who can beat the odds. High levels of self-confidence can also lure in potential investors to a new business venture. Likewise, one of the essential skills for a political leader or CEO is confidence. Doubts about one's leadership abilities can lead to a buck-passing approach and are likely to be picked up by potential voters.[42] To be effective, a leader must be both capable and willing to take action rather than giving the responsibility to someone else. But what happens if a leader lacks the necessary skills or experience but is nonetheless very willing? If a leader fails to realise their extent of their own ignorance they are less likely to pass the problem on to someone with the knowledge to be able to solve the problem. Instead, they will stick at it and forge ahead.

As we have seen in Chapter 2, power can have curious and cognitively debilitating effects on holders of high office. One of the paradoxes of confidence is that top corporate decision-makers persistently over-estimate their own skills relative to others. As a result they tend to be overly optimistic about the outcomes of their decisions.[43] For example, three failed launch attempts in the early stages of Elon Musk's Space X project between 2006 and 2008 almost ended the company.[44]

As well as the BTAEs and DKEs, there are a number of other factors that may lead to inflated levels of confidence amongst senior leaders:

(1) *self-serving attributions*: these are where someone (not necessarily a leader) attributes successful outcomes to their own actions whilst attributing failures to the actions of others or to sheer bad luck;

(2) *base-rate neglect*: this is where someone over-estimates their abilities by comparing themselves to the average. For example, CEOs may compare themselves to senior managers whom they are likely to meet on a daily basis and whom they are, by definition, likely to surpass in CEO qualities. Instead, they ought to be comparing themselves to the average CEO with whom they are less likely to meet and interact on a daily basis.

These sources of over-confidence can be amplified when a CEO achieves 'superstar' status, as in the various awards from magazines such as *Forbes* and *Fortune*. Researchers have found that award-winning CEOs subsequently under-perform both relative to their performance before the award and relative to a matched sample of non-award winning CEOs. Award winners also tend to extract higher levels of compensation from their organisations and spend more time on external public and private activities such as taking seats on the boards of other companies, writing business books, and CEO autobiographies.[45] The downside of having a CEO who achieves superstar status is that it can end up being counter-productive for the firm that they lead.

Most people are, by definition, about average, but few of us believe it about ourselves. We're prone to self-enhancement bias and to interpreting the world in a way that makes us feel better about ourselves and helps us to envisage positive outcomes. The chances of over-estimating our knowledge, skills, and abilities are likely to be elevated when a leader or manager has achieved significant power and/or has had a run of successes. Many extraordinary people tend, regrettably, only to be extraordinary in their own estimation.[46] The problem with leadership is that power amplifies our predisposition to think that we are above average. This can have significant consequences for leader behaviours and ultimately predispose them to the recklessness that leads to hubristic incompetence and unintended negative consequences.

Avoiding Exposure to the Self-deception Hazard

When a decision is inconsequential, such as what to choose from a restaurant menu, we can afford to take a risk, for example, by trying a novel dish. Likewise, trainee airline pilots can take as many risks as they like in a flight simulator because there are no negative consequences (other than possibly failing the course) of their risky actions. If a trainee pilot in a simulator over-estimates their level of skill there are no dire consequences for passenger safety. As far as risky activities in the real world, such as driving a car, flying a plane, or leading a country or business, are concerned there are consequences to one's actions. Believing that you're more skilled and safer as a driver than is the case is likely to influence driving behaviours and precipitate risk-taking and even recklessness. Self-deception is a significant hazard when taking decisions that are consequential.

Likewise with leadership. The more capable a leader thinks they are the more likely they are to take risks. This leads to overly optimistic behaviours. Leaders who deceive themselves under-estimate the chances of bad things happening, whilst simultaneously over-estimating the chances of good things happening. Taken to extreme, their self-deception may lead them to believe that bad things never happen to them but only happen to other people. When leaders have the power to influence the economy of a nation and the livelihoods of citizens, and they think that they are more capable than they actually are, then the risks of bringing about unintended negative consequences are high. A wider repercussion is that politicians' hubristic incompetence further undermines the frailty of trust that people have in political leaders. Hubristic incompetence is an enemy of trust.[47]

Self-deception, be that amongst politicians or business leaders, is a hubris risk factor. Fortunately, there are a number of ways in which exposure to self-deception can be avoided or abated. Being a prime minister or a CEO must be a lonely and isolating existence. Not only that, but also people who are at the top of their particular tree are, by definition, going to be dealing with people who are 'beneath them', so to speak, on a daily basis. The danger is that if they habitually benchmark themselves against subordinates with whom they come into regular contact rather than their peers then this is likely to elevate levels of self-evaluation and cause them to be upwardly biased. For a more realistic evaluation of their capabilities CEOs and prime ministers ought to be encouraged by those around them (for example, confidantes, coaches, mentors, friends, parents, partners, etc.) to benchmark themselves against other CEOs and heads of government for a more realistic assessment.

Gut feelings (the subject of Chapter 4) are paradoxical in that they can both help and hinder leaders' decision-making. One of the invidious effects of our intuitions is that they can seriously warp numerical judgements and inferences and lead us into self-deception. Such errors of judgement, which seem to be 'wired' in to the human brain, can have significant consequences. For example, someone starting up a business venture might overestimate their chances of success as a result of ignorance of the base rates of business failures (i.e. many start-ups fail to make it to the end of their first year). Likewise retail investors in the stock market can significantly underestimate their chances of losing money in the absence of a knowledge of the base rates of retail investors' success (i.e. many retail investors lose money). A little knowledge, which is often easily obtained, can go a long way in debiasing our decisions and protecting us against the risks of self-deception.

Often self-deception can be down to something as simple as a lack of knowledge. This is easy to fix so long as the potential self-deceiver is open to learning. Unfortunately one of the hallmarks of hubris is a contempt for advice even when it's presented as friendly and constructive criticism from which a leader might learn. On the other hand, one of the hallmarks of humility is an openness to comment and criticism and a willingness to learn from it. It may be a tall order, but if a potential hubrist is willing to practise a little more humility, for example, by being open to having their opinions and beliefs challenged, they may be less prone to the destructive effects of self-deception.

Over-confidence and self-deception can be particularly invidious when they occur within groups; for example, in politics this can lead to groups of ideologues having zero tolerance for naysayers. Groupthink is a feeling of optimistic invulnerability which pervades when a group of like-minded, powerful individuals arrive at a consensus, will not entertain critical thinking from within the ranks, and naysayers' loyalty is questioned.[48] Inoculating an organisation against groupthink is possible but depends crucially on creating and maintaining a culture in which:

(1) the group is aware of and accepts the perils of groupthink;
(2) members are encouraged to proactively share information and openly debate ideas from outside the group's orbit;
(3) bringers of bad news are listened to and there is no 'shooting the messenger';
(4) devil's advocacy is encouraged and integrated into decision-making processes;
(5) decisions are documented for future reference.[49]

Organisational cultures that are infected with groupthink are a breeding ground of self-deception and hubristic leadership; creating a culture that is antithetical to groupthink is one way of protecting organisations from exposure to the perils of self-deceit, intentional or otherwise. A hubristic tone at the top of a business organisation or political institution can be conducive to groupthink.

Needless to say, when intentional deceit by people who are consciously making things up, in a deliberate attempt to deceive others, comes to light it should not be tolerated by boards and shareholders or cabinets and the electorate. Unfortunately, it seems as though, in the epidemic of hubris that is sweeping through business and politics, the bar for the tolerance of deceit is regrettably high. All roads in these discussions seem to lead to Donald Trump. In 2021 the *Washington Post* fact-checker reported that in four years Donald Trump made an astounding 30,573 false or misleading claims, including "We just got seventy five million votes. And that's a record in the history of sitting presidents" (in fact: Trump received 74 not 75 million votes; Biden earned more than 81 million, a margin of 4.5 percentage points which was larger than Barack Obama's victory in 2012 and George W. Bush's victory in 2004). Trump is on record as having repeated this claim at least 19 times.[50] Facts seem to come lower down the list of priorities for hubrists who believe that "rather than being accountable to the mundane court of colleagues or public opinion, the court to which they answer is history or God" (HS, Symptom 9).[51]

Self-deception: Signs to Look Out For

(1) Leader is unskilled and unaware of how unskilled they are;
(2) Leader refuses to seek help or advice;
(3) Leader is steadfast and stubborn in the light of obvious shortcomings in performance;
(4) Leader welcomes favourable information and rejects unfavourable information;
(5) Leader ignores criticisms;
(6) Mistakes are increasingly discounted by leader;
(7) Other people or circumstances beyond leader's control are blamed for failings;
(8) Decisions are taken increasingly from position of in-group solidarity.

Notes

1 Svenson, O. (1981). Are we all less risky and more skilful than our fellow drivers? *Acta Psychologica*, 47(2), 143–148.

2 Zell, E., Strickhouser, J. E., Sedikides, C., & Alicke, M. D. (2020). The better-than-average effect in comparative self-evaluation: A comprehensive review and meta-analysis. *Psychological Bulletin*, 146(2), 118–149.

3 Gignac G. E., & Zajenkowski, M. (2019). People tend to overestimate their romantic partner's intelligence even more than their own. *Intelligence*, 73 (2019), 41–51.

4 Alicke, M. D., & Sedikides, C. (2009). Self-enhancement and self-protection: What they are and what they do. *European Review of Social Psychology*, 20:1–48.

5 Von Hippel, W., & Trivers, R. (2011). The evolution and psychology of self-deception. *Behavioral and Brain Sciences*, 34(1), 1–16, p.5.

6 Roll, R. (1986). The Hubris Hypothesis of corporate takeovers. *Journal of Business*, 59(2), 197–216, p.197.

7 Sadler-Smith, E. (2019). *Hubristic leadership*. London: SAGE.

8 This quip is usually attributed to the British Prime Minister Harold Wilson, circa 1964.

9 Islam, F. (2022). Prime Minister Liz Truss was the author of her own demise. BBC, October 20. Available at: https://www.bbc.co.uk/news/business-63330243

10 Demianyk, G. (2023). 'Political vandals': George Osborne's brutal verdict on Liz Truss's government. *The Huffington Post*, April 25. Available at: https://www.huffingtonpost.co.uk/entry/political-vandals-george-osborne-liz-truss_uk_644826cfe4b011a819c41b82

11 Rentoul, J. (2022). Liz Truss is a warning to us all about the danger of overconfidence. *The Independent*, October 28. Available at: https://www.independent.co.uk/independentpremium/voices/liz-truss-overconfidence-mini-budget-demise-b2212742.html

12 Helm, T., & Inman, P. (2022). Revealed: The £30bn cost of Liz Truss's disastrous mini-budget. *The Guardian*, November 12. Available at: https://www.theguardian.com/politics/2022/nov/12/revealed-the-30bn-cost-of-liz-trusss-disastrous-mini-budget

13 Toynbee, O. (2023). The 'left-wing economic establishment' did not bring Liz Truss down. Reality did. *The Guardian*, February 6. Available at: https://www.theguardian.com/commentisfree/2023/feb/06/leftwing-economic-establishment-liz-truss-small-state

14 Darwin, C. (1871). *The descent of man*. London: John Murray, p.3.

15 Applebaum, B. (2016). Needing not to know: Ignorance, innocence, denials, and discourse. *Philosophy of Education Archive*, 448–456.

16 Medina, J. (2013). Colour blindness, meta-ignorance, and the racial imagination. *Critical Philosophy of Race*, 1(1), 38–67.

17 BTAE differs from other self-evaluation biases such as 'unrealistic optimism' in that the latter is concerned with judgements of things that might happen in the future whereas BTAE is concerned with one's current abilities and traits. BTAE overlaps with this and other self-evaluation biases including self-esteem (see below).

18 Dunning, D. (2011). The Dunning–Kruger effect: On being ignorant of one's own ignorance. *Advances in Experimental Social Psychology*, 44, 247–296.

19 Kruger, J., & Dunning, D. (1999). Unskilled and unaware of it: How difficulties in recognizing one's own incompetence lead to inflated self-assessments. *Journal of Personality and Social Psychology*, 77(6), 1121–1134.

20 Dunning, D. (2011). The Dunning-Kruger effect. On being ignorant of one's own ignorance. *Advances in Experimental Social Psychology*, 44, 247–296.

21 Dunning, D. (2011). The Dunning-Kruger effect. On being ignorant of one's own ignorance. *Advances in Experimental Social Psychology*, 44, 247–296, p.250.

22 The ability to think critically about one's own thinking processes.

23 McIntosh, R. D., & Della Salla, S. (2022). The persistent irony of the Dunning-Kruger effect. *The Psychologist*, February 7. Available at: https://www.bps.org.uk/psychologist/persistent-irony-dunning-kruger-effect

24 Devega, C. (2020). Our Dunning-Kruger president: Trump's arrogance and ignorance are killing people. *Salon*, April 2. Available at: https://www.salon.com/2020/04/02/our-dunning-kruger-president-trumps-arrogance-and-ignorance-are-killing-people

25 Snyder, C. R. (1985) cited in Brown, A. D., & Jones, M. (2000). Honourable members and dishonourable deeds: Sensemaking, impression management and legitimation in the 'Arms to Iraq Affair'. *Human Relations*, 53(5), 655–689.

26 Brown, A. D., & Jones, M. (2000). Honourable members and dishonourable deeds: Sensemaking, impression management and legitimation in the 'Arms to Iraq Affair'. *Human Relations*, 53(5), 655–689, p.665.

27 Sackeim, H. A., & Gur, R. C.(1979). Self-deception, other-deception, and self-reported psychopathology. *Journal of Consulting and Clinical Psychology*, 47(1), 213–215.

28 Brown, A. D., & Jones, M. (2000). Honourable members and dishonourable deeds: Sensemaking, impression management and legitimation in the 'Arms to Iraq Affair'. *Human Relations*, 53(5), 655–689.

29 The Decision Lab (no date). *Niccolò Machiavelli: Why good politicians can't always be loved.* Available at: https://thedecisionlab.com/thinkers/political-science/niccolo-machiavelli

30 Trivers, R. (2000). The elements of a scientific theory of self-deception. *Annals of the New York Academy of Sciences,* 907(1), 114–131.

31 Von Hippel, W., & Trivers, R. (2011). The evolution and psychology of self-deception. *Behavioral and Brain Sciences,* 34(1), 1–16.

32 Lord, C. G., Ross, L., & Lepper, M. R. (1979). Biased assimilation and attitude polarization: The effects of prior theories on subsequently considered evidence. *Journal of Personality and Social Psychology,* 37, 2098–2109.

33 D'Argembeau, A., & Van der Linden, M. (2008). Remembering pride and shame: Self-enhancement and the phenomenology of autobiographical memory. *Memory,* 16, 538–547.

34 Trivers, R. (2000). The elements of a scientific theory of self-deception. *Annals of the New York Academy of Sciences,* 907(1), 114–131, p.129.

35 Atir, S., Rosenzweig, E., & Dunning, D. (2015). When knowledge knows no bounds: Self-perceived expertise predicts claims of impossible knowledge. *Psychological Science,* 26(8), 1295–1303.

36 Sadler-Smith, E., & Cojuharenco, I. (2021). Business schools and hubris: Cause or cure? *Academy of Management Learning & Education,* 20(2), 270–289.

37 Pennycook, G., Ross, R. M., Koehler, D. J., & Fugelsang, J. A. (2017). Dunning–Kruger effects in reasoning: Theoretical implications of the failure to recognize incompetence. *Psychonomic Bulletin & Review,* 24(6), 1774–1784.

38 Pennycook, G., Ross, R. M., Koehler, D. J., & Fugelsang, J. A. (2017). Dunning–Kruger effects in reasoning: Theoretical implications of the failure to recognize incompetence. *Psychonomic Bulletin & Review,* 24(6), 1774–1784, p.1783.

39 Dunning, D. (2011). The Dunning-Kruger effect. On being ignorant of one's own ignorance. *Advances in Experimental Social Psychology,* 44, 247–296.

40 ITV-X (2022). Mini-budget: Eight things you need to know as huge tax cuts announced. ITV News, September 23. Available at: https://www.itv.com/news/2022-09-23/mini-budget-eight-things-you-need-to-know-as-huge-tax-cuts-announced

41 McLoughlin, B. (2022). Liz Truss admits mistakes were made in mini-Budget preparation. *Evening Standard,* October 2. Available at: https://www.standard.co.uk/news/politics/liz-truss-tax-cut-mini-budget-bbc-laura-kuennsberg-kwasi-kwarteng-b1029600.html

42 Kipnis, D., & Lane, W. P. (1962). Self-confidence and leadership. *Journal of Applied Psychology,* 46(4), 291–295, p.294.

43 Malmendier, U., & Tate, G. (2005). Does overconfidence affect corporate investment? CEO overconfidence measures revisited. *European Financial Management*, 11, 649–659, p.651.

44 Kay, G., & McFall-Johnsen, M. (2023). 14 big moments in the history of Elon Musk's SpaceX – from nearly going bankrupt in 2008 to the fiery Starship explosion. *Insider*, April 23. Available at: https://www.business insider.com/spacex-history-biggest-moments-elon-musk-2022-12?r=US&IR=T#between-2006-and-2008-spacex-had-three-failed-launch-attempts-that-musk-has-said-almost-ended-the-company-3

45 Malmendier, U., & Tate, G. (2009). Superstar CEOs. *The Quarterly Journal of Economics*, 124, 1593–1638.

46 Cited in Hiller, N. J., & Hambrick, D. C. (2005). Conceptualizing executive hubris: The role of (hyper-) core self-evaluations in strategic decision-making. *Strategic Management Journal*, 26(4), 297–319, p.297.

47 Galford, R. M., & Seibold Drapeau, A. (2003). The enemies of trust. *Harvard Business Review*, February. Available at: https://hbr.org/2003/02/the-enemies-of-trust

48 Reynolds, C., & Bogan, S. (no date). How did Liz Truss and Kwasi Kwarteng get it so wrong – and how can psychology explain their downfall? *Pearn Kandola*. Available at: https://pearnkandola.com/diversity-and-inclusion-hub/leadership/how-did-liz-truss-and-kwasi-kwarteng-get-it-so-wrong-and-how-can-psychology-explain-their-downfall

49 Quast, L. (2016). Groupthink: 7 Tips to prevent disastrous decisions. *Forbes*, April 18. Available at: https://www.forbes.com/sites/lisaquast/2016/04/18/groupthink-7-steps-to-prevent-disastrous-decisions/

50 Fact Checker. (2021). In four years, President Trump made 30,573 false or misleading claims. *The Washington Post*, January 20. Available at: https://www.washingtonpost.com/graphics/politics/trump-claims-database

51 Owen, D., & Davidson, J. (2009). Hubris syndrome: An acquired personality disorder? A study of US presidents and UK prime ministers over the last 100 years. *Brain*, 132(5), 1396–1406.

7

LACK OF CHECKS AND BALANCES

Corporate Governance and Hubris

Lord David Owen, one of the originators of the idea of the hubris syndrome, has commented that above all else good leaders accept that the inbuilt checks and balances of corporations and governments should be scrupulously respected and that there should be no attempt whatsoever to circumvent them. He also noted that whilst interpersonal factors such as partners, colleagues, friends, and mentors and intrapersonal factors such as humour, cynicism, self-criticism, and humility may help to curb hubristic tendencies there can be no substitute for institutional frameworks which legitimate and enforce the checks and balances which are necessary to constrain hubris.[1]

Democratic societies have developed mechanisms such as cabinets, parliament, collective responsibility, and the media to constrain leaders in an attempt to immunise nation states against the excesses of individual

DOI: 10.4324/9781003128427-7

leaders,[2] whilst in business corporate governance is the system by which companies are directed and controlled so that they can deliver long-term success. Good corporate governance is embodied in a set of basic principles which the board of directors and the business managers should abide by in order to deliver on the company's mission and balance the interests of all its stakeholders and which they can be held accountable to by its stakeholders.[3] The principles of good corporate governance exist to ensure that effective decision-making processes, financial and other controls, and risk management systems are in place.

In business, a company's board of directors is responsible for the corporate governance of a firm since it is they who have the ultimate responsibility for the success or failure of a business. What the board does and the values it embodies are at the heart of good corporate governance.[4] Some of the basic principles of effective corporate governance from the UK's Corporate Governance Code[5] are shown in Table 7.1.

Good governance is a key issue in managing the risks associated with the hubris hazard not least because having a hubrist in the top team can be an existential risk to a business as attested to by the numerous examples

Table 7.1 Basic Principles of Corporate Governance

Principle	Description
Mission	The company should be led by an effective board whose role is to promote the long-term success of the business, deliver value for its stakeholders, and contribute to wider society.
Conduct	An effective board should establish the business's purpose, values, and strategy and align these with the culture of the organisation. The members of the board should act with integrity and lead by example.
Resources	The board should ensure that the necessary resources are in place to deliver on the business's mission.
Control	The board should establish a framework of effective controls which enable risk to be recognised, assessed, and managed.
Engagement	In order to act responsibly towards its stakeholders the board should ensure that there's effective engagement with, and participation from, the business's stakeholders.
People policies and practices	The board should ensure that its workforce policies and practices fit with the company mission and values, that these support long-term success and sustainability, and that employees are able to raise issues of concern.

cited in this book and to be found almost daily in the news media. What are the consequences for individuals, and for the organisations that they lead, when the basic principles of good corporate governance are ignored or even absent in the first place? In the living laboratory of hubris that is business, the case of Sam Bankman-Fried is a salutary tale of what can go wrong when there are 'no adults in the room' to keep a lid on a leader's hubristic exuberances.

Sam Bankman-Fried and FTX

At the time of writing, Sam Bankman-Fried (often referred to as SBF), the 31-year-old co-founder and ex-CEO of the now bankrupt cryptocurrency company FTX, is at the centre of one of the most significant scandals to rock the corporate world. His trial commenced in October 2023 in a Federal Court in Manhattan, and at the time of writing the outcome is unknown. SBF has pleaded not guilty to seven counts of fraud and conspiracy in connection with the collapse of FTX. The case was described by the US Attorney of the Southern District of New York as potentially "one of the biggest financial frauds" in history.[6] A guilty verdict could result in a prison sentence for SBF of 115 years.[7] SBF, who ticked all the boxes for the unconventional, eccentric, entrepreneurial hero even down to his trademark attire of tee shirt, cargo shorts. and trainers, became like Elizabeth Holmes before him (see Chapter 3) the centre of attention for the business and popular press in the USA. His image adorned the covers of *Fortune* and *Forbes* magazines.[8] From a standing start in 2019 FTX grew to be one of the world's biggest cryptocurrency exchanges. In early 2022 it was valued at $32 billion. According to *Forbes*, at its peak SBF's personal wealth is estimated to have been $26.5 billion. Less than a year later SBF told the *New York Times* that his total wealth had plummeted to a relatively modest $100,000.[9]

The Rise of SBF

SBF was born on March 5, 1992 the son of two Stanford University Law School professors, Joe Bankman and Barbara Fried. At high school SBF was mathematically gifted. He graduated from Massachusetts Institute of Technology (MIT) as a physics major with mathematics. After graduating he worked as an intern at Jane Street Capital, one of the world's biggest trading firms. He left Jane Street to join the Centre for Effective Altruism (CEA) briefly as its Director of Development in October 2017 and then left the following November to form his own cryptocurrency trading firm Alameda Research with Tara MacAulay. Effective altruism is a philanthropy movement which espouses the 'Robin Hood' ideal of trying to make as much money as possible so as to be able to maximise one's charitable donations.[10]

In 2019 SBF founded a sister company to Alameda Research; he called it FTX (short for 'Futures Exchange'). FTX was a crypto derivatives exchange fund based on the principle of buying cryptocurrencies in one market and selling them in another as a way to make "quick and easy money".[11] FTX very quickly became one of the world's leading cryptocurrency exchanges. It struck a "long-term partnership" deal with Formula 1 Motor Racing with its logo prominently displayed on Mercedes F1 cars and on the apparel of its number-one driver, Lewis Hamilton.[12] FTX featured in TV advertisements featuring the star American former football quarterback Tom Brady. The marking strategy was aimed directly at retail investors with the strap line 'FTX: The most trusted way to buy and sell crypto' and 'FTX: don't miss out on crypto. The next big thing'.[13] Beyond the retail sectors FTX attracted high-profile investors including SoftBank and the world's biggest investment company, BlackRock. On September 22, 2022 one of the leading venture capital firms, Sequoia Capital, published a 13,000-word profile of SBF in which he was described as a billionaire who had achieved no less than "the status of legend" at the tender age of 30.[14] In early 2022 FTX's value peaked at around $40 billion, worth more than Deutsche Bank.[15]

On the ground, FTX was run from 'The Albany', a 600-acre luxury compound in Nassau the Bahamas (owned in part by Tiger Woods and Justin Timberlake).[16] The Bahamian government had developed bespoke regulations to attract cryptocurrency firms and welcomed FTX.[17] The main company office was a 12,000-square-foot, five-bedroom penthouse which housed SBF, Caroline Ellison who was also Alameda's co-CEO, Gary Wang his Chief Technology Officer (CTO) and former MIT room-mate, and Nishad Singh FTX Director of Engineering and a high school friend of SBF's brother. The penthouse set-up has been described as being more like a college dormitory than the headquarters of one of the world's largest cryptocurrency firms.[18] SBF was dubbed the King of Crypto[19] and only months before FTX collapsed he shared the stage with various luminaries including Bill Clinton and Tony Blair.

The Fall of SBF

After a meteoric rise following the founding of FTX in 2019, SBF's and FTX's precipitous downfall occurred over a few short weeks between November 2022 and December 2022. The key event was on November 2, 2022 when CoinDesk, a news site specialising in bitcoin and digital currencies, published an exclusive report revealing some perplexing balance-sheet details for Alameda which showed that a substantial proportion of its $14.6 billion of assets was heavily invested in FTX's Token 'FTT' (in effect a share in FTX with a buy-back promise):

> Bankman-Fried's trading giant Alameda rests on a foundation largely made up of a coin that a sister company invented, not an independent asset like a fiat currency[20] or another crypto. The situation adds to evidence that the ties between FTX and Alameda are unusually close.[21]

One finance expert commented that "It's fascinating to see that the majority of the net equity in the Alameda business is actually FTX's own centrally controlled and printed-out-of-thin-air token".[22] Even though they were supposed to be separate, FTX's sister company Alameda apparently held over $5 billion in FTT (i.e., FTX's 'loyalty' tokens).[23] The *Financial Times* described the relationship between the two companies that were supposed to be separate as not only close but "incestuous".[24] The CoinDesk report raised significant questions about the state of Alameda's financial health and raised the spectre of a potential liquidity crisis. On November 6 in response to the CoinDesk scoop, the CEO of FTX's main rival Binance, Changpeng Zhao (CZ), tweeted that he would be selling his holdings of FTT tokens: "Due to recent revelations that have came [sic] to light, we have decided to liquidate any remaining FTT on our books" (3:47pm Nov. 6, 2022); CZ added that "we will try to do so in a way that minimizes market impact" and tried to assure the markets that this wasn't a "move against a competitor".[25] Binance's stake in FTX had amounted to $580 billion.[26] In the subsequent 24 hours the price of FTX's token plummeted and customers struggled to withdraw their money.[27]

On Tuesday November 8 Binance tweeted that it wanted to buy FTX and had signed a non-binding letter of intent (LOI) with SBF subject to due diligence (DD):

> This afternoon, FTX asked for our help. There is a significant liquidity crunch. To protect users, we signed a non-binding LOI, intending to fully acquire http://FTX.com and help cover the liquidity crunch. We will be conducting a full DD in the coming days.
>
> (4:09pm Nov. 8, 2022)

CZ, who subsequently faced legal difficulties of his own, commented further that "there's a lot to cover and it will take some time" and drew attention to the fact that Binance "has the discretion to pull out from the deal at any time".[28] The next day, Wednesday November 9, having looked 'under the bonnet' at FTX's books, Binance scrapped the deal and walked away. In a statement to CoinDesk, a Binance spokesperson said: "As a result of corporate due diligence, as well as the latest news reports regarding mishandled customer funds and alleged U.S. agency investigations, we have decided that we will not pursue the potential acquisition of FTX.com".[29]

Then, on Thursday November 10, SBF suddenly announced that Alameda was winding down with a promise that he'd use every penny of its assets to repay users of the tokens. He began his 21-tweet long announcement with "1) I'm sorry. That's the biggest thing. I f***ed up, and should have done better." (1/21) and ended with what can only be described as Twitter-babble (in mixed upper and lower case):

> 21) NOT ADVICE, OF ANY KIND, IN ANY WAY. I WAS NOT VERY CAREFUL WITH MY WORDS HERE, AND DO NOT MEAN ANY OF THEM IN A TECHNICAL OR LEGAL SENSE; I MAY WELL HAVE NOT DESCRIBED THINGS RIGHT though I'm trying to be transparent. I'M NOT A GOOD DEV AND PROBABLY MISDESCRIBED SOMETHING.
>
> (21/21; 2:13pm Nov. 10 2022)

At around 10pm that same day it was announced that the Bahamian Securities Commission had frozen the assets of FTX and applied to the Supreme Court of the Bahamas for the appointment of an attorney to act as liquidator for FTX.[30] As events gathered momentum the very next day, Friday November 11, it was announced that the FTX group (including

Alameda Research and its 'jungle' of 130 affiliated companies) was filing for bankruptcy protection in the USA under Chapter 11 bankruptcy proceedings (a form of bankruptcy involving the reorganisation of a debtor's business affairs, debts, and assets). The impact on investors was significant to say the least. Sequoia Capital, who it may be recalled previously described SBF as a "legend", marked down its $214-million investment to zero.[31] SBF resigned and John J. Ray III was appointed as the new CEO to oversee the bankruptcy proceedings.[32] Ray has over 40 years of legal and restructuring experience having been the Chief Restructuring Officer or CEO in "several large and vexing corporate failures involving allegations of criminal activity and malfeasance, including the Enron bankruptcy".[33]

On Sunday November 13 Reuters reported that SBF had "moved" $10 billion in funds from FTX to Alameda, that between "$1billion and $2billion in client money is unaccounted for", and that executives set up a "bookkeeping back door that thwarted [internal compliance or accounting] red flags"; moreover the "whereabouts of the missing funds is unknown".[34] In an attempt at mitigation SBF commented that "We didn't secretly transfer. We had confusing internal labelling and misread it."[35]

On November 30, against the advice of his lawyers, SBF gave an interview to the New York Times in which he claimed that these issues stemmed from sloppy accounting, a market crash, and not from any unlawful activity. He claimed to be ignorant of what was going on between FTX and Alameda Research and said neither he nor anyone else, to the best of his knowledge, oversaw the compliance of the two entities and that this was "a failure [of corporate governance] he now regrets". In the same interview in response to a question about whether he'd co-mingled FTX and Alameda Research funds, SBF said that he didn't "knowingly" do so.

Things went from bad to worse for SBF when on December 12, 2022 the Bahamian police arrested him. He initially resisted extradition to the USA, but after spending nine nights in a Bahamian jail, he was extradited on December 21. He appeared before a Federal judge on December 22 and was granted bail of $250 million secured against his parents' home in Palo Alto to which he was confined wearing an ankle monitor as part of this bail conditions.[36]

Hours after SBF was handed over to the US authorities more unwelcome news followed. His former FTX colleague and MIT room-mate Gary Wang pleaded guilty to charges of wire fraud, conspiracy to commit wire fraud, conspiracy to commit commodities fraud, and conspiracy to commit securities fraud. Caroline Ellison, his former girlfriend and Alameda's ex-CEO, pleaded guilty to two counts of wire fraud, two counts of conspiracy to commit wire fraud, conspiracy to commit commodities fraud, conspiracy to commit securities fraud, and conspiracy to commit money laundering.[37] As part of their deal with the Southern District of New York both Ellison and Wang agreed to 'cooperate fully' with investigators and to "truthfully and completely disclose all information concerning all matters' related to FTX".[38] Then in February 2023, FTX's former engineering director, Nishad Singh, admitted six charges, which included three counts of conspiracy to commit fraud, as part of his bargain with the authorities. Singh also agreed to cooperate with the prosecutors.[39]

On Tuesday January 3, 2022 at the Manhattan Federal court, eight charges were made against SBF including wire fraud, conspiracy to commit commodities and securities fraud, conspiracy to commit money laundering, and campaign finance violations. The Assistant US Attorney alleged that SBF had also "laundered money through political donations and charitable donations" and that the unlawful activities "took place with the defendant's knowledge and at his direction".[40] In court, not in his trademark cargo shorts but in a blue suit, white shirt, and spotted tie, SBF pleaded not guilty to the charges of defrauding FTX customers and investors, defrauding lenders to Alameda, and violating US political campaign finance laws.

The plot thickened when on March 16, 2023 the *Financial Times* (FT) reported that SBF and "five members of his inner circle transferred $3.2billion in total to their personal account in the form of 'payments and loans' " and that the funds came primarily from Alameda Research. Then on March 29, 2023 the same newspaper also reported that "US prosecutors accused SBF of sending a bribe to regain access to trading accounts that had been frozen by law enforcement in China". The FT described this payment as being "roughly $40million".[41]

Reflecting on the case Katie Martin, Markets Editor of the FT commented that "If you're a nerd and you're working with a bunch of other nerds and you're changing the world through sheer nerdery, you feel pretty powerful".[42] Against the advice of his lawyers, SBF continued to give interviews to the press. In conversation with George Stephanopoulos for the TV show *Good Morning America* he admitted that "[H]onestly, if I look back on myself I think I got a little cocky, I mean more than a little bit, um, and I think part

[of] me like you know felt, um, like um we'd made it".[43] In an interview with the FT published on February 9, 2023, whilst still awaiting trial, SBF reflected that: "It felt to me like everyone around me had lost their minds all at once ... I did feel sort of like there were no adults left in the room".[44]

Ironically, immediately prior to his arrest SBF was actively engaged in lobbying in Washington for a regulatory framework for cryptocurrency.[45] Had he not been arrested by the Bahamian police he would have made a scheduled appearance at the US House Financial Services Committee on December 13. According to the script of his planned testimony, which was obtained by *Forbes*, he was intending to say somewhat gnomically: "When all is said and done, I'll judge myself by one metric: whether I have eventually been able to make customers whole".

Corporate Governance at FTX

The FT described FTX as a multi-billion-dollar business "unlike any other": it didn't have a board; there was nobody overseeing what was going on; and there were no risk management procedures.[46] The expert appointed to oversee the administration of FTX, John J. Ray, identified numerous shortcomings in corporate governance at FTX including lack of formal board meetings, lack of formal lists of bank accounts and account signatories, lack of documentation for key transactions, etc. FTX employees used 'QuickBooks' for the accounts (a package more suited to a one-person business and small and medium-sized enterprises) and the 'Slack' app for filing expenses.[47] Table 7.2 summarises Ray's testimony to the House Financial Services Committee on December 13, 2002.

Ray also commented that whilst there is much that we do not know and perhaps never will know about FTX, a number of fundamentals appear to be self-evident:

> Customer assets from FTX.com were commingled with assets from the Alameda trading platform; Alameda used client funds to engage in margin trading which exposed customer funds to massive losses; FTX went on a spending binge in late 2021 through 2022, during which approximately $5billion was spent buying a myriad of businesses and investments many of which may be worth only a fraction of what was paid for them; Loans and other payments were made to insiders in excess of $1billion.[48]

Table 7.2 John J. Ray III's Summary of Unacceptable Management Practices at FTX

Failure	Description
Access to customer assets	Use of computer infrastructure that gave senior management access to systems that stored customer assets, without security controls to prevent them from redirecting those assets
Ineffective security controls	Storing of private keys to access hundreds of millions of dollars in crypto assets without effective security controls or encryption
Borrowing by Alameda from FTX	Ability of Alameda to borrow funds from FTX for its own trading or investments without any effective limits
Comingling of assets	The commingling of Alameda and FTX assets
Lack of documentation	Lack of complete documentation for investment transactions involving FTX Group funds and assets
Audit failures	Absence of audited or reliable financial statements
Risk management	Lack of financial and risk management functions
Governance	Absence of any form of independent governance throughout the FTX Group

In an interview for CoinDesk TV on the back of the December 13 meeting of the House Financial Services Committee, the New York Democrat Congressman Ritchie Torres, who has been critical of crypto regulation, pointed out that decisions about the disbursement of funds were made in an on-line chat with personalised emojis.[49] The Congressman also commented that "FTX had the corporate governance of a fraternity [and] it would be laughable were it not so serious".[50] As a veteran of the Enron bankruptcy, in his preliminary report Mr Ray spoke very directly:

> Never in my career have I seen such a complete failure of corporate controls and such a complete absence of trustworthy financial information as occurred here. From compromised systems' integrity and faulty regulatory oversight abroad, to the concentration of control in the hands of a very small group of inexperienced, unsophisticated and potentially compromised individuals, this situation is unprecedented.[51]

In its analysis of the bankruptcy report which exposed FTX as one of the most comprehensive failures of corporate governance, *Forbes* identified the numerous defects including:

(1) *Non-existent board of directors*: the board, which never had any board meetings, in effect consisted of SBF, the only other two members had

dropped off the board months before the collapse and hadn't been replaced;

(2) *Conflicts of interest*: the company was rife with conflicts of interest and self-dealings in its alleged funnelling of money from FTX to prop-up Alameda, SBF told the FT that FTX had "accidentally given $8billion of its customers' funds to Alameda";

(3) *Lack of financial controls*: there was no centralised control of cash flows and balances, and because of historical cash management failures the exact amount of cash that the FTX Group held may never be known.

Forbes summarised the FTX episode as one of governance failures that were "vast and severe".[52] The financial journalist Ollie Smith, writing for the American financial services firm Morning Star, identified 'key man [person] risk' as central to the FTX case.[53] Smith noted that organisations expose themselves to many potential leadership derailments when they become too dependent on one individual and the risk is magnified where there's an absence of checks and balances that could help to hold potentially hubristic leaders to account. John J. Ray III's initial report, released in April 2023, offered the following summarisation: "while the FTX Group's failure is novel in the unprecedented scale of harm it caused in a nascent industry, many of its root causes are familiar: hubris, incompetence, and greed". [54]

Corporate Governance and Hubris

The presence of good corporate governance can and should alleviate the negative effects of CEO hubris; the absence of good corporate governance, on the other hand, will exacerbate the negative effects of CEO hubris. Good governance should protect an organisation's stakeholders and its assets from being exposed to the hubris hazard. This basic principle was put to the test by a group of researchers in South Korea led by Jong-Hun Park in a study of the relationship between CEO hubris, CEO power, governance, and firm performance in a sample of over 600 Korean firms between 2001 and 2008. Park and his colleagues measured CEO hubris indirectly using a media praise for the CEO (based on newspaper reports), CEO awards, and levels of confidence in the language that CEOs used in their letters to shareholders. CEO power was measured by CEOs' years of tenure (i.e. how 'entrenched' they were) and their level of ownership of the firm. Board vigilance was measured in terms of the proportion of outside members of the board (i.e. the 'outsider ratio') and whether or not the CEO was the chair of the board (i.e. 'duality' where CEO holds both positions, and 'non-duality' where CEO is not the chair). Firm performance was measured using two-year, industry-adjusted return-on-assets (ROA).[55] Park and his colleagues found that:

(1) CEO hubris was negatively related to firm performance, i.e. firms led by high hubris CEOs underperformed compared to those led by low hubris CEOs;
(2) the effect of hubris on firm performance was mitigated when there was low CEO ownership, CEO non-duality, and high outsider ratio, i.e. the negative effects of CEO hubris are not as bad when effective governance is in place (i.e. non-duality and high outsider ratio), see Figure 7.1.

The Korean researchers concluded that separating out the roles of CEO and chairperson so that one person cannot occupy both (i.e. non-duality) and having a higher proportion of outside directors on the boards of companies are simple and straightforward ways in which corporate governance could be used to combat the detrimental effects of a hubristic CEO on

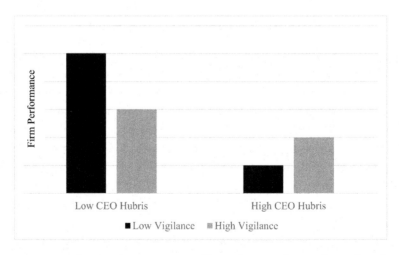

Figure 7.1 Generalised and Approximate Effects of CEO Hubris and Board Vigilance on Firm Performance

firm performance. However, they also noted that board vigilance can only reduce the negative effects of CEO hubris, it cannot change a hubrist's negative influence into a positive one.

In the case of FTX, SBF rose quickly to the status of CEO celebrity, however celebrity status is often associated with hubris and related negative effects. For example, researchers discovered that CEOs who had won 'CEO of the Year' awards tended to extract higher compensation from their business in the form of stock and options.[56] Not only that, but award winners also engaged in distractions and non-value-adding activities such as sitting on outside boards, writing popular business books, playing more golf, etc., all of which brought little benefit to the firm itself.[57] The same study also found that long-term under-performance of superstar CEOs and unrestrained increases in their equity-based compensation were typical of firms with weak corporate governance. This resonates with the Boston Consulting Group's (BCG's) suggestion that better control can be leveraged over potentially hubristic CEOs through better management of executive compensation and rewards. Another route for managing CEO hubris is by limiting their term in office in much the same say as functioning democracies do with prime ministers and presidents, such as the two four-year terms for US presidents. The BCG recommends that CEOs should not serve more than ten years (whilst acknowledging that there are always bound to be exceptions, for example, Ingvar Kamprad at IKEA and Jack Welch at GE). BCG's recommmendations for combatting CEO and top management team hubris through the remuneration and tenure routes include:

(1) remuneration and bonus payments for top managers should be such that CEOs still have 'skin in the game';
(2) CEOs and boards should ask 'Is CEO compensation in line with performance?';
(3) CEOs who've failed to deliver should face negative consequences — consequences for fraud should be proportionate and severe;
(4) CEOs should regularly shake up the top management team, especially when the top management team (TMT) is unwilling/incapable of challenging leader/status quo;
(5) CEOs' tenures, like those of politicians in functioning democracies, should be time limited;

(6) most CEOs, in the spirit of stewardship, should step aside after no more
     than ten years in office.

BCG acknowledge that in any walk of life knowing when to 'move on' or
'hang up one's boots' is one of the most difficult professional decisions. But
it's perhaps better for a CEO, or head of government, to leave on a high and
quit while they're ahead rather than become encumbered with the trappings of power and success and fall prey to hubris.[58]

Under the shareholder model of corporate governance there is typically
a single-tier board structure, comprised of executive and non-executive
directors (NEDs). The stakeholder model, on the other hand, can involve
a two-tier structure of a supervisory board and a management board (for
example, in Germany companies such as Volkswagen have an *Aufsichtsrat* and
the *Vorstand* filling these two roles respectively).[59] NEDs differ from executive directors in that they are essentially 'outsiders' to a company who are
detached from day-to-day operations; as such their role is to contribute to
the board by providing independent oversight and constructive challenges
to the CEO and other executive directors.[60]

To be effective the board of a company needs to have an NED team on
the board with two essential and related capabilities: first, the requisite
knowledge and experience to understand the business; and, second, the
courage and social skills to be able to challenge executives.[61] Furthermore,
in terms of some basic moral guidelines for shaping governance principles,
a major US technology company set down the following ethical questions
that could be used as a check and balance on corporate behaviour:

1) Is the action legal?
2) Does it comply with our values?
3) Would it make you feel bad if you did it?
4) How would it look in the newspaper?
5) Do you know in your heart of heart that it's wrong?
6) Are you sure about it? If you're not then you should ask.[62]

Many of the hubristic business failures documented in this book have their
roots in weakness at the corporate and institutional levels and a lack of
the necessary checks and balances to curtail a hubristic leader's behaviour
which exposes a business, industry, or nation state to the hubris hazard.

The governance principle of executive restraint applies to politics also, but the potential mechanisms for containing a hubristic prime minister or president are somewhat different.

Every Hubrist Needs a Toe-holder

Margaret Thatcher (1925–2013) was prime minister of the UK from 1979 to 1990. Views on her premiership still bitterly divide opinion in the UK. She was responsible for huge swathes of privatisation of public sector business including telecoms and gas, she diminished (or reined in depending on your point of view) the power of trade unions, particularly the coal miners' union, widened home ownership by selling off council-owned properties, successfully stood up to the Argentinian invasion of the Falkland Islands, and through her friendship with Ronald Reagan and Mikhail Gorbachev was instrumental in hastening the end of the Cold War and the break up of the Soviet Union. There can be no doubt that she was one of the most influential politicians of the 20th century, on both the national and international stages.

Thatcher's fall from grace is almost as well known as her rise to power and her achievements. David Owen, in his book *The Hubris Syndrome: Bush, Blair and the Intoxication of Power* (2007), referred to Thatcher's premiership as a "model case of a political leader succumbing to hubris syndrome".[63] During her initial period in office she was not hubristic. The inflexion point seems to have come following her success in the Falklands War in 1982. After this she began to be dismissive of her critics and surrounded herself with like-minds and created an echo chamber for her own views. She became dangerously confident of her own judgement and contemptuous of other people's opinions. The gradient of her upwards hubristic trajectory steepened in 1988 when William Whitelaw, who had been her deputy prime minister, confidante, and restraining influence, stepped down. A prominent member of Thatcher's government, the former Chancellor of the Exchequer Nigel Lawson, said of the Thatcher-Whitelaw relationship:

> He was irreplaceable. It was not simply that he was a wise elder statesman of immense experience and acute political instinct, unfailingly loyal and devoid of personal ambition, to whom Margaret could always turn. He also resolved many of the tensions that arise between

Cabinet colleagues in any government before they even reached Margaret. And when she was involved, it was he alone who could sometimes, although inevitably not always, prevail upon her to avoid needless confrontations or eschew follies.[64].

Lawson commented that the late 1980s, which was the time when Thatcher's hubris was in its ascendency, could not have been a worse time for her to lose Whitelaw's good counsel. His departure was part of her hubristic decline and fall: "when she needed him most she ignored him completely, and instead retreated even further into her Downing St bunker".[65] Indeed, earlier in her career Thatcher explicitly recognised how invaluable Whitelaw was to her premiership when she remarked (in private, but it leaked out, and she seemed to be unaware of any innuendo) that "Every Prime Minister needs a Willie".[66] Whitelaw's main task was to scan for problems before they materialised and recommend prompt action to avoid them. The beginning of the end for Thatcher coincided with Whitelaw's resignation at the end of 1987 after he suffered a stroke.[67] David Owen remarked that one person who could have been her 'toe-holder' and prevented her recklessness from spiralling out of control and into full-blown hubris was shut out of her life. Thatcher was humiliatingly removed from office by her own MPs in 1990 in another dramatic demonstration of how nemesis follows hubris in political life.

Tony Blair, in a moment of self-reflection, recognised hubris as a potential inevitability of political life. He remarked in his autobiography that during his last summer as prime minister in the wake of various controversies, including the Iraq invasion, and amidst mounting pressure for his resignation: "I had my determination to comfort me, and by and large it did (which is what happens to leaders when the final *hubris* overwhelms them)".[68] It's been argued that at the time of the Iraq invasion Blair might have benefitted from a trusted confidante who could have challenged him more effectively in his support for Bush's decision to invade. David Owen observed that Blair did not appear to have that many close ministerial colleagues. His Foreign Secretary, Robin Cook, resigned but there did not seems to be anyone who was capable of or prepared to step forward in effectively curtailing his enthusiasm for the invasion.

A 'toe-holder' (or 'foil') is a trusted adviser who isn't dependent on the leader for favours or patronage, who can hold up a metaphorical mirror to the leader, and help them to reflect on their behaviours critically and objectively.[69] The term itself appears to have been first applied to Louis Howe, President Franklin D. Roosevelt's (FDR's) trusted adviser, to whom FDR gave "licence to dissent"[70] and for whom Howe "provide[d] the toe-weights".[71] FDR showed clear signs of hubris, but was self-aware enough to put an important check and balance in place in the form of Howe's wise counsel.[72] As Secretary to the President, Louis Howe, was FDR's 'streetwise sidekick'.[73] Howe lived in the White House, wherever FDR went Howe also went; he was allowed to speak frankly to the President, be on first-name terms with him.[74] FDR chose Howe because he was prepared to argue, and he had permission from FDR to do so. FDR encouraged and even expected dissent from Howe, and he got it: "You damned fool", "Goddammit Franklin, you can't do that", and "That is the stupidest idea I've ever heard of". Howe was the President's 'no man'. Howe realised how important he had been to FDR when he remarked shortly before his untimely death in 1936 that "Franklin is on his own now".[75] Following Howe's passing, the President brought other toe-holders into his immediate orbit deliberately, including his wife Eleanor, his Secretary of Commerce Harry Hopkins, and Personal Secretary to the President, Marguerite 'Missy' Le Hand, to help keep his hubristic inclinations in check. A later US president who succumbed to hubris, George W. Bush (see Chapter 4), had at his disposal at the time of the Iraq invasion a potential toe-holder in the form of his Secretary of State General Colin Powell. However, the interpersonal dynamics of Bush's top team of Condoleezza Rice, Dick Cheney, and Donald Rumsfeld meant that any 'cautious restrainer' role that Powell might have been able to fulfil was thwarted.[76] Cabinet colleagues and senior civil servants are the most obvious candidates for toe-holders, but the leader must be amenable to restraint in the first place for this process to be effective.

It's said that in Ancient Rome when a victorious general returned home he was accompanied in his victory parade by a slave whose job it was to whisper into his ear "Remember you will die" (a memento mori) to keep any political ambitions that he may have had and his ego in check.[77] The lessons of FTX in business and Margaret Thatcher and others in politics highlight the importance for senior leaders of having in place a seasoned colleague who has no unfulfilled personal ambitions or particular axe to grind and who can therefore help to keep their hubris in check by being their toe-holder, foil, or wise warner.[78]

Avoiding Exposure by Putting Checks and Balances in Place

The good news is that precisely because hubris is an acquired, state-like condition, unlike narcissism which is more trait-like and fixed, it's amenable to intervention, prevention, and containment. The cases discussed in this chapter illustrate the problems that can arise when there are no checks and balances in place to contain a leader's behaviours. One of the main checks and balances recommended by Mathew Hayward in his book *Ego Check* (2007) is that every executive should have at least one 'foil'. A foil in business is like a toe-holder in politics; it's a trusted ally or confidante who has complementary capabilities, is free of competing ambitions, and who's capable and willing to present the facts openly and honestly to a CEO who might be at risk of developing hubris. He puts Steve Job's disastrous decision after he left Apple to launch the NeXT computer prematurely in 1988 down to, at least in part, Jobs not having a foil who might've persuaded him to call off the launch.

Hayward calls the inability that hubrists have to rein in and get over themselves as 'getting in our own way'. He suggests that pride is one of the main causes of CEOs getting in their own way which makes it a major obstacle to prudent decision-making. Pride has two sides, a brighter and more positive aspect and a darker more pernicious face:

(1) hubristic pride is an egotistical pride involving self-aggrandisement based on feelings of pomposity, being stuck-up, conceit, snobbishness, egotism, arrogance, and smugness – it's been found to be related to narcissism, aggression, rejection sensitivity, insecurity, anxiety, and Machiavellianism;[79]
(2) authentic pride, on the other hand, is a non-egotistical, much more humble form of pride which involves effort and achievement, and satisfaction at a job well done based on feelings of accomplishment, success, achievement, fulfilment, self-worth, confidence, and productivity.[80]

Hayward's rule-of-thumb for getting out of our own way is recognising when we do things from the undesirable position of hubristic pride rather than from the preferred position of authentic pride. Hayward suggests that if a self-aware leader begins to sense that they're doing things for the sake of hubristic pride then that's the time to 'back off' and ask their foil for their opinion. Hayward argues that with a trusted foil to hand they'll probably be in a much better position to keep their inauthentic hubristic pride in check and, in the bargain, learn some lessons, which may not always be comfortable, about how to deal with the self-aggrandisement that is the thin end of the hubristic wedge.[81]

Former CEO of Calor Group plc, John Harris, in observing that as a chief executive he had status, authority, a PA, a car and chauffeur, no need to carry money or organise his travel or manage his time, and a team dedicated to meeting his every whim, commented ruefully that perhaps we should not be surprised that "hubris is an inevitable consequence" of such position and privilege.[82] A further consequence for CEOs, presidents, and prime ministers of being the most powerful person in their organisation or institution is that they're also likely to be the most isolated, and possibly the loneliest. In his book *Pariahs: Hubris, Reputation and Organizational Crises* (2016), Matt Nixon points to isolation as a crucial factor which can contribute to the emergence of hubris. Nixon notes that it's hard for CEOs, presidents, and prime ministers to avoid the isolating effects of their office. Their position, fame, and wealth, allied to the very real need for protection and security, means that in practice they tend—although there are exceptions—not to mix with regular employees or voters except under the most controlled or contrived conditions such as walkabouts and photo opportunities. Moreover, as a result of their isolation, it's inevitable that CEOs will compare their day-to-day performance with that of other executives and senior managers in their immediate orbit who, by definition and position, may not be so capable or have achieved as much, hence their self-perception may become blurred.[83] Symptom 11 of hubris syndrome is "loss of contact with reality; often associated with progressive isolation".[84] Nixon argues that senior leaders' isolation can warp how leaders make sense of their world. The damage that a distorted reality field around a CEO can bring about is illustrated by the case of SBF and his small and select leadership team who worked and lived commune-style inside a gated, luxury compound on a tropical island. SBF might have benefitted from 'getting out more' and taking a reality check against genuine peers in order to ground himself and bring the business back down to Earth before things spiralled out of control.

Making the most of opportunities for CEOs to compare themselves to other CEOs rather than employees in general could buffer overly positive self-evaluations. By benchmarking against genuine peers, CEOs may come to see themselves as less remarkable than they think they are in the rarefied atmosphere of the C-suite. Taking opportunities to meet regularly and informally with a trusted peer group of executives or with an executive coach could provide CEOs with the opportunity to step out of role and discuss concerns, hopes, and fears without compromising themselves. But for an honest self-appraisal CEOs need to look in several directions at once: as well as looking sideways they also need to reach out to people lower down the corporate hierarchy.

Nixon suggests the "complex enemy" that is hubris can be tackled by using the necessary checks and balances to create a culture that's unfriendly to hubris.[85] This means—on the basis that an ounce of prevention is better than a pound of cure—keeping those who are prone to hubris away from power; but it also involves making organisations safer places in themselves. In terms of governance this is likely to involve not having the same person occupying the chair and CEO roles (i.e. non-duality), and having in place strong boards, non-executive directors, and chairpersons who are prepared to face down a potential hubrist. Boards can also create a culture that's antithetical to hubris by soliciting feedback from employees and external stakeholders via anonymous surveys or consultants. A strong sign of hubris is when adverse feedback is greeted with rejection.[86] Perhaps the ultimate sign of a hubristic leader is an unwillingness to acknowledge that they may be hubristic. The current Governor of the Bank of England Andrew Bailey, who spoke eloquently about the need to identify and manage the hubris risk in banking, argues that corporate culture can never be an issue for regulators; the change has to be instigated and managed from within (see Chapter 1). Boards, be they in banks or any other corporate entities, who are incapable of instilling an anti-hubris culture may be failing in one of their principal professional duties and moral responsibilities.

Lack of Checks and Balances: Signs to Look Out For

(1) Decisions taken by a small, privileged, and isolated inner circle;
(2) Members of inner circle have close/conflicting/compromised interests;
(3) Organisation overly dependent on high-profile, lauded individual ('key person' risk);
(4) Absence of leader toe-holder/foil;

(5) Ineffective governance mechanisms and reporting systems;

(6) Lack of financial controls and poor risk management procedures;

(7) Opaque and inequitable leader remuneration package;

(8) Leader purges top team of critics.

Notes

1 Owen, D. (2008). Hubris syndrome. *Clinical Medicine*, 8(4), 428–432.

2 Garrard, P. (2013). Dangerous link between power and hubris in politics. *The Conversation*, November 26. Available at: https://theconversation.com/dangerous-link-between-power-and-hubris-in-politics-20169

3 Chartered Governance Institute UK and Ireland. (no date). *What is corporate governance?* Available at: https://www.cgi.org.uk/about-us/policy/what-is-corporate-governance

4 Institute of Chartered Accountants of England and Wales. (no date). *What is corporate governance?* Available at: https://www.icaew.com/technical/corporate-governance/principles/principles-articles/does-corporate-governance-matter

5 Based on: *The UK Corporate Governance Code*. London: Financial Reporting Council. Available at: https://www.frc.org.uk/getattachment/88bd8c45-50ea-4841-95b0-d2f4f48069a2/2018-UK-Corporate-Governance-Code-FINAL.PDF

6 Rosenberg, E. (2023). Who is Sam Bankman-Fried? *Investopedia*, February 18. Available at: https://www.investopedia.com/who-is-sam-bankman-fried-6830274

7 Sweet, K. (2022). The DOJ threw the book at Sam Bankman-Fried, who could face up to 115 years in jail. *Fortune*, December 13. Available at: https://fortune.com/2022/12/13/how-much-jail-time-sam-bankman-fried-up-to-115-years-fraud-ftx-crypto

8 Faux, Z. (2022). A 30-year-old crypto billionaire wants to give his fortune away. *Bloomberg Markets*, April 3. Available at: https://www.bloomberg.com/news/features/2022-04-03/sam-bankman-fried-ftx-s-crypto-billionaire-who-wants-to-give-his-fortune-away

9 Reuters. (2023). FTX's ex-engineering director agrees to plead guilty to US criminal charges. *The Guardian*, February 28. Available at: https://www.theguardian.com/business/2023/feb/28/ftx-nishad-singh-agrees-plead-guilty-criminal-charges

10 Taiwo, O. O., & Stein, J. (2022). Is the effective altruism movement in trouble? *The Guardian*, November 16. Available at: https://www.theguardian.com/commentisfree/2022/nov/16/is-the-effective-altruism-movement-in-trouble

11 *Financial Times* Film. (2023). *FTX: The legend of Sam Bankman-Fried.* Available at: https://www.ft.com/video/f7a7fad1-f3ed-41ee-94a7-e1311989aa7e

12 AMG Petronas Formula One Team. (no date). FTX and Mercedes F1 team announce long-term partnership. Available at: https://www.mercedesamgf1.com/news/ftx-and-mercedes-f1-team-announce-long-term-partnership

13 https://www.ft.com/video/f7a7fad1-f3ed-41ee-94a7-e1311989aa7e

14 Nguyen, B. (2022). FTX investor Sequoia removed its glowing 13,000-word profile of Sam Bankman-Fried and replaced it with sombre note after its investment cratered to $0. *Insider*, November 10. Available at: https://www.businessinsider.com/ftx-investor-sequoia-removes-sam-bankman-fried-profile-2022-11?r=US&IR=T

15 Forbes Profile. (2023). Sam Bankman-Fried. *Forbes*, May 9. Available at: https://www.forbes.com/profile/sam-bankman-fried/

16 Schwartz, L. (2022). Inside Sam Bankman-Fried's extravagant penthouse lifestyle in the Bahamas, where the T-shirt-clad FTX founder lived like royalty. *Fortune Crypto*, November 22. Available at: https://fortune.com/crypto/2022/11/22/sbf-ftx-bahamas-house-lifestyle

17 Oliver, J. (2023). 'Sam? Are you there?!' The bizarre and brutal final hours of FTX. *Financial Times Magazine*, February 9. Available at: https://www.ft.com/content/6e912f25-f1b7-4b19-b370-007fbc867246

18 Griffith, K. (2022). Inside Sam Bankman-Fried's $256.3M Bahamas property empire that the island nation is now trying to claw back – including $16M vacation home he bought for his Stanford Law professor parents. *Daily Mail*, December 13. Available at: https://www.dailymail.co.uk/news/article-11533065/Inside-Sam-Bankman-Frieds-300M-Bahamas-property-empire.html

19 Smith, O. (2023). All the governance issues at stake in the FTX case. *Morning Star*, January 16. Available at: https://www.morningstar.co.uk/uk/news/230830/all-the-governance-issues-at-stake-in-the-ftx-case.aspx

20 According to Investopedia: "Fiat money is a government-issued currency that is not backed by a commodity such as gold. Fiat money gives central banks greater control over the economy because they can control how much money is printed. Most modern paper currencies, such as the U.S. dollar, are fiat currencies." https://www.investopedia.com/terms/f/fiat-money.asp

21 Allison, I. (2022). Divisions in Sam Bankman-Fried's crypto empire blur on his trading titan Alameda's balance sheet. *CoinDesk*, November 6. Available at: https://www.coindesk.com/business/2022/11/02/divisions-in-sam-bankman-frieds-crypto-empire-blur-on-his-trading-titan-alamedas-balance-sheet

22 Allison, I. (2022). Divisions in Sam Bankman-Fried's crypto empire blur on his trading titan Alameda's balance sheet. *CoinDesk*, November 6. Available at: https://www.coindesk.com/business/2022/11/02/divisions-in-sam-bankman-frieds-crypto-empire-blur-on-his-trading-titan-alamedas-balance-sheet

23 *Good Morning America*. (no date). FTX founder Sam Bankman-Fried denies 'improper use' of customer funds. *GMA*. Available at: https://www.youtube.com/watch?v=oHxf4Vf54PI

24 *Financial Times* Film. (2023). FTX: The legend of Sam Bankman-Fried. Available at: https://www.ft.com/video/f7a7fad1-f3ed-41ee-94a7-e1311989aa7e

25 Twitter Account of CZ Binance. (2022). Available at: https://twitter.com/cz_binance/status/1589283421704290306

26 Berwick, A. (2022). Exclusive: At least $1 billion of client funds missing at failed crypto firm FTX. *Reuters*, November 13. Available at: https://www.reuters.com/markets/currencies/exclusive-least-1-billion-client-funds-missing-failed-crypto-firm-ftx-sources-2022-11-12

27 Wang, T., & Baker, N. (2022). FTX agrees to sell itself to rival Binance amid liquidity scare at crypto exchange. *CoinDesk*, November 8. Available at: https://www.coindesk.com/business/2022/11/08/ftx-reaches-deal-with-binance-amid-liquidity-scare-sam-bankman-fried-says

28 Huang, K. (2022). Why did FTX collapse? Here's what to know. New York Times, November 18. Available online at: https://www.nytimes.com/2022/11/10/technology/ftx-binance-crypto-explained.html

29 Reynolds, K. (2022). Binance walks away from deal to acquire FTX. *CoinDesk*, November 9. Available at: https://www.coindesk.com/business/2022/11/09/binance-walks-away-from-ftx-deal-wsj

30 Twitter Account of Eyewitness News Bahamas. (2022). Available at: https://twitter.com/ewnewsbahamas/status/1590840936946634753

31 Nguyen, B. (2022). FTX investor Sequoia removed its glowing 13,000-word profile of Sam Bankman-Fried and replaced it with sombre note after its investment cratered to $0. *Insider*, November 10. Available at: https://www.businessinsider.com/ftx-investor-sequoia-removes-sam-bankman-fried-profile-2022-11?r=US&IR=T

32 Twitter Account of FTX. (2022). Available at: https://twitter.com/ftx_official/status/1591071832823959552

33 House Financial Services Committee. (2022). Testimony of Mr. John J. Ray II. *House Financial Services Committee*, December 13. Available at: https://democrats-financialservices.house.gov/uploadedfiles/hhrg-117-ba00-wstate-rayj-20221213.pdf

34 Berwick, A. (2022). Exclusive: At least $1 billion of client funds missing at failed crypto firm FTX. *Reuters*, November 13. Available at: https://www.reuters.com/markets/currencies/exclusive-least-1-billion-client-funds-missing-failed-crypto-firm-ftx-sources-2022-11-12

35 Berwick, A. (2022). Exclusive: At least $1 billion of client funds missing at failed crypto firm FTX. *Reuters*, November 13. Available at: https://www.reuters.com/markets/currencies/exclusive-least-1-billion-client-funds-missing-failed-crypto-firm-ftx-sources-2022-11-12

36 Rosenberg, E. (2023). Who is Sam Bankman-Fried? *Investopedia*, February 18. Available at: https://www.investopedia.com/who-is-sam-bankman-fried-6830274

37 Sigalos, M., & Goswami, R. (2022). FTX's Gary Wang, Alameda's Caroline Ellison plead guilty to federal charges, cooperating with prosecutors. *CNBC*, December 22. Available at: https://www.cnbc.com/2022/12/22/ftxs-gary-wang-alamedas-caroline-ellison-plead-guilty-to-federal-charges-cooperating-with-prosecutors.html

38 Steib, M. (2022). The Feds flipped two of SBF's top lieutenants. *Intelligencer*, December 22. Available at: https://nymag.com/intelligencer/2022/12/sbf-lieutenants-caroline-ellison-and-gary-wang-plead-guilty.html

39 BBC. (2023). FTX's Nishad Singh pleads guilty to fraud charges. *BBC News*, February 28. Available at: https://www.bbc.co.uk/news/business-64803468

40 Benny-Morrison, A., & Dolmetsch, C. (2023). Bankman-Fried pleads not guilty, faces trial in October. *Bloomberg Crypto*, January 3. Available at: https://www.bloomberg.com/news/articles/2023-01-03/bankman-fried-s-not-guilty-plea-sets-up-path-to-fraud-trial?leadSource=uverify%20wall

41 *Financial Times*. (2023). The case against SBF grows thicker. *Financial Times*, March 29. Available at: https://www-ft-com.ezp.lib.cam.ac.uk/content/69971bb9-a084-4229-9cf4-9451d0768679

42 FT Film. (2022). The legend of Sam Bankman Fried. Available online at: https://www.ft.com/video/f7a7fad1-f3ed-41ee-94a7-e1311989aa7e

43 *Good Morning America*. (no date). FTX founder Sam Bankman-Fried denies 'improper use' of customer funds. *GMA*. Available at: https://www.youtube.com/watch?v=oHxf4Vf54PI

44 Oliver, J. (2023). 'Sam? Are you there?!' The bizarre and brutal final hours of FTX. *The Financial Times*, February 9. Available at: https://www.ft.com/content/6e912f25-f1b7-4b19-b370-007fbc867246

45 Piper, K. (2022). Sam Bankman-Fried tries to explain himself. *Vox*, November 16. Available at: https://www.vox.com/future-perfect/23462333/sam-bankman-fried-ftx-cryptocurrency-effective-altruism-crypto-bahamas-philanthropy

46 *Financial Times* Film. (2023). *FTX: The legend of Sam Bankman-Fried.* Available at: https://www.ft.com/video/f7a7fad1-f3ed-41ee-94a7-e1311989aa7e

47 Chittum, M. (2022). Sam Bankman-Fried's FTX had the corporate governance of a college fraternity, congressman says. *Insider*, December 22. Available at: https://markets.businessinsider.com/news/currencies/ftx-had-the-corporate-governance-of-a-college-fraternity-congressman-2022-12

48 House Financial Services Committee. (2022). Testimony of Mr. John J. Ray III. House Financial Services Committee, December 13. Available at: https://democrats-financialservices.house.gov/uploadedfiles/hhrg-117-ba00-wstate-rayj-20221213.pdf

49 Velasquez, F. (2022). Sam Bankman-Fried was a 'pathological liar': Congressman. *CoinDesk*, December 14. Available at: https://www.coindesk.com/policy/2022/12/14/sam-bankman-fried-was-a-pathological-liar-congressman

50 Velasquez, F. (2022). Sam Bankman-Fried was a 'pathological liar':1 Congressman. *CoinDesk*, December 14. Available at: https://www.coindesk.com/policy/2022/12/14/sam-bankman-fried-was-a-pathological-liar-congressman

51 Smith, O. (2023). All the governance issues at stake in the FTX case. *Morning Star*, January 16. Available at: https://www.morningstar.co.uk/uk/news/230830/all-the-governance-issues-at-stake-in-the-ftx-case.aspx

52 Calhoun, G. (2022). FTX and ESG: A panorama of failed governance (pt 1 – the internal failures). *Forbes*, November 21. Available at: https://www.forbes.com/sites/georgecalhoun/2022/11/21/ftx-and-esg-a-panorama-of-failed-governance-pt-1--the-internal-failures/

53 Smith, O. (2023). All the governance issues at stake in the FTX case. Morning Star, January 16. Available online at: https://www.morningstar.co.uk/uk/news/230830/all-the-governance-issues-at-stake-in-the-ftx-case.aspx

54 Cavaliere, V. (2023). FTX failure rooted in 'hubris,' 'greed,' debtors report says. *Bloomberg Crypto*, April 9, emphasis added. Available at: https://www.bloomberg.com/news/articles/2023-04-09/

55 Park, J. H., Kim, C., Chang, Y. K., Lee, D. H., & Sung, Y. D. (2018). CEO hubris and firm performance: Exploring the moderating roles of CEO power and board vigilance. *Journal of Business Ethics*, 147, 919–933.

56 Malmendier, U., & Tate, G. (2009). Superstar CEOs. *The Quarterly Journal of Economics*, 124, 1593–1638.

57 Malmendier, U., & Tate, G. (2009). Superstar CEOs. *The Quarterly Journal of Economics*, 124, 1593–1638.

58 Bürkner, H-P. (no date). *Fighting corporate hubris*. Boston Consulting Group. Available at: https://web-assets.bcg.com/img-src/Fighting_Corporate_Hubris_June_2013_tcm9-97860.pdf

59 Johnson, G. et al. (2017). *Exploring strategy*. London: Pearson.

60 Institute of Directors. (2018). *What is the role of the non-executive director?* Available at: https://www.iod.com/resources/factsheets/company-structure/what-is-the-role-of-the-non-executive-director

61 Fitzsimmons, A. (2018). How to help non-executive directors see through a chief's charms. *Financial Times*, May 17. Available at: https://www.ft.com/content/2877e126-47ae-11e8-8ee8-cae73aab7ccb

62 Johnson, G. et al. (2017). *Exploring strategy*. London: Pearson.

63 Owen, D. (2007). *The hubris syndrome. Bush, Blair and the intoxication of power*. London: Politico, p.8.

64 Owen, D. (no date). Margaret Thatcher's hubris and her relations with William Whitelaw and other Cabinet colleagues. Lecture notes. Available online at: https://www.lorddavidowen.co.uk/wp-content/uploads/2020/05/5.6.2013-IoP-speech.pdf

65 Owen, D. (no date). Margaret Thatcher's hubris and her relations with William Whitelaw and other Cabinet colleagues. Lecture notes. Available online at: https://www.lorddavidowen.co.uk/wp-content/uploads/2020/05/5.6.2013-IoP-speech.pdf

66 Owen, D. (2013). *Margaret Thatcher's hubris and her relations with William Whitelaw and other Cabinet colleagues*. Institute of Psychiatry, June 5.

67 O'Flynn, B. (2021). Boris needs a wise old owl to watch for political pitfalls. *Daily Express*, November 6. Available at: https://www.express.co.uk/comment/columnists/patrick-o-flynn/1517410/boris-johnson-cabinet-members-political-pitfalls

68 Blair, T. (2010). *A journey*. London: Hutchinson, p.600, emphasis added.

69 Owen, D. (2016). Hubris syndrome. *Enterprise Risk Winter*, 20–24, p.23.

70 Owen, D. (2018). cited in Sadler-Smith, E. (2019). *Hubristic leadership*. London: SAGE, p.167.

71 Owen, D. (2018) cited in Sadler-Smith, E. (2019). *Hubristic leadership*. London: SAGE, p.64.

72 Sadler-Smith, E. (2019). *Hubristic leadership*. London: SAGE.

73 Sadler-Smith, E. (2019). *Hubristic leadership*. London: SAGE.

74 Hoogenboezem (2007) cited in Sadler-Smith, E. (2019). *Hubristic leadership*. London: SAGE, p.145.

75 Owen, L. D. (2018). Heads of government, 'toe-holders' and time limits. In P. Garrard (ed.) *The leadership hubris epidemic: Biological roots and strategies for prevention*. Cham, Switzerland: Palgrave Macmillan, pp. 165–78, p.167.

76 Sadler-Smith, E. (2019). *Hubristic leadership*. London: SAGE.

77 Titus, Contributing Writer. (2020). Memento mori in the ancient world. *Classical Wisdom*, November 6. Available at: https://classicalwisdom.com/culture/memento-mori-in-the-ancient-world

78 Sadler-Smith, E. (2019). *Hubristic leadership*. London: SAGE.

79 Machiavellianism denotes cunning and manipulativeness; it's part of the so-called 'dark triad' along with psychopathy and narcissism. Tracy, J. L., Cheng, J. T., Robins, R. W., & Trzesniewski, K. H. (2009). Authentic and hubristic pride: The affective core of self-esteem and narcissism. *Self and Identity*, 8(2–3), 196–213.

80 Tracy, J. L., & Robins, R. W. (2004). Putting the self into self-conscious emotions: A theoretical model. *Psychological Inquiry*, 15(2), 103–125.

81 Hayward, M. (2007). *Ego check*. Sydney: Kaplan, p.90.

82 Harris, J. (2016). Tales from the road – encounters with hubris? In Garrard, P., & Robinson, G. (eds.). (2016). *The intoxication of power: Interdisciplinary insights*. Basingstoke: Palgrave Macmillan, pp.117–134.

83 Sadler-Smith, E., Robinson, G., Akstinaite, V., & Wray, T. (2018). Hubristic leadership: Understanding the hazard and mitigating the risks. *Organizational Dynamics*, 48(2), 8–18.

84 Owen, D., & Davidson, J. (2009). Hubris syndrome: an acquired personality disorder? A study of US Presidents and UK Prime Ministers over the last 100 years. *Brain*, 132, 1396–1406.

85 Nixon, M. (2016). *Pariahs: Hubris, reputation and organizational crises*. Faringdon: Libri, p.95.

86 Reed, A. (2023). Three ways a board can help identify and mitigate executive hubris. *Forbes*, April 18. Available at: https://www.forbes.com/sites/forbescoachescouncil/2023/04/18/three-ways-a-board-can-help-identify-and-mitigate-executive-hubris

8

NARCISSISTIC TENDENCIES

Echo and Narcissus

A persistent theme in hubris is that the Ancients, and particularly the Ancient Greeks, knew about it and the risks that it (i.e. *hybris* as they referred to it) posed both to the individual hubrist themselves (the *hybristes*)[1] and to the well-being of the citizens of the Greek city state (the *polis*). Little appears to have changed in the intervening two-and-a-half millennia: hubristic leaders still pose a threat not only to themselves but, arguably more importantly, to the well-being of the organisations and institutions that they lead.

As already noted in Chapter 1, the Ancient Greeks captured their wisdom in morality tales in the form of myths to warn against the dangers of 'thinking big' and showing contempt towards others;[2] for example, in the myths of Icarus (who had the temerity to use his new-found, and God-like, power of flight to fly too close to the sun ignoring his father Daedalus' wise

DOI: 10.4324/9781003128427-8

warning to avoid excess) and Phaethon (who had the audacity to ride the chariot of the sun across the sky, and was struck down by Zeus as punishment for aspiring to be god-like).

Narcissism, the subject of this chapter, is closely related to hubris and has its origins in Ancient Greece. One way in which hubris and narcissism are related is that narcissistic tendencies can predispose a leader to hubristic behaviours. Another is that the pathological form of narcissism, narcissistic personality disorder (NPD), also overlaps with hubris syndrome because the latter includes a narcissistic propensity to see the world as an arena to exercise power and seek glory as one of its 14 symptoms. It comes as no surprise therefore to find that the Ancient Greeks had a morality tales to warn against the perils of narcissism as well as of hubris.

The Roman poet Publius Ovidius Naso (43 BCE–17/18 AD), known to us simply as 'Ovid', re-told almost 250 of the Ancient Greek myths in his epic poem from the year 8CE, *Metamorphóses*. Many of the heroes and heroines and victims and villains in these various tales undergo different types of transformations (hence the poem's title); for example, humans are metamorphosed into trees, flowers, stars, etc. The myth of Echo and Narcissus is to be found in Book 3 of Ovid's 25 book magnum opus. It's the origin of the term 'narcissism'. As with many of the myths, they're open to different interpretations and there are several narrative themes running in parallel within this particular story; for our purposes its essence is as follows.

The most handsome youth Narcissus refused the romantic entreaties of the "fairest of all" the nymphs, Echo, because he deemed her to be undeserving of his attention: "I will die before I give you power over me".[3] His contempt proved to be prophetic. Echo went away to pine and eventually perish until all that remained of her was an echo. As punishment for the way in which he treated her, Narcissus was condemned by the Gods to fall into an intoxicating love (*narkōtikos*) with himself.[4] In Ovid's re-telling of the myth Narcissus arrived hot and exhausted from the hunt at a "clear, un-muddied pool of silvery shimmering water". Thirsty for the water he started to drink but was overwhelmed by a vision of beauty; he gazed in amazement at his own reflection with its rippling golden curls "like the locks of a god" and "fell in love with an empty hope, a shadow mistaken for substance".[5] Narcissus became enslaved by his reflected image, a thing that he could never have as an object of physical affection. Only death could free him from his intoxication with his own self:[6] "He laid down his weary head in the green grass, death closing those eyes that had marvelled at their lord's [his] beauty" but when his funeral pyre was being prepared a body couldn't be found: "they came upon a flower, instead of his body, with white petals surrounding a yellow heart".[7] Narcissus' tragic and impossible-to-fulfil, phobic self-obsession led to his demise and transformation into a beautiful flower, the narcissus.

Narcissism is intoxication with the self in its rawest form. The myth is a cautionary tale from the classical world against the seeds of self-destruction that lurk within all-consuming self-love and self-obsession.[8] Self-love can be particularly potent, and especially perilous, when it is combined with the power that comes with high office.[9]

Much has been written about the former UK Prime Minister Boris Johnson. A persistent question in the popular press is 'Is Boris Johnson a narcissist?'[10] The right-of-centre British newspaper that Johnson worked for and was fired from, The Daily Telegraph, asked in a headline whether he's "Narcissist, Fantasist or … Psychopath?' and questioned 'How dark does [his personality] get?'[11] Readers will no doubt come to their own view on this question.

Dr Supriya McKenna MD, former GP, educator in the field of narcissistic relationships and author of Divorcing a Narcissist (2021) and Narcissism and Family Law (2021), singled out no less than ten aspects of personality that might signal narcissistic tendencies in a leader:

(1) narcissistic leaders present a 'false' persona to the world which they need the world to believe in so that they can believe in it themselves;

(2) narcissistic leaders have a strained relationship with the truth, Dr McKenna also comments that the truth to a narcissist is whatever they say at the time that they're saying it;

(3) narcissistic leaders shift the blame because they can't take responsibility for their own mistakes as doing so would weaken their narcissistic persona;

(4) narcissistic leaders exploit others to achieve personal gain; Dr McKenna describes interpersonal exploitation as a "hallmark of narcissism";

(5) narcissistic leaders are unwilling or unable to empathise with the feelings, wants, and needs of others;

(6) narcissistic leaders are fixated on the fantasies of power and success; this is the driving force of external validation; the so-called 'narcissistic supply', which in practice is inexhaustible, gives a narcissist the endorsement that they crave;

(7) narcissistic leaders believe they're exempt from normal rules—their world is governed by a sense of entitlement

(8) narcissistic leaders need to believe that they're superior;

(9) narcissistic leaders require continual admiration from others—Dr McKenna describes a narcissist's needs for admiration and affirmation as being like a "bucket with a hole in it" that continually needs to be topped up with narcissistic supply by others;

(10) narcissistic leaders deprecate former acolytes and treat them with contempt.[12]

Whether or not Boris Johnson is narcissist would entail a close examination not only of whether he meets the relevant criteria but also of relevant aspects of his childhood and subsequent development by a skilled clinician. Johnson's biographer Tom Bower, in *Boris Johnson: The Gambler*, says that to understand Johnson requires "forensic examination"[13] of his relationship with his father both as a child and an adult. In commenting on his childhood relationships with his siblings Johnson himself is reported to have said: "I've always known that my position is unchallengeable. It is the fixed point about which my cosmos is organised. I smile indulgently on everybody else's attempts to compete with me. Bring it on, I say."[14] His classics master at Eton College remarked that as a boy Johnson believed that he "should be free of the network of obligation which binds everyone else".[15] Johnson's childhood ambition to be 'World King' has been widely reported. This prompted Matthew Flinders of the Bernard Crick Centre for the Public Understanding of Politics, at the University of Sheffield, to point out that hubris syndrome is an acquired disorder linked to the pressures of holding high political office; hubris is more state-like than trait-like (see below). The fact that Johnson's over-weening ambition appears to have been ever-present prompts Flinders to wonder if there is "a deeper malady at play".[16]

Narcissism

Narcissism is a personality trait characterised by an inflated self-view, grandiosity, self-absorption, vanity, low empathy, and an incessant need for
adulation and power.[17] It's been recognised as a risk to individual and collective well-being across history and cultures back at least as far as the
Narcissus myth. The English psychologist Havelock Ellis (1859–1939) was
the first person to use the term 'Narcissus-like' in a clinical setting in the
late 1890s to link the myth to the condition being experienced by one of
his patients.[18] Sigmund Freud published his famous essay On Narcissism: An
Introduction in 1914. In it Freud argued that people normally go through a
phase of what he termed 'primary narcissism' in which they're egocentric
and can't take the other's perspective. According to Freud, healthy development involves an inflexion point after which a person is able to invest
their libidinal energies in others rather than primarily in themselves. With
this comes with a consequent, but healthy, diminishment of self-regard.
Freudian 'secondary narcissism' is an unhealthy state in which individuals regress to loving themselves as compensation for when a love object
is unable or unwilling to return their love.[19] Freud also commented that
people with a narcissistic personality "are especially suited to … take on
the role of leaders, and to give fresh stimulus to cultural development or
damage the established state of affairs".[20] Narcissism is typically thought of
as a disorder, however the Austrian-American psychoanalyst Heinz Kohut
(1913–1989) suggested that narcissism isn't necessarily pathological; in its
healthy form it can produce constructive behaviours such as humour and
creativity.[21]

Given its effects on psychological well-being and its prevalence amongst
the rich and powerful, narcissism is an important psychological and psychiatric phenomenon. There's a vast literature on the subject, added to
which narcissists themselves are, even according to the analyst par excellence, Sigmund Freud, notoriously difficult to analyse.[22] A helpful way to
approach the complex topic of narcissism is to think of it in terms of three
inter-related components, self, relationships, and strategies:

(1) the narcissistic self: positivity, specialness and uniqueness, grandiosity,
    vanity, a sense of entitlement, and a desire for power, success, and
    esteem;

(2) *narcissistic relationships*: low levels of empathy and emotional intimacy, numerous shallow, exciting, engaging, manipulative, and exploitative relationships;

(3) *narcissistic strategies*: ways in which the narcissist maintains their over-inflated self-views, for example, by narcissistic supply (see above) to compensate, metaphorically speaking, for the leaky tyre or the hole-in-the-bucket of their ego,[23] see Figure 8.1.

Narcissists tend to gravitate towards occupations where they can showcase themselves and exercise control over other people. So leadership, whether it be in business or politics, presents an ideal platform. Moreover, narcissists appear to be skilled at attaining leadership positions, and those who do so are often admired and followed, at least initially. However, they're more likely to falter over time because their narcissism itself fuels poor decision-making. Even though narcissists often have the requisite social skills to attain power, they may not have the leadership skills necessary to execute the role and stay the course.[24]

As alluded to above, narcissism is a trait in that it's stable over time and has its likely origins in early childhood experiences which influence subsequent personality development.[25] This aspect of narcissism is one of the primary differences between it and hubris. Unlike narcissism, which

Narcissistic self

- Positivity, specialness and uniqueness, grandiosity, vanity, a sense of entitlement, and desire for power, success and esteem

Narcissistic relationships

- Low levels of empathy and emotional intimacy, numerous shallow, exciting, engaging, manipulative and exploitative relationships

Narcissistic strategies

- Ways in which the narcissist maintains their over-inflated self-views (including narcissistic supply)

Figure 8.1 Three Components of Narcissism

is trait-like, hubris is more state-like; its on-set appears to be a result of a particular set of circumstances, for example, significant power, a run of successes, praise from followers and the press, and a conducive context. It may also be a reaction to stressful events and understood as a coping mechanism in the face of impending threats.[26]

Psychologists have speculated that narcissism may be disproportionally present at the most influential levels of society[27] and also that it may be something of a 'first-world problem' in that people who are pre-occupied with meeting their basic physiological and safety needs don't have the luxury of the spare mental and emotional resources that are needed to be narcissistic. It may also be more of a feature of individualistic cultures (such as in North America and Western Europe) rather than collectivist cultures (such as in the Far East), more prevalent amongst the professions (including law, medicine, sport, business, and entertainment), and more typical of males, perhaps because traditional male behaviours such as exercising power and aggression and status-seeking are more in keeping with narcissism.[28] Interestingly, researchers also have found a positive relationship between narcissism and basal testosterone levels in a sample of young males.[29] This research is consistent with other work discussed in Chapter 5 in which it was found that testosterone may represent a biological marker of a dominant, cold, and antisocial, interpersonal leadership style. Indeed when we think of narcissism an image of familiar stereotypes of dysfunctional men in politics, business, and entertainment is often conjured up. For example, the eminent psychiatrist Allen Frances (who wrote the diagnostic criteria for NPD, see below) described Donald Trump in a letter to the New York Times in 2017 as a "world class narcissist" and referred to Trump's grandiosity, self-absorption, and lack of empathy as prime evidence.[30]

Researchers distinguish between two forms of the condition: a pathological (i.e. diseased) form of narcissism, and a personality trait variant of narcissism. NPD is the pathological form of narcissism and reference to it draws our attention to a divide between two strands of research in this area.[31] The first strand is the clinical and is concerned with narcissism as a recognisable mental disorder or pathology, i.e. NPD. NPD is included in the latest version of the *Diagnostic and Statistical Manual of Mental Disorders* (DSM-V) published by the American Psychiatric Association (APA). It's described in *DSM-V* as a "pervasive pattern of grandiosity (in fantasy or behaviour), a constant need for admiration, and a lack of empathy".

The second strand of research is the personality trait variant of narcissism, often referred to as 'grandiose narcissism'.[32] When people refer to narcissism in business, politics, and public life they're generally referring to the grandiose form of narcissism rather than the pathological (NPD) form. Grandiose narcissism is a personality trait with levels that range from very high to very low. It's measurable using validated questionnaires such as the 'Narcissistic Personality Inventory' (NPI). The NPI, which exists in various longer and shorter versions, includes items such as "I really like to be the centre of attention", "I am an extraordinary person", "I like having authority over other people", etc.[33]

Leadership researchers have also tended to focus on grandiose narcissism. A typical image of a typical leader or CEO with grandiose narcissism as "someone who is over-confident, extraverted, high in self-esteem, dominant, attention-seeking, interpersonally skilled and charming, but also unwilling to take criticism, aggressive, high in psychological entitlement, lacking in true empathy, interpersonally exploitative and grandiose or even haughty".[34] The relative intensity of these characteristics and the ability to be self-aware and self-regulate is one of the things that separates grandiose narcissism from NPD.[35] Only a trained physician is qualified to say whether narcissism is pathological or not.

Too Much, or Too Little, of a Good Thing

Debates about narcissism, especially in leadership, tend to focus on the question of "is narcissism a good or a bad thing?".[36] In this respect, it can be thought of as having two manifestations, one of which is 'adaptive' (i.e. it has a valuable function in everyday life) and another which is 'maladaptive' (i.e. it mitigates against normal functioning).[37] Whether Trump's narcissism is maladaptive probably depends on your political point of view, but whether it is pathological (i.e. shows evidence of an illness or mental problem) is a scientific and, in the absence of a formal diagnosis, open question. Allen Frances (the author of the American Psychiatric Associations' criteria for NPD) doesn't think that Trump is psychologically ill as result of his narcissism because he doesn't seem to be suffering from any associated psychological distress or impairment, indeed much of the distress caused by Trump's narcissism is experienced by other people. For this reason, in Allen's view, Trump doesn't qualify for a diagnosis of NPD.[38]

As well as existing in adaptive and maladaptive forms, narcissism can also be conceptualised as existing on a spectrum from 'healthy' to 'disordered'. In keeping with this idea, the eminent scholar of personality disorders Theodore Millon (1928–2013),[39] regarded narcissism as a 'personality style' in which a fine line divides normal self-confidence from a pathologically inflated sense of self-worth. Millon's idea acknowledges that narcissism can be useful (i.e. adaptive or productive) in some situations, which aligns with Freud's view that we can all be somewhat narcissistic.[40] Seen in this way, too little self-worth (i.e. a deficiency) can be almost as bad as too much self-worth (i.e. an excess). Too little manifests as feelings of "incompetence, ineffectiveness, incompetence and inferiority", whilst too much manifests as "superiority, arrogance, grandiosity and lack of empathy".[41] Both conditions can be dysfunctional and paralysing: the first by lack of action and ineffectuality; the second by an excess of action and misplaced feelings of omnipotence. In Millon's model of narcissism the relationship between narcissism and its dysfunctional manifestations is U-shaped, see Figure 8.2. The optimum for normal everyday functioning is at the midpoint of neither deficiency (i.e. inferiority, incompetence, and importance) nor excess (i.e., superiority, arrogance and omnipotence).

On the wider point of human excess, the Italian sociologist, Carlo Bordoni, has argued the desire to constantly improve and go beyond Homo sapiens' limits, has been vital in furthering human progress.[42] On the other hand, the historian and political philosopher Hannah Arendt (1906–1975) remarked in her book The Human Condition (1958) that it's precisely because human beings can "perform miracles" they should "retain a sense of moderation".[43] We return to a discussion of the relationship between excess and deficiency in Chapter 9.

Context can't be ignored because it can determine where the optimum lies. For example, in the upper echelons of business and politics a self-confident, assertive, sometimes bordering-on-narcissistic, leadership style may be a requirement because business organisations and political institutions need to be inspired and led to follow a grand vision. CEOs and heads of government need to have faith in themselves (but without denigrating or belittling others), have a powerful vision that they are instrumental in delivering (but which acknowledges that others also have a role and contribution), and an enthusiasm, zeal, and charisma (which others find appealing, are attracted to, and can be inspired by). These behaviours can

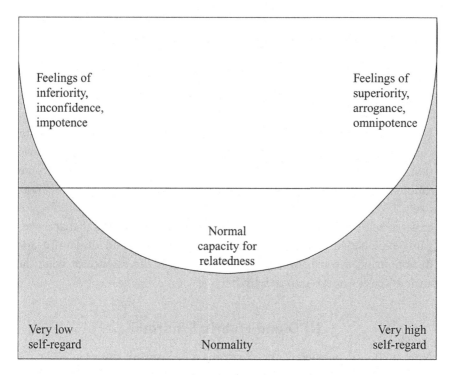

Figure 8.2 Narcissism as a Personality Style with Deficiency, Optimum, and Excess

Source: Million, T. et al. (2004). *Personality Disorders in Modern Life*. Hoboken, NJ: John Wiley & Sons, p.335. Reproduced by permission of John Wiley & Sons.

manifest as narcissism but it need not be maladaptive, and in certain circumstances it may actually be adaptive.

According to Dutch psychoanalyst and leadership scholar Manfred Kets de Vries, a moderate amount of narcissism is necessary for organisational success but "like everything else, it is a matter of degree" and the avoidance of excess (see Chapter 9).[44] Narcissism when taken to excess presents a threat which can derail leaders and their organisations. The eminent psychologist Adrian Furnham of University College London believes that managers often derail not because they have too little of something (i.e. because they're incompetent) but most often they "fail and derail" because they have too much of something.[45] Leaders in business and politics may often have to err on the side of excess (otherwise they might not achieve great things) but in doing so they also have to stay 'within range' by using their practical judgement and wisdom to ascertain where the fine line between adaptive and maladaptive narcissism lies. Being able to anchor within the acceptable range of a leadership capability, be that confidence or ambition, is a vital skill because going out of range can be an Achilles' heel for a leader.

Narcissism becomes maladaptive when it deviates rightwards from the bottom of the U (Figure 8.2) tipping over into an over-confident and exaggeratedly assertive style in which excesses of boldness, ambition, audacity, cunning, and entitlement are beyond what is merited by the leader's position, achievements, or capabilities and which ultimately create the conditions that make undesirable, and possibly destructive, outcomes more likely.[46] When the Rubicon which separates normality from pathology is crossed, self-regard is taken to its extreme form. Behaviours that are arrogant, exploitative, controlling, scheming, irrational, and disdainful and dishonouring towards others follow suit: this is the essence of what the ancient Greeks referred to as *hybris*.[47]

NPD and Hubris Syndrome

From a clinical perspective narcissism is a personality disorder, NPD, the markers of which are grandiosity, a need for admiration, and a lack of empathy. NPD emerges before adulthood and in the American Psychiatric Association's diagnostic manual, *DSM-V*, narcissism has nine diagnostic criteria including: a grandiose sense of self-importance; a fixation with fantasies of unlimited success, control, brilliance, and beauty; a desire for unwarranted admiration; no form of empathy, etc. It starts in early adulthood. The presence of NPD is signified by the existence of five out of the nine *DSM-V* criteria.

In the *DSM-V* NPD comes under the same umbrella of 'Cluster B' personality disorders as antisocial personality disorder, histrionic personality disorder, and borderline personality disorder. Cluster B personality disorders are 'dramatic' disorders, Cluster A disorders are 'odd' disorders, such as paranoid and schizoid disorders, and Cluster C disorders are 'anxious' disorders such as obsessive compulsive disorder.[48] Cluster B disorders typically present as overtly emotional and unpredictable behaviour, and persons with NPD can often present with impairments both in their working and their interpersonal relationships.[49] The prevalence of narcissistic traits amongst the general population is much larger than the prevalence of

NPD.[50] As alluded to earlier, Donald Trump is not deemed mentally ill in the terms set out in DSM's criteria for NPD because, according to Allen Frances:

> Instead of experiencing distress himself, Trump causes severe distress in others and has been rewarded richly for doing so, not least by the honour of being elected to the high office of President of the United States of America.

However, other psychiatrists have arrived at a different view. For example, Dr John Zinner, a former head of the Unit on Family Therapy Studies at the National Institute of Mental Health (NIMH), has said that Trump does have NPD and that psychiatrists have a responsibility to speak out.[51] For psychiatrists this issue is problematic because it's contrary to the so-called 'Goldwater Rule' which prevents APA members from commenting publicly on the psyche of living persons who they've not examined in a clinical setting. Others see no need to comment; one psychiatrist remarked that "If we make pronouncements about Donald Trump, nothing is gained. [By analogy] you don't need a doctor to tell you that the guy on the plane with a hacking cough is sick."[52]

NPD overlaps with hubris syndrome as defined by David Owen and Jonathan Davidson (see Chapter 2). Owen and Davidson proposed 14 clinical features of, five of which are unique and four are shared with NPD, see Table 8.1.

Owen and Davidson suggest that to make a 'diagnosis' of hubris syndrome, three or four out of the 14 symptoms should be present, and at least one of these must be from the five unique hubris syndrome symptoms (i.e. HS.5, HS.6, HS.10, HS.12, and HS.13). But they also note that more is required than simply checking off the symptoms. For a diagnosis of hubris syndrome, as well as the person showing the requisite symptoms (one unique plus at least two others), they must have held substantial power for a significant length of time.

As alluded to already, unlike NPD which appears in early adulthood, hubris syndrome is an acquired condition the appearance of which postdates the acquisition of considerable power and a run of successes as a leader. This last point helps to clarify and reinforce the distinction between hubris and narcissism as follows. Hubris is an acquired, state-like condition characterised by an intoxication with power and success and which normally remits once power is lost (Owen often cites the case of George

Table 8.1 Symptoms Shared Between NPD and Hubris Syndrome

Hubris Syndrome Symptom (HS)	Shared or Unique
A narcissistic propensity to see their world primarily as an arena in which to exercise power and seek glory (HS.1)	NPD.6
A predisposition to take actions which seem likely to cast the individual in a good light, i.e. in order to enhance image (HS.2)	NPD.1
A disproportionate concern with image and presentation (HS.3)	NPD.3
A messianic manner of talking about current activities and a tendency to exaltation (HS.4)	NPD.2
Excessive confidence in the individual's own judgement and contempt for the advice or criticism of others (HS.7)	NPD.9
Exaggerated self-belief, bordering on a sense of omnipotence, in what they personally can achieve (HS.8)	NPD.1&2
A belief that rather than being accountable to the mundane court of colleagues or public opinion, the court to which they answer is History or God (HS.9)	NPD.3
An identification with the nation, or organisation to the extent that the individual regards his/her outlook and interests as identical (HS.5)	Unique
A tendency to speak in the third person or use the royal 'we' (HS.6)	Unique
An unshakable belief that in the court of History or God they will be vindicated (HS.10)	Unique
Restlessness, recklessness, and impulsiveness (HS.12)	Unique
A tendency to allow their 'broad vision', about the moral rectitude of a proposed course, to obviate the need to consider practicality, cost, or outcomes (HS.13)	Unique
Loss of contact with reality; often associated with progressive isolation (HS.11)	APD.3&5
Hubristic incompetence, where things go wrong because too much self-confidence has led the leader not to worry about the nuts and bolts of policy (HS.14)	HPD.5

Note: APD, antisocial personality disorder; HPD, histrionic personality disorder

Source: Reprinted from Garrard, P., Rentoumi, V., Lambert, C., & Owen, D. (2014). Linguistic biomarkers of Hubris syndrome. *Cortex*, 55, 167–181 with permission from Elsevier.

W. Bush's hubris syndrome remitting once he left office). Narcissism, on the other hand, is a trait-like condition characterised by an intoxication with the self which does not remit in the same way (for example, many of Trump's narcissistic behaviours predated his time in office as president and have continued unabated since he left office in 2021).

Narcissism and Leadership

Narcissism has been an attribute of powerful leaders throughout history. Narcissists such as Alexander the Great, Napoleon Bonaparte, and Adolph Hitler have shaped human destinies. A study in the *Journal of Conflict Resolution* found that between 1897 and 2007 US presidents who scored above average for narcissism spent an average of 613 days at war, compared to an average of 136 days for those leaders who scored below average, of course, the causality of this relationship, i.e. its direction, is ambiguous.[53] In contemporary business and politics leaders often use their power and influence to support and sustain a deep-seated, grandiose image of themselves, one need look no further than leaders such as Donald Trump and Elon Musk (see Chapter 9) who've both been described as manifestations of a unique type of 21st-century leader personality: "the wildly disruptive narcissist".[54]

A position of power is an attractive proposition to a narcissistic leader because it can help to alleviate, but never satiate, their vanity and desire for grandiosity. Being a leader magnifies the narcissist's already inflated self-confidence, further inflates vanity and pride, creates numerous opportunities for self-aggrandisement, immodest behaviours, and exhibitionism, and helps to reinforce their sense of superiority. Leadership, be it in business or politics, is the ideal apparatus with which to reinforce a swollen self-view and top up the 'leaky bucket' of self-esteem.[55] The scent of power draws narcissistic individuals towards leadership positions,[56] but the evidence suggests that when they attain significant power and influence, they often fail to deliver as effective leaders.[57] All too often narcissists tend to rise to, and sometimes abuse, positions of power; they then fall from grace leaving collateral damage in their wake.[58]

A number of commentators have argued that Boris Johnson's aspirations for power played an important role in the stance that he took on the UK's membership of the European Union (EU). He came out in favour of Brexit. However, CNN revealed that he drafted an unpublished column (just two days before he came out in favour of Brexit) in which he urged Britain to stay in the EU. In it he's reported to have said that "Britain is a great nation, a global force for good. It is surely a boon for the world and for Europe that she should be intimately engaged in the EU." He warned that Brexit would cause an "economic shock" that could lead to the "break-up" of the UK.[59] One of his former colleagues said that Johnson's leave position was "all about the leadership" and a "cynical bet he made in order to win over Conservative party members and become prime minister".[60] Whether or not Johnson's position paid off for himself or the country, or whether narcissism played any role in the process, is open a question that will continue to be debated.

Narcissism is paradoxical in leadership because it can be both a leader's strength and weakness. In the words of the American psychoanalyst and anthropologist the late Michael Maccoby (1933–2022), narcissism in leadership has some "incredible pros" (he calls this 'productive narcissism') but also has "inevitable cons" (he calls this 'unproductive narcissism').[61] According to Maccoby, two of the pros of narcissism for business leaders are that narcissists have vision (because it's in their nature to see the bigger picture) and they can attract followers (because through their charisma and rhetoric they're able to persuade people to follow their vision).[62] Other research has also identified positives: narcissistic business leaders are willing to take risks, they don't tend to be put off by weak performance, they lead their firms to faster recovery after economic crises, they're prepared to undertake extensive, organisation-wide change, and having a narcissistic leader at the helm appears to especially useful when the external environment is characterised by change, disruption, and discontinuity.[63]

But Maccoby also notes that a narcissist's strengths may contain the seeds of their destruction; for example, the adulation that a narcissist's rhetoric creates feeds and exacerbates their feelings of invincibility which can eventually turn toxic. Amongst the more overt cons identified by Maccoby is that narcissists tend to be thin-skinned and hyper-sensitive to criticism. As well as being ill at ease with their own emotions they're also uncomfortable with others expressing negative views especially when such criticisms are directed at them. As a buffer they tend to surround themselves with those who will echo their own views rather than be a sounding board. Narcissists' sensitivity to criticism also makes them poor listeners, especially when they feel they're being threatened, confronted, or exposed.[64] For narcissists, empathy is a one-way street: they crave being liked and need empathy from others, but they're distinctly unempathetic themselves. This point aligns with other findings which suggest that high-testosterone leaders lack empathy and, like narcissists, have an intense and relentless desire to compete, win, and attain status (see Chapter 5). This suggests that a high-testosterone, narcissistic male leader occupying a position of power in an unstable situation creates a potentially destructive combination.

Narcissism and the Emergence of Hubris

It's been argued here and elsewhere that hubris and narcissism overlap (for example, in the symptoms of hubris syndrome and NPD, see above) and are distinct (for example, hubris is a more state-like intoxication with power and success whilst narcissism is a more trait-like intoxication with the self). However, they're also related in that narcissism has been identified as a factor that can drive the emergence of hubris.[65] In many of the examples of hubristic leaders in this book, power, influence, charisma, and rhetoric have been mobilised to support personal vanity and a grandiose vision in which the narcissist themself is the centre of attention.

Although the focus in this chapter has been mainly on men from Narcissus to Johnson and Trump, the grandiosity and over-ambition that is associated with narcissism isn't confined to men; we need only think of Elizabeth Holmes (see Chapter 3). Indeed some have speculated that Holmes, with her sense of entitlement and exceptionalism, is narcissistic.[66] Self-adulation can drive hubrists to pursue ever-more ambitious projects that eventually end in disaster, for example, Holmes' vision to transform the blood-testing industry with Theranos' Edison machine. Hubris tends to manifest in people already prone to the combined effects of narcissism, a string of successes, and media praise, and who has the support of acolytes who are willing to provide narcissistic supply, all of which catalyse hubristic behaviours.[67] If a leader who is infected with excessive self-love finds themself in a context that enables or allows over-confident and reckless behaviour it's highly likely that at some stage they'll be over-taken by hubris. That said, it's entirely possible for a leader to be a hubrist without being a narcissist: for example, George W. Bush isn't rated highly on narcissism[68] but he is deemed by many to have been hubristic in his decision to invade Iraq in 2003.[69]

Even if narcissism predisposes a leader to hubris, a key distinction between hubris and narcissism is the energising role that power plays in a leader's psyche. Narcissists derive their power from being at the centre of attention, and their decisions are focused largely on enhancing a positive self-image. Hubristic leaders, on the other hand, don't need a stage on which to shine or seek out opportunities for getting attention in order to bolster their self-image and self-esteem. More substantial issues are at stake. For the hubrist, power is used in the service of a bigger-than-themselves project which could be anything from the geopolitical to the entrepreneurial, but they have in common that they have an extrinsic and ambitious goal to be pursued. For a narcissist, on the other hand, the goal is intrinsic and power is used in the service of the self and ego inflation.[70] The commonalities and differences between hubris and narcissism are summarised in Table 8.2.

Nick Bouras, Professor of Psychiatry at King's College, University of London, remarked that there's a common misconception that hubris is indistinguishable from narcissism but while excessive narcissism might lead to or co-exist with hubris they are fundamentally distinct. Bouras delineates them with precision and simplicity:

(1) narcissism is expressed with a blatantly attention seeking, grandiose sense of self-importance, and a persistent and burdensome search for admiration, and lack of empathy;

(2) hubris is characterised by over-confidence, over-ambition, arrogance, and excessive pride.[71]

Table 8.2 Comparison of Hubris and Narcissism

Comparison	Narcissism	Hubris
Narcissists and hubrists are over-confident	Narcissists are prone to making more favourable assessments of their decision-making accuracy and regard their knowledge and capabilities as higher than others	Hubristic executives are over-confident, for example, in their financial estimates of the value of firms during mergers and acquisitions
Narcissism is trait-like and hubris is state-like.	Narcissism is an enduring trait that emerges before adulthood	Hubris emerges under environmental conditions (e.g. power and success)
Hubris and narcissism are both disorders	Narcissism represents a character disorder	Hubris is a reactive or adjustment disorder in response to a situation or events
Hubris and narcissism are both associated with power	Narcissistic leaders reflect a preoccupation with fantasies of personal power to garner the approval and admiration of others and bolster and enhance ego	Hubrists exercise power to achieve overly ambitious goals, both personal and organisational

Irrespective of the similarities and differences between hubris and narcissism—and it's undeniable that more research is needed to understand their relationship[72]—it's beyond dispute that either singly or in combination they have the potential to create conditions for, or to directly bring about, negative and sometimes catastrophic unintended outcomes for organisations and wider society.[73]

Avoiding Exposure to Leaders' Narcissistic Tendencies

Managing a narcissist at the top of a business corporation or government is, to say the least, a significant challenge. Manfred Kets de Vries noted that it's unfortunate that the normal systems of checks and balances in organisations only seem to pick up the danger signs once the damage is in progress or has already been done.[74] He thinks that one solution is recognising the problem in good time, i.e. prior to or during the selection process. In the selection process it's been found that even experienced interviewers and assessment centre evaluators can evaluate narcissists more favourably than other applicants.[75] Making the mistake of hiring a narcissist could be an unintended consequence of seeking a stereotypical strong, confident, and ambitious leader.

The psychoanalyst Michael Maccoby noted that one of the main problems with trying to coach a narcissistic leader out of their maladaptive behaviours is that because of their very nature they're unlikely to be inclined to self-reflection or be open to criticism, even when it's meant to be constructive. A second problem Maccoby noted is that psychoanalysts are unlikely to be able to get anywhere near a narcissistic CEO or head of government. Nonetheless he offers a couple of suggestions to narcissists themselves for how they might avoid the leadership trap posed by their own personality. The first is to get a trusted sidekick to act as a toe-holder or anchor. One of the biggest challenges facing a leader who's prone to narcissism is judging where the fine line between adaptive and maladaptive narcissism lies. An external opinion from an acceptable and trusted source, for example a coach, mentor, therapist, colleague, peer executive, senior civil servant, partner, etc., can help to anchor a narcissist to the right side of the line. Kets de Vries suggests that an organisational 'fool' (as in the fool in Shakespeare's *King Lear*) can act as a foil to a narcissistic or hubristic leader through the use of wit and humour to defuse situations and protect narcissists from themselves. The second is that narcissistic leaders should, if they can bear it, 'get into analysis' because tools such as psychoanalysis and therapy can help them to work on themselves. As far as therapeutic solutions are concerned, Theodore Million noted that most narcissists strongly resist psychotherapy, but when they do engage one of the biggest pitfalls is when the therapist becomes too reinforcing, thus encouraging a narcissist to want to stay in therapy even if its effects on the root causes are limited. Million also noted that for therapy to work with a narcissist there has to be a strong working relationship between the client and the therapist that allows for behaviours to be faced in the right way and at the right time.

Maccoby suggests that it's possible to work with a leader's narcissism by always empathising with them but not expecting any empathy in return, by giving ideas but letting the narcissistic boss take credit for them, and by organising your time management skills so as to be available whenever a narcissistic boss makes the call. The ethics and practicalities of some of these suggestions are dubious. On the other hand, avoidance can work by transferring the narcissist out of harm's way or keeping vulnerable subordinates out of their reach. As noted above, a preemptive avoidance tacit is to not appoint a narcissist in the first place.[76] However, the latter is likely to be challenging because narcissists can be both ingratiating in the selection process and manipulative once they're in post.

Jennifer Chatman of UC Berkely Haas Business School offered some suggestions for how to head off narcissistic leadership:

(1) simply don't hire them by putting in place measures to screen for narcissistic personalities at the selection stage;
(2) use 360-degree evaluations to help surface self-absorbed leaders and weed them out before they rise too far up the hierarchy;
(3) use the best efforts of the board, especially non-executives and chairs, to rein in a narcissist;
(4) as a containment strategy, base a significant part of a narcissist's compensation on the development and the performance of the team so that they can't avoid or circumvent sharing credit or working with others.

Chatman noted that if a narcissist leader gets a foothold in an organisation but is eventually removed there's bound to be a lot of repair work required to restore the organisation to business as usual.[77] Given the risks that come with having a narcissist at the helm, all necessary steps should be taken to try to exclude, divert, or contain them before they're able to inflict serious harm on the organisation and its stakeholders.

Narcissistic Tendencies: Signs to Look Out For

(1) Leader displays inflated self-view, grandiosity, self-absorption, vanity, incessant need for adulation, sense of entitlement, and low empathy;
(2) Leader is charismatic and energetic; initially impresses but falters over time and is unable to execute the role over the longer term;
(3) Leader prefers followers to be an echo chamber for their own views rather than a sounding board to test ideas.

Notes

1 Robertson, H. G. (1955). The hybristes in Homer. *The Classical Journal*, 51(2), 81–83.
2 Cairns, D. L. (1996). Hybris, dishonour, and thinking big. *The Journal of Hellenic Studies*, 116, 1–32.
3 Ovid, *Metamorphoses*, Book 3.
4 Everly, G. S. (2019). The three faces of narcissism: A new look at an old problem. *Psychology Today*, July 1. Available at: https://www.psychologytoday.com/gb/blog/when-disaster-strikes-inside-disaster-psychology/201907/the-three-faces-narcissism-new-look-old
5 Ovid, *Metamorphóses*, Book 3, line 421.
6 Stolorow, R. D. (1975). Narcissus revisited. *American Journal of Psychoanalysis*, 35(3), 286–286.
7 Poetry in Translation. (no date). Book III:474–510 *Narcissus is changed into a flower*. Available at: https://www.poetryintranslation.com/PITBR/Latin/Metamorph3.php#anchor_Toc64106194
8 Sadler-Smith, E. (2019). *Hubristic leadership*. London: SAGE.
9 McKenna, S. (no date). Should narcissists lead the country? When pathological narcissism meets high political office. Opinion. *The Life Doctor*. Available at: https://www.thelifedoctor.org/should-narcissists-lead-the-country-when-pathological-narcissism-meets-high-political-office

10 Veljanovski, L. (2022). Boris Johnson won't quit as he behaves like a narcissist, says psychologist. *The Daily Mirror,* July 22. Available at: https://www.mirror.co.uk/news/politics/boris-johnson-wont-quit-because-27412673; Purnell, S. (2022). Reality is closing in on Boris Johnson, a narcissist scared of what he has unleashed. *The Guardian,* June 25. Available at: https://www.theguardian.com/commentisfree/2022/jun/25/reality-is-closing-in-on-boris-johnson-narcissist

11 Taylor, S. (2022). Narcissist, fantasist or ... psychopath? How Boris's last days as PM showed his darker side. *The Daily Telegraph,* July 8. Available at: https://www.telegraph.co.uk/news/2022/07/08/boris-johnson-psychopath

12 McKenna, S. (no date). Should narcissists lead the country? When pathological narcissism meets high political office. Opinion. *The Life Doctor.* Available at: https://www.thelifedoctor.org/should-narcissists-lead-the-country-when-pathological-narcissism-meets-high-political-office

13 Bower, T. (2020). *Boris Johnson: The gambler.* London: W. H. Allen, p.xi.

14 Mount, H. (2013). *The wit and wisdom of Boris Johnson.* London: Bloomsbury, pp.1–2.

15 Gant, J. (2022). Boris seems affronted when criticised for what amounts to a gross failure of responsibility. *The Daily Mail,* January 14. Available at: https://www.dailymail.co.uk/news/article-10398617/Letter-PMs-Eton-classics-master-emerges.html

16 Flinders, M. (2022). Boris Johnson: A terminal case of hubris syndrome. The Conversation, July 6. Available online at: https://theconversation.com/boris-johnson-a-terminal-case-of-hubris-syndrome-186495

17 Campbell, W. K., Hoffman, B. J., Campbell, S. M., & Marchisio, G. (2011). Narcissism in organizational contexts. *Human Resource Management Review,* 21(4), 268–284; Rosenthal, S. A., & Pittinsky, T. L. (2006). Narcissistic leadership. *The Leadership Quarterly,* 17(6), 617–633.

18 University of Michigan. (no date). *A brief history of narcissism.* Available at: https://deepblue.lib.umich.edu/bitstream/handle/2027.42/57606/skon-rath_2.pdf;jsessionid=6E44AA452143BA81A179509DED73E7FF?sequence=2

19 University of Michigan. (no date). *A brief history of narcissism.* Available at: https://deepblue.lib.umich.edu/bitstream/handle/2027.42/57606/skon-rath_2.pdf;jsessionid=6E44AA452143BA81A179509DED73E7FF?sequence=2

20 Freud cited in Maccoby, M. (2000). Narcissistic leaders. *Harvard Business Review,* 78(1), 68–77, p.70.

21 Rosenthal, S. A., & Pittinsky, T. L. (2006). Narcissistic leadership. *The Leadership Quarterly,* 17(6), 617–633.

22 Freud cited in Maccoby, M. (2000). Narcissistic leaders. *Harvard Business Review*, 78(1), 68–77, p.70.

23 Campbell, W. K., Hoffman, B. J., Campbell, S. M., & Marchisio, G. (2011). Narcissism in organizational contexts. *Human Resource Management Review*, 21(4), 268–284.

24 Rosenthal, S. A., & Pittinsky, T. L. (2006). Narcissistic leadership. *The Leadership Quarterly*, 17(6), 617–633.

25 Thomaes, S., Bushman, B. J., De Castro, B. O., & Stegge, H. (2009). What makes narcissists bloom? A framework for research on the etiology and development of narcissism. *Development and Psychopathology*, 21(4), 1233–1247.

26 Russell, G. (2011). Psychiatry and politicians: The 'hubris syndrome'. *The Psychiatrist*, 35(4), 140–145.

27 Tempany, A. (2010). When narcissism becomes pathological. *Financial Times Magazine*, September 4. Available at: https://www.ft.com/content/5ff67be2-b636-11df-a784-00144feabdco

28 Million, T., Millon, C. M. & Meagher, S. E. (2004). *Personality disorders in modern life*. Hoboken, NJ: John Wiley & Sons; Tempany, A. (2010). When narcissism becomes pathological. *Financial Times Magazine*, September 4. Available at: https://www.ft.com/content/5ff67be2-b636-11df-a784-00144feabdco

29 Pfattheicher, S. (2016). Testosterone, cortisol and the Dark Triad: Narcissism (but not Machiavellianism or psychopathy) is positively related to basal testosterone and cortisol. *Personality and Individual Differences*, 97, 115–119.

30 Frances, A. (2017). Letter: An eminent psychiatrist demurs on Trump's mental state. *The* New York Times, February 1. Available online at: https://www.nytimes.com/2017/02/14/opinion/an-eminent-psychiatrist-demurs-on-trumps-mental-state.html

31 Asad, S., & Sadler-Smith, E. (2020). Differentiating leader hubris and narcissism on the basis of power. *Leadership*, 16(1), 39–61.

32 Miller, J. D., Hoffman, B. J., Gaughan, E. T., et al. (2011). Grandiose and vulnerable narcissism: A nomological network analysis. *Journal of Personality*, 79(5), 1013–104; Reina, C. S., Zhang, Z., & Peterson, S. J. (2014). CEO grandiose narcissism and firm performance: The role of organizational identification. *The Leadership Quarterly*, 25(5), 958–971.

33 Ames, D. R., Rose, P., & Anderson, C. P. (2006). The NPI-16 as a short measure of narcissism. *Journal of Research in Personality*, 40(4), 440–450.

34 Campbell, W. K., Hoffman, B. J., Campbell, S. M., & Marchisio, G. (2011). Narcissism in organizational contexts. *Human Resource Management Review*, 21(4), 268–284, p.270.

35 Pincus, A. L. & Roche, M. J. (2011). Narcissistic grandiosity and narcissistic vulnerability In: Campbell, W. K., & Miller, J. D. (eds.). *The handbook of*

narcissism and narcissistic personality disorder. Hoboken, NJ: John Wiley and Sons, pp.31–40.

36 Rosenthal, S. A., & Pittinsky, T. L. (2006). Narcissistic leadership. *The Leadership Quarterly*, 17(6), 617–633.

37 Pincus, A. L., & Lukowitzky, M. R. (2010). Pathological narcissism and narcissistic personality disorder. *Annual Review of Clinical Psychology*, 6, 421–446.

38 Frances, A. (2017). An eminent psychiatrist demurs on Trump's mental state. *The New York Times* (letters), February 14. Available at: https://www.nytimes.com/2017/02/14/opinion/an-eminent-psychiatrist-demurs-on-trumps-mental-state.html

39 Everly, G. S. (2019). The three faces of narcissism: A new look at an old problem. *Psychology Today*, July 1. Available at: https://www.psychologytoday.com/gb/blog/when-disaster-strikes-inside-disaster-psychology/201907/the-three-faces-narcissism-new-look-old

40 Maccoby, M. (2000). Narcissistic leaders. *Harvard Business Review*, 78(1), 68–77, p.70.

41 Million, T. et al. (2004). *Personality disorders in modern life.* Hoboken, NJ: John Wiley & Sons, p.334.

42 Bordoni, C. (2019). *Hubris and progress.* Abingdon: Routledge.

43 Arendt, H. (1958). Cited in Canovan, M. (1997). *Hannah Arendt as a conservative thinker,* pp.11–32. In May, L., & Kohn, J. (eds.). (1997). *Hannah Arendt: Twenty years later.* Cambridge, MA: MIT Press, p.19.

44 Kets de Vries, M. (1993). *Leaders, fools and imposters.* San Francisco: Jossey Bass, p.34.

45 Daedalus Trust. (2014). *Conference 2014 Video. Prof Adrian Furnham: The psychology of derailment.* The Daedalus Trust. Available at: http://www.daedalustrust.com/conference-2014-video-prof-adrian-furnham-the-psychology-of-leadership-derailment

46 Million, T. et al. (2004). *Personality disorders in modern life.* Hoboken, NJ: John Wiley & Sons, p.336.

47 Everly, G. S. (2019). The three faces of narcissism: A new look at an old problem. *Psychology Today*, July 1. Available at: https://www.psychologytoday.com/gb/blog/when-disaster-strikes-inside-disaster-psychology/201907/the-three-faces-narcissism-new-look-old

48 Tempany, A. (2010). When narcissism becomes pathological. *Financial Times Magazine*, September 4. Available at: https://www.ft.com/content/5ff67be2-b636-11df-a784-00144feabdc0

49 Mitra, P., & Fluyau, D. (2023). *Narcissistic personality disorder.* National Library of Medicine. Available at: https://www.ncbi.nlm.nih.gov/books/NBK556001

50 Campbell, W. K., Hoffman, B. J., Campbell, S. M., & Marchisio, G. (2011). Narcissism in organizational contexts. *Human Resource Management Review*, 21(4), 268–284.

51 Crump, J. (2020). Unfit: Damning documentary argues Trump is a malignant narcissist. *The Independent*, August 27. Available at: https://www.independent.co.uk/news/world/americas/us-politics/damning-documentary-unfit-claims-trump-suffers-from-mental-disorders-a9692176.html

52 Mayer, J. (2017). Should psychiatrists speak out against Trump? *The New Yorker*, May 15. Available at: https://www.newyorker.com/magazine/2017/05/22/should-psychiatrists-speak-out-against-trump

53 Georgiou, A. (2022). The most narcissistic presidents in modern U.S. history ranked. *Newsweek*, September 16. Available at: https://www.newsweek.com/most-narcissistic-presidents-modern-united-states-history-ranked-1743670; Harden, J. P. (2021). All the world's a stage: US presidential narcissism and international conflict. *International Studies Quarterly*, 65(3), 825–837.

54 Reich, R. (2022). Trump and Elon Musk are dangerous narcissists tailored to 2022 America. *The Guardian*, November 8. Available at: https://www.theguardian.com/commentisfree/2022/nov/08/trump-and-elon-musk-are-dangerous-narcissists-tailored-to-2022-america

55 Brunell, A. B., Gentry, W. A., Campbell, W. K., Hoffman, B. J., Kuhnert. K. W., & DeMarree, K. G. (2008). Leader emergence: The case of the narcissistic leader. *Personality and Social Psychology Bulletin*, 34(12), 1663–1676.

56 Glad, B. (2002). Why tyrants go too far: Malignant narcissism and absolute power. *Political Psychology*, 23(1), 1–37.

57 Grijalva, E., Harms, P., Newman, D., & Gaddis, B. (2015). Narcissism and leadership: A meta-analytic review of linear and nonlinear relationships. *Personnel Psychology*, 68(1), 1–47.

58 Mead, N. L., Baumeister, R. F., Stuppy, A., & Vohs, K. D. (2018). Power increases the socially toxic component of narcissism among individuals with high baseline testosterone. *Journal of Experimental Psychology: General*, 147(4), 591–596.

59 Bloom, D., & Veselinovic, M. (2016). Boris Johnson's secret pro-EU article revealed. *CNN*, October 16. Available at: https://edition.cnn.com/2016/10/16/europe/britain-brexit-boris-johnson-eu-column/index.html

60 Bienkov, A. (2019). Boris Johnson said he was a fan of the EU and wanted to stay in the single market. *Insider*, July 24. Available at: https://www.businessinsider.com/boris-johnson-fan-of-eu-wanted-stay-single-market-brexit-2019-7?r=US&IR=T

61 Maccoby, M. (2000). Narcissistic leaders. *Harvard Business Review*, 78(1), 68–77.

62 Maccoby, M. (2000). Narcissistic leaders. *Harvard Business Review*, 78(1), 68–77.

63 Asad, S., & Sadler-Smith, E. (2020). Differentiating leader hubris and narcissism on the basis of power. *Leadership*, 16(1), 39–61.

64 Maccoby, M. (2000). Narcissistic leaders. *Harvard Business Review*, 78(1), 68–77.

65 Kroll, M. J., Toombs, L. A., & Wright, P. (2000). Napoleon's tragic march home from Moscow: Lessons in hubris. *Academy of Management Perspectives*, 14(1), 117–128.

66 O'Reilly, C. A., & Chatman, J. A. (2020). Transformational leader or narcissist? How grandiose narcissists can create and destroy organizations and institutions. *California Management Review*, 62(3), 5–27.

67 Kroll, M. J., Toombs, L. A., & Wright, P. (2000). Napoleon's tragic march home from Moscow: Lessons in hubris. *Academy of Management Perspectives*, 14(1), 117–128.

68 Harden, J. P. (2022). Looking like a winner: Leader narcissism and war duration. *Journal of Conflict Resolution*, https://doi.org/10.1177/00220027221123757 (in press).

69 Owen, D. (2007). *The hubris syndrome: Bush, Blair and the intoxication of power*. London: Politicos.

70 Asad, S., & Sadler-Smith, E. (2020). Differentiating leader hubris and narcissism on the basis of power. *Leadership*, 16(1), 39–61.

71 Bouras, N. (2018). Foreword. In Garrard, P. (ed.) *The leadership hubris epidemic: Biological roots and strategies for prevention*. Basingstoke: Palgrave Macmillan, p.x.

72 Asad, S., & Sadler-Smith, E. (2020). Differentiating leader hubris and narcissism on the basis of power. *Leadership*, 16(1), 39–61.

73 Asad, S., & Sadler-Smith, E. (2020). Differentiating leader hubris and narcissism on the basis of power. *Leadership*, 16(1), 39–61.

74 Kets de Vries, M. (1993). Leaders, *fools and imposters*. San Francisco: Jossey-Bass Publishers.

75 Campbell, W. K., Hoffman, B. J., Campbell, S. M., & Marchisio, G. (2011). Narcissism in organizational contexts. *Human Resource Management Review*, 21(4), 268–284.

76 Rosenthal, S. A., & Pittinsky, T. L. (2006). Narcissistic leadership. *The Leadership Quarterly*, 17(6), 617–633.

77 Butts, M. (2020). How narcissistic leaders infect their organizations' cultures. *Berkley Haas Newsroom*, October 3. Available at: https://newsroom.haas.berkeley.edu/research/how-narcissistic-leaders-infect-their-organizations-culture

9

EXCESS

Nothing to Excess

The Sanctuary of Apollo at Delphi is one of the most famous archaeological sites in the whole of Greece. It's a genuine wonder of the ancient world, standing near to the summit of Mount Parnassus in Central Greece and dating back to at least the 6th century BC. For the Ancient Greeks Delphi was the navel (*omphalos*, ὀμφᾰλός) of the world. In the Sanctuary itself the Temple of Apollo, son of Zeus and God of harmony, knowledge, light, prophecy, and truth, was the focal point. It was in the Temple to Apollo that the high priestess (known as the 'Pythia' or 'Oracle', hence the 'Oracle of Delphi') delivered her pronouncements. She did so in a frenzied state thought to have been induced by mind-altering vapours arising from a chasm in the rock. The Oracle was the mouthpiece of Apollo, and the Temple was a fount of wisdom for the Ancient Greeks. Three pithy maxims

DOI: 10.4324/9781003128427-9

are said to have been inscribed on the Temple (opinion is divided as to exactly where):

(1) know thyself;
(2) nothing to excess;
(3) give a pledge—ruin follows.[1]

The first and second are well known, the third is less so and is more ambiguous. The maxim of 'nothing to excess' (*meden agan*, μηδὲν ἄγαν), or in other words 'moderation', is one of the Platonic virtues espoused by the Ancient Greeks (the others included courage, justice, and wisdom). It can be found in other philosophies, wisdom traditions and teachings, for example, in Buddhism the 'middle way' refers to avoiding the extremes of self-denial and self-indulgence.[2] The Ancient Greeks' characterising of virtue as a middle way between the extremes of deficiency and excess following the Oracle's maxim was an important moral principle for healthy communal living.[3] Although the so-called 'doctrine of the mean' was not Aristotle's invention, it was made famous in his great ethical work *The Nicomachean Ethics* (hereafter the *Ethics*) named after his son Nicomachus.

For Aristotle, the *Ethics* is an exposition of a 'practical science' in the sense of a work that seeks to inform its readers about how to act in order to achieve the highest human good.[4] Aristotle's other work of practical science is *The Politics*. Together they make up a philosophical system where "so much depends on particular circumstances that only general rules can be given" and forms the basis for individual judgement on how to act in a specific situation.[5] In Book II of the *Ethics* Aristotle makes a point which is fundamental to his system of virtue: "it is in the nature of moral qualities that they are destroyed by deficiency and excess".[6] This is the first appearance in the *Ethics* of the doctrine of the mean, or the as it has come to be known 'the golden mean', although the epithet 'golden' is not Aristotle's.[7] He illustrates this with reference to the virtue of 'courage' which is "destroyed by excess and deficiency and preserved by the mean":[8] "The man who shuns and fears everything and stands up to nothing becomes a coward; the man who is afraid of nothing at all, but marches up to every danger, becomes foolhardy".[9]

In a modern application of this principle, the distinguished British psychologist, Adrian Furnham, argues that leaders tend to fail and derail not because they have too little of something (i.e. because they are incompetent), rather because they have too much of something else or "too much of a good thing".[10] For example, ambition in moderation on the part of a leader is functional, but too much ambition exercised by the wrong leader in the wrong circumstances can become dysfunctional. Some of the cases given earlier in this book illustrate what can happen when a laudable vision, for example for economic growth or potentially revolutionary medical technology, becomes grossly exaggerated.

This idea of an ordinarily beneficial aspect of leader behaviour causing harm when taken too far has been referred to as the 'to-much-of-a-good-thing effect' (TMGT effect) in which the relationship between the variable of interest and outcomes has a curvilinear shape, see Figure 9.1.[11] For example, in the relationship between formal planning and new venture survival and success there is an inflexion point (the top of the inverted U): up to this point, increased formal planning contributes to the long-term survival and success of new firms, whereas after the top of the inverted U increased planning has no benefit and may even have detrimental effects because there are diminishing returns from devoting additional resources to formal planning.[12]

A similar, but slightly different, idea is to be found in Confucianism: "too much can be worse than too little".[13] But is too much of something, for example, confidence or ambition, always bad? As far as excess is concerned there

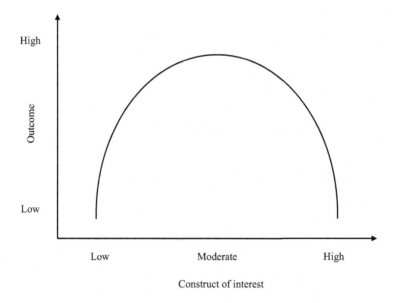

Figure 9.1 Curvilinear Relationship Between Construct of Interest and Outcome

are a number of subtly different issues that are pertinent to hubris. Leaders, both in politics and business, face two challenges: the first is treading the fine line between deficiency and excess thus adhering to the Aristotelian golden mean as shown in the inflexion point in inverted U-shape shown in Figure 9.1; the second, which in some ways seems at odds with the first, is in deciding when excess is appropriate on the basis that excess can sometimes be not only desirable but also essential for human progress. In this respect the Italian sociologist Carlo Bordoni has referred to hubris as "the engine of history".[14] An implication of this is that hubris might have a 'bright side' as a well as the dark side that has been so much of the focus of this book. A business leader who is notable for many things, including his walking of the "hubris tightrope"[15] but not least for his embracing of grandiose visions in his ambitions both for himself and humanity, is Elon Musk.

Elon Musk

Is Musk a hubrist who's guilty of serial excesses, is he an iconic business venturer who, for the most part, has successfully trodden the fine line between deficiency and excess, or is he a complex and paradoxical embodiment of all these things?[16] His acquisition of Twitter is a case in point. In October 2022, the billionaire entrepreneur, 'maverick', and one of the world's richest people acquired the social media platform Twitter for $44 billion. He signed a binding merger agreement originally for a bid of $54.2 million, and then tried to back out of the deal. Twitter sued Musk and compelled him to close on the agreement.[17] Shortly before the acquisition he posted a video of himself entering the company's San Francisco lobby carrying a sink and posted a Tweet "Entering Twitter HQ – let that sink in!".[18] The *Sydney Morning Herald* called these shenanigans "unconventional at best, foolhardy at worst", The *Harvard Gazette* concurred, calling the process "erratic and even foolhardy",[19] with others describing it as "peak hubris".[20] According to Musk's own Twitter feed he "had a car named Hubris once".[21]

Musk's stated aim was to make Twitter a haven for any kind of free speech so long as it was "within the bounds of the law". But there have been a number of unanticipated negative consequences of Musk's acquisition of Twitter, for example, it's reported that more than 500 major advertisers paused spending, and daily revenues dropped by 40 per cent.[22] The impact on the value of the company was substantial. When Musk made his offer to buy the firm, Twitter's share price was $45.08; by April 25, 2022 when the board accepted Musk's offer it had risen to $51.70.[23] By July 8 when Musk tried to pull out of the deal the price had dropped to $36.81. Following this roller coaster ride, as of October 2022 Twitter stock is not available for purchase on the stock market. In January 2023 *Fortune* reported that more than half of Twitter's value had been destroyed in a little over two months[24] and *Time* reported that Musk's net worth dropped by $9 billion following the deal. In August 2023 Musk announced that Twitter would no longer be called Twitter but instead would be referred to simply as X which reflected his fondness for the letter 'x' more generally.

Elon Musk is an intriguing character. He was born in Pretoria, South Africa in 1971. He has a bachelor's degree in economics and physics from the University of Pennsylvania. He moved to Stanford University in 1995 and, like Jobs and Holmes before him, dropped out of university to found his own company; in the case of Musk it was the software company Zip2 which he founded with his brother Kimbal. Musk is a self-made billionaire and one of the most successful entrepreneurs of all time.[25] He's said to be a 'difficult' person to work with; he has a reputation as a micromanager but has also been described as a 'visionary' and brilliant workaholic.[26] Musk's biographer Ashlee Vance summarised the arc of his career in the authorised biography *Elon Musk: How the Billionaire CEO of SpaceX and Tesla is Shaping Our Future* (2015):

(1) Musk was part of the dot com mania in the mid-1990s. He founded a company called Zip2 one of the first internet maps and direction services which was bought for Compaq for $307 million;

(2) He invested the $22 million he made from that deal into his next business venture PayPal, the world's leading internet payment system;

(3) When eBay acquired PayPal in 2002 for $1.5 billion Musk became fantastically wealthy even by Silicon Valley standards;

(4) On the back of this deal he invested the best part of $200 million in founding SpaceX entering into what has been described as a battle with not only Lockheed Martin and Boeing but also with Russia and China no less;

(5) He was an early investor in Tesla Motors and became its chairperson, chief product architect and CEO in 2008.[27]

His other ventures include Neuralink which is developing ultra-high-bandwidth brain-machine interfaces with the aim of connecting the human brain to computers, and The Boring Company which combines tunnelling technology with electric transportation to "alleviate soul-crushing urban congestion".[28] The consistency and unity of principle behind Musk's two main businesses (SpaceX and Tesla) is that they're trying to "achieve the impossible" in order to save humanity from itself.[29]

Throughout his life and career boldness and brashness have been amongst Musk's most noteworthy attributes. In an interview with Wired's journalist Chris Anderson, Musk commented that "There's a tremendous bias against taking risks. Everyone is trying to optimise their ass-covering."[30] The British-American journalist, Nick Bilton, writing in Vanity Fair, and predating the Twitter debacle, described Elon Musk as being on numerous missions: a mission to Mars; a mission to save humanity from its reliance on fossil fuels; a mission to save us from artificial intelligence (AI) going rogue and destroying humanity by accident; a mission to transport people from Los Angeles to San Francisco in giant air tubes; a mission to dig tunnels underground to alleviate traffic jams; and a mission to inhabit other planets and star systems.[31] In an interview with Gillian Tett in the Financial Times, Walter Isaacson, who got close to Musk during the writing of his biography Elon Musk (2023), noted that "Musk goes through manic mood swings, and deep depressions and risk-seeking highs.[32] Isaacson believes that if Musk didn't have that kind of personality he would not have achieved remarkable things; Isaacson thinks that Musk's diabolical 'demons' are, paradoxically, his inspirational angels', but also that Musk continually lives close to the edge.

Musk's ambitions for the human race are perhaps grounded in annihilation anxieties about humanity's future.[33] The high ambition of his vision is best exemplified by his mission for human beings to colonise Mars, which Musk sees as the first step towards Homo sapiens becoming a multiplanetary species. Inside the headquarters of SpaceX in California there are said to be two giant posters of Mars hanging side by side: one depicts Mars in its natural, red, cold, dusty, and barren state; the other depicts it following the Red Planet's Muskian makeover with emerald green landmasses surrounded by azure blue oceans. Musk thinks the colonisation of Mars feasible for five quite simple reasons:

(1) Mars is about half as far again from the Sun as Earth is, so it still has "decent sunlight";
(2) even though Mars is "a little cold" we can still "warm it up";

(3) the Martian atmosphere is mainly comprised of CO_2 so "we can grow plants on Mars just by compressing the atmosphere";

(4) gravity on Mars is about one-third that of the Earth so we'd "be able to lift heavy things and bound around";

(5) the length of the Martian day is virtually the same as that of Earth at 24 hours and 37 minutes.[34]

Musk's vision is to build enough rockets to be able to have a million people living on Mars by 2050.[35] Just for the record he himself wouldn't mind dying on Mars "so long as it wasn't on impact".[36]

The Mars project is an example of the grandiosity of Musk's ambitions. But his Mars plans have been criticised roundly by some: first, the presence of humans could contaminate Mars with Earthly microbes; second, robots are better suited to exploring Mars than humans; third, the Martian environment is totally inhospitable to human beings and always will be; and fourth, the money spent on the exploration and colonisation of Mars would be better spent on fixing the Earth itself.[37] Undeterred by the critics Musk has said that:

> You want to wake up in the morning and think the future is going to be great – and that's what being a spacefaring civilization is all about. It's about believing in the future and thinking that the future will be better than the past. And I can't think of anything more exciting than going out there and being among the stars.[38]

Musk's biographer, Ashlee Vance, seems as perplexed by Musk as the rest of us: on the one hand, he's "a well-intentioned dreamer" and "card-carrying member of Silicon Valley's techno-utopian club",[39] on the other, he's a pragmatist who actually built a rocket factory in the middle of Los Angles, flew a supply capsule to the International Space Station, and brought the rocket back down to Earth, and he delivered the Tesla Model S and made the company one of the world's biggest automobile manufacturers.[40] These are colossal achievements.[41] However, a commentator on the Bloomberg website also remarked that even though he's capable of doing remarkable things the biggest risk to Musk "may be his own hubris".[42]

Whether or not Musk is, in the words of Ben Laker and colleagues in their book *Too Proud to Lead* (2021), a "hubristic megalomanic"[43] for whom an "air of infallibility has crept in" or a "visionary environmentalist"[44] who will make a "real difference to the fight against global warming",[45] it's safe to say that Musk is a character of extremes and excesses. *Vanity Fair's* Nick Bilton summed him up as follows:

> Every once in a while, a human comes along and propels us forward by leaps and bounds ... but, at the same time, those humans are imperfect, even if we don't want them to be they're flawed [and] absolute extremes of themselves.[46]

Perhaps what comes with the territory and job description for individuals who thrive on extreme ambition is a courage of conviction that's rooted in a self-evaluation which is positive to the extent that it verges on excess. Musk and his achievements are without doubt extraordinary. As far as extraordinariness is concerned the 28th President of the USA, Woodrow T. Wilson (1856–1924), once remarked that "All the extraordinary men I have known were extraordinary in their own [self-]estimation".[47] The same is true of many of the leaders, both men and women, discussed in this book, they all appear to hold themselves in the highest regard.

Hyper Core Self-evaluation

Whether we're a president, a prime minister, a CEO, or just an ordinary citizen going about our business we all need a certain amount of conviction about ourselves—a positive 'self-concept'—in order to function effectively in the world. A positive self-concept helps to give a person some certainty about their self-worth, a trust in their knowledge and skills, and a belief in their ability get things done without becoming overly anxious. Without the foundation of a positive core self-concept we'd all probably be ineffectual, not to mention demotivated, demoralised, and depressed people..

The need for positive self-belief steps up a level as far as leaders are concerned: they need a strong, positive self-concept to give them the energy and effort that's required to be effective in taking decisions, solving problems, inspiring others, marshalling resources, dealing with difficult people, delegating, troubleshooting, etc. But being an effective leader involves a fine balancing act between, on the one hand, having enough self-assurance to be able to make the most of opportunities and rise to challenges, and, on the other hand, not falling into the trap of taking excessive risks fuelled by inflated self-worth and over-confidence. In order to walk this tightrope leaders need to be able to make accurate self-assessments in terms of a number of core aspects of their psyche, and then to behave accordingly.

A group of behavioural scientists led by Tim Judge of Ohio State University attempted to explain why some people were very satisfied and successful in their jobs whilst others were less so. Judge and colleagues identified four traits which they grouped under the umbrella of 'core self-evaluation' (CSE). These four aspects of CSE are the "fundamental, bottom-line evaluations that individuals hold about themselves" and are amongst the most widely studied traits in psychology.[48] They are:

(1) *Self-esteem*: a person's overall approval of themself and the degree to which they see themself as capable, significant, successful and worthy, essentially it is a person's self-liking, self-acceptance, and self-respect;
(2) *Self-efficacy*: a person's belief in their capability to successfully perform difficult and novel tasks and to cope with adversity in demanding situations;
(3) *Locus of control*: a person's beliefs about their ability to control their situation and how much influence they have over what happens to them;
(4) *Emotional stability*: a person's freedom from worry, fear, stress, and feelings of helplessness.[49]

This combination of self-esteem, self-efficacy, locus of control, and emotional stability is an 'integrative personality trait' in that someone who has high self-esteem is also likely to have high self-efficacy and feel that they're in control of events, they're also likely to have little to worry or be anxious about. In terms of bottom-line outcomes, a person with high CSE will tend to be more satisfied with and perform better in their job, be more successful in their career, have lower levels of stress and anxiety, cope better with setbacks, and be able to make the most of advantages and opportunities,[50] see Figure 9.2. On the other hand, having a deficiency of CSE is a liability and especially so for a leader given the challenges and demands that are associated with leadership roles.

In terms of how they feel about themselves, a person with the requisite levels of CSE will have healthy self-esteem (for example, they'll have the feeling that 'I am worthy'), self-efficacy (they'll have the confidence

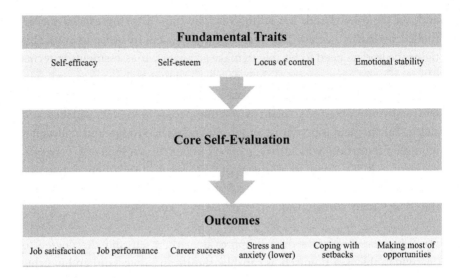

Figure 9.2 CSE and Its Relationship to Outcomes

Table 9.1 Bright-side (CSE) and Dark-side (Dark Triad) Leader Personality Traits

Bright side traits (CSE)	Dark-side traits (Dark Triad)
Emotional stability: freedom from worry, fear, stress, and feelings of helplessness	Machiavellianism: a manipulative personality
Locus of control: beliefs about one's ability to control situations	Narcissism: grandiosity, entitlement, dominance, superiority, and lack of empathy
Self-efficacy: belief in one's capability to successfully execute and perform tasks	Psychopathy: high impulsivity/thrill-seeking coupled with low empathy/anxiety; socially malevolent character with tendencies towards self-promotion, emotional coldness, duplicity, and aggressiveness
Self-esteem: overall approval of oneself	

that 'I succeed at tasks'), and locus of control (they'll have an attitude that 'life's events are within my control') combined with a freedom from anxiety (they'll have the sense that 'I'm free from excessive fears, worries, or anxieties'). Core self-evaluation is a bright-side leadership trait, unlike narcissism, Machiavellianism, and psychopathy which are dark-side leader personality traits and part of the so-called Dark Triad,[51] see Table 9.1.

Positive self-evaluations are an important psychological resource for leaders. They support capability, performance, resilience, and strength in the face of hardships and difficulties. CSE is a good thing for a leader to have. Leaders with the requisite levels of self-esteem, self-efficacy, locus of control, and emotional stability are more likely to:

(1) advance in their careers;
(2) overcome setbacks;
(3) be persistent and competitive;
(4) seize opportunities;
(5) give off an aura of confidence;
(6) inspire others to follow them.

But it's not necessarily the case that senior leaders will uniformly exhibit elevated levels of CSE. As with any trait, there are likely to be individual differences in CSE amongst senior leaders. Differences are more likely to be found at the excessive end rather than the deficient end of the CSE spectrum, this is because aspirant leaders deficient in CSE would have been weeded out and are unlikely to have made it to a senior level in the first place.

Management researchers Nathan Hiller and Donald Hambrick pointed out that while researchers have focused on understanding the effects on a person's behaviour of having the requisite amount or a deficiency of CSE, they've tended to ignore the implications of having an excess of CSE or too-much-of-a-good-thing (the 'TMGT effect').[52] As already noted, leaders at the top of their organisations are likely to have elevated levels of CSE because this would probably have been a contributory factor to them attaining a senior leadership position in the first place. However, problems arise when levels of CSE are taken to excess.

An important question for senior leaders who appear to have CSE in abundance, such as Elon Musk, is how much self-efficacy, self-esteem, locus of control, and freedom from anxiety is enough, given the risk that TMGT might translate into over-confident and even reckless behaviours (crossing from the top of the inverted U in Figure 9.1 over to the right-hand side). As we know from the Ancient Greeks, 'nothing to excess' is a helpful guiding principle, however, as will be discussed below, it may not necessarily be a cardinal rule. But for now an implication of the Delphic Oracle's 2,500-year-old maxim is that more CSE may not necessarily be better. For example, taken to the extreme, a leader with excess CSE might be confident to the extent that they feel 'I am the most worthy', 'I can succeed at anything

I set out to do', '*everything* is within my control', and 'I am an *anxiety-free zone*'. An epitome of an excess of CSE is to be found, perhaps predictably, in Donald Trump as illustrated in his infamous 'stable genius' tweet:

> Actually, throughout my life, my two greatest assets have been mental stability and being, like, really smart. Crooked Hillary Clinton also played these cards very hard and, as everyone knows, went down in flames. I went from VERY successful businessman, to top T.V. Star to President of the United States (on my first try). I think that would qualify as not smart, but genius . . . and a very stable genius at that![53]

Donald Trump and his idiosyncrasies aside, Hiller and Hambrick offer a brief portrayal of what a hyper-CSE leader might look like:

> Exceedingly confident and full of self-regard and self-worth. They are sure of their abilities, and they believe deeply that the application of their abilities will bring positive outcomes. They are free of anxiety and have little concern about negative outcomes because they possess a core conviction that they can surmount adversity and repair all problems. In short, hyper-CSE executives are sure they will prevail.[54]

Being sure that one will prevail comes dangerously close to the arrogance and conceit which may open the door to hubris. The risk associated with hyper core-self-evaluation (hCSE) is that it may seduce leaders into taking over-confident, over-ambitious, grandiose, self-serving actions that are contemptuous of advice and criticism based on an arrogant assumption that they know best, that they can do no wrong, and they can fix all the world's wrongs. These are the hallmarks of hubris, and the links to hubris syndrome (HS) are palpable:

(1) excessive confidence in the individual's own judgement and contempt for the advice or criticism of others (HS Symptom 7);
(2) exaggerated self-belief, bordering on a sense of omnipotence, in what they personally can achieve (HS Symptom 8).[55]

Hiller and Hambrick proposed that exceptionally high CSE or hCSE aligns with what is "colloquially called 'hubris' ".[56]

In terms of that most fundamental aspect of the executive's role, decision-making, leaders with hyper core self-evaluation are more likely to mistakenly believe they know more than they actually do and eschew the exhaustive gathering of information to justify their decisions. This, in turn, is likely to make them more susceptible to act instinctively by simply 'going-with-their-gut' at the expense of the finer details of planning and implementation (see Chapter 4). They may also end up deceiving themselves (see Chapter 6). Moreover, excessive CSE is also more likely to convince a leader they are the one who is capable of overcoming any problems that might arise. As a consequence they're more likely to be prone to taking ill-conceived, arbitrary decisions that simply 'feel right' (as in the case of George W. Bush's decision to invade Iraq in 2003) without due regard for the nuts and bolts of the practicalities and policies and longer-term outcomes. David Owen and Jonathan Davidson refer to this as 'hubristic incompetence' (HS Symptom 14).

That said, Hiller and Hambrick identify several other manifestations of hCSE which are not necessarily bad for leaders who have to take actions in volatile, uncertain, complex, and ambiguous situations, including:

(1) faster decision-making inspired by high levels of self-confidence and potency;
(2) more centralised decision-making based on a belief in the uniqueness of their capabilities;
(3) greater willingness to undertake large-scale, more radical, higher-risk projects;
(4) less need to conform to industry or institutional norms;
(5) more committed to an idea if it is their personal brain-child;
(6) be more persistent in pursuing strategies that they chose personally and are committed to.[57]

All of the above, when exercised by the right person, in the right circumstances, and to the right amount, have the potential to be beneficial, for example, in making radical rather than incremental innovations, or seizing the initiative in challenging and difficult circumstances such as political instability or military conflict. The challenge for any leader, be they in business or politics, is having the nous to be able to judge whether or not they're the right person to be taking the decision, if the circumstances are right, and what the right amount of any given leader behaviour is.

In the *Ethics* Aristotle distinguished between two types of 'excellence' with regard to intelligence (sometimes called 'intellectual virtues'): the first excellence of intelligence is 'theoretical', for example, to be good at mathematics; the second type of excellence of intelligence is 'practical' and is sometimes referred to as 'practical intelligence' or 'practical wisdom'. This second type is an excellence in "deciding on the right way to behave and getting the right thing done".[58] Excellence in judging the right amount of a particular leader behaviour, for example, how much ambition is needed to get the right thing done, is a fundamental aspect of a leader's practical wisdom; without it a leader's decision-making lacks excellence.[59] This is a topic to which we shall return shortly, but first we need to explore a fundamental paradox that seems to be at work in hubristic leader behaviours.

Strengths-into-Weaknesses Paradox

We typically think of an abundance of leader qualities (for example, confidence, ambition, pride, etc.) as unequivocally and unconditionally a 'good thing'. However, a corollary of the hCSE concept is that it's possible to have TMGT.[60] For example, when taken to excess the four CSE traits of self-esteem, self-efficacy, locus of control, and emotional stability can morph from leader strengths into leader weaknesses. Similarly, leader behaviours such as confidence, ambition, pride, benign influence, positive alignment, and healthy energy when taken to excess become likewise transformed, see Table 9.2.

As discussed briefly in Chapter 1, the management researcher Danny Miller of the HEC Graduate Business School in Montreal wrote a book about this phenomenon. He called it *The Icarus Paradox* (1990), named after Icarus whose new-found power of flight was transformed by his over-confidence, recklessness, and wild abandon into his greatest, and ultimately fatal, weakness. Miller observed that this same paradox often applies to leaders when hubris takes hold: "their victories and their strengths often seduce them into the excesses that cause their downfall".[61] The process is shown in Figure 9.3 below, and Miller's 'Icarus Paradox' works like this:

(1) leaders have free will, therefore they are capable of being volitionally over-confident, careless, or contemptuous whilst not necessarily intending to bring about destructive outcomes;

Table 9.2 Leader Strengths When Taken to Excess Morph into Weaknesses

Strength when practised to right amount	Weakness when practised to excess
Self-esteem	Becomes arrogant over estimation of one's worth, e.g. 'I am the most worthy'
Self-efficacy	Become hubristic over-confidence, e.g. 'I can succeed at anything I set out to do'
Locus of control	Becomes an illusion of omnipotence, e.g. 'everything is within my control'
Emotional stability	Becomes an emotional smoke screen, e.g. 'I am an anxiety-free zone'
Benign influence	Becomes a narcissistic propensity to see the world as an arena for exercising power and seeking glory, e.g. 'It's all about me'
Positive alignment	Becomes an over-identification with the organisation or institution, e.g. 'I am this company or administration'
Healthy energy	Becomes messianic manner and tendency to exaltation, e.g. using the 'royal we
Sound judgement	Becomes excessive reliance on gut feelings, e.g. 'just trust me, I know'
Proper ambition	Becomes exaggerated self-belief, bordering on omnipotence, e.g. 'I can lead us to do anything we choose'

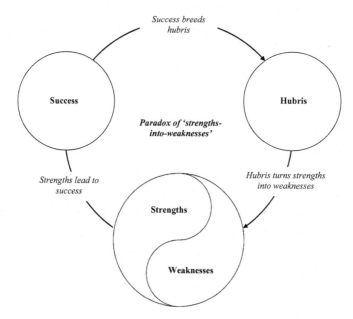

Figure 9.3 The Paradox of Strengths into Weaknesses in the Hubristic Leadership Process (Sadler-Smith, 2019)

(2) in over-extending their strengths volitionally they're not engaging in deliberately destructive behaviours but they may be inadvertently creating the conditions for negative outcomes to arise;

(3) nevertheless, they are complicit of hubristic incompetence, albeit unintentionally, and must take their share of the responsibility for any damaging outcomes which ensue in the form of unintended negative consequences.

In this paradox, a leader's strengths and weaknesses co-exist as two sides of the same coin. In practical terms this can mean, for example, that a leader who is a growth-driven, entrepreneurial 'builder' can morph into an impulsive, greedy 'imperialist' who expands their businesses helter-skelter into areas they know little about such as a self-declared 'excellent engineer' (i.e., Musk) seeking to become a social media mogul; the strength of being able to build a successful electric vehicle or space rocket business morphs into the weakness of gratuitous over-expansion.[62] Miller argued that the leaders of business organisations can be caught in a downward spiral as a result of a self-created 'leadership trap' which leads them into:

(1) making overconfident decisions based on prior success;
(2) becoming prone to self-satisfaction, over-ambition, and complacency;
(3) taking too much pride in, and taking the credit for, successes that may be attributable to others or sheer luck;
(4) taking too seriously the praise of acolytes and admirers;
(5) believing their own press;
(6) creating an echo chamber for their own views;
(7) becoming deaf to naysayers, devil's advocates, and critics.

In a similar vein, the occupational psychologists Joyce and Robert Hogan have identified a number of what they term 'leadership derailers' (i.e. things that cause successful leaders to 'fall off the tracks' metaphorically) including: 'boldness', its strengths are ambition and self-confidence, whilst its weaknesses are being self-absorbed, cocky, and unwilling to admit mistakes; 'excitableness', its strengths are charisma and excitement for people and projects, whilst its weaknesses are moodiness, sensitivity to criticism, and volatility; and 'mischievousness', its strengths are charm and friendliness, whilst its weaknesses are manipulativeness, impulsivity, and risk-seeking behaviours.[63]

For anyone, and for leaders especially, being positive, confident, and ambitious is a good thing. It helps them to initiate decisive action and motivate themselves and colleagues to achieve remarkable things. But this is only true up to a point; when excess kicks in trouble may start to loom. Any leadership attribute, or virtue for that matter, has a requisite amount for a given set of circumstances. For example, crossing the line which divides the requisite amount of confidence from its excess brings about reckless, irresponsible, naive, and foolish behaviours. When the line is crossed from the requisite amount to the corresponding excess or deficiency, a virtue (for example, courage) becomes a vice (for example, recklessness or cowardice).

The paradox of 'strengths-into-weaknesses' and the idea that a strength if over-exercised can become a weakness, and the related idea of the TMGT effect, is contrary to the prevalent 'abundance model' of leader traits and behaviours, i.e. that more is always better. It is not. Leaders have to be skilled, i.e. practically intelligent, in identifying where to draw the line between the requisite amount of behaviour, such as confidence, ambition, or pride, and its excess. Knowing where the Rubicon lies is the essence of a leader's practical wisdom.

Practical Wisdom

In Aristotle's moral philosophy, practical wisdom (also known as prudence, and in Greek phronēsis, φρόνησις) is the skill of knowing how to exercise one's judgement in particular cases.[64] In the Bible's Book of Proverbs, the same verse that warns us about 'pride going before a fall' also counsels that "The wise in heart shall be called prudent". As such, prudence, or simply practical wisdom, determines the suitable means for achieving a desired end.[65] Practical wisdom doesn't imply a moral act in itself; the morality depends on the ends to which the act is directed. More specifically, practical wisdom is a refined capacity to come to an intuitive grasp of the most important features of a problem or decision and the ability to craft a way forward driven by the pursuit of the common good.[66] It's essentially a tool for navigating volatile, uncertain, complex, and ambiguous situations.

Leaders, by definition, have more discretion than most about what they do, hence their judgements are consequential both for themselves and those whom they lead.[67] Practical wisdom entails the ability to judge what is the requisite, or 'right', level of a particular leader behaviour. But how are leaders to judge what is the right amount given the risk that too much self-confidence or ambition may lead them into hubristic excess and create the conditions for negative unintended consequences to arise?

At the beginning of this chapter the Aristotelian doctrine of the mean was introduced. It has a connotation as some kind of 'magic formula' for deciding what the right amount (the mean) of a particular virtue is. But this is an inaccurate interpretation of the *Ethics*. In an appendix to the *Ethics* Aristotle specifies the excess, mean, and deficiency for selected virtues; for example, the mean for 'fear and confidence' is 'courage', whilst its excess and deficiency are 'rashness' and 'cowardice' respectively. Leadership researchers have developed this idea further by specifying character strengths for leaders and their respective virtuous means, excesses, and deficiencies; for example, on either side of the leadership virtuous mean of 'creativity' lie the deficiency of 'unoriginality' and the excess of 'impracticality'; likewise on either side of 'compassion' are 'unfeeling' (the deficiency) and 'indulgent' (the excess). These efforts at identifying virtue as the middle, and hence the 'best', way can be taken to imply that the mean is a literal midpoint for a given virtue (e.g. the halfway point between 'stinginess' and 'profligacy' is 'generosity').[68]

Thought of in this way the mean becomes a *quantitative* standard that divides too little from too much. However, moral judgement is not a quantitative matter, it is a *qualitative* appraisal or evaluation that must be made according to the circumstances pertaining at the time. Take the example of bravery: there are likely to be circumstances in which hiding from danger (the deficiency) to live and fight another day might be the prudent, but risk-averse, thing to do; on another occasion rushing forward headlong (i.e. the excess) to seize the initiative might be the prudent, but risk-seeking, thing to do. In either case the 'mean' as a literal mid-point makes little sense. That veering towards an extreme (either deficiency or excess) may, on occasion, be the best thing to do is acknowledged by Aristotle in his insistence that the mean is always relative and hence does not always occupy the middle ground. This is encapsulated in the *Ethics*: "[the best way involves doing things] at the right times, on the right grounds, towards the right people for the right motive and in the right way".[69] This isn't a cop-out: for a leader, the judgement as to what constitutes the right amount of ambition, confidence, or pride will vary according to the circumstances pertaining at that time. The ability to do so is a matter of experience, and effective leaders have the requisite levels of self-esteem, self-efficacy, locus of control, and emotional stability (i.e. CSE) to confidently make the right judgement call most of the time.

Practical wisdom is especially pertinent to contemporary leadership because leaders in the 21st century have to deal with unprecedented levels of volatility, uncertainty, complexity, and ambiguity. Practical wisdom can help leaders to deliver long-term benefits and "infuse virtue" (in the sense of the right action at the right time for the right reasons) into decision-making.[70] Following this line of thought, leadership researcher Bernard McKenna and his colleagues argue that wise leaders must:

(1) be rational and deep thinkers with the cognitive complexity to be able to deal with uncertainty and ambiguity;
(2) display creativity and be capable of drawing on non-rational (i.e. intuitive) ways of knowing as appropriate;
(3) have a long-term vision that they are able to articulate and reach people through their words and through their deeds.[71]

If practical wisdom is such a precious asset for organisations and institutions, especially when it comes to balancing excesses and deficiencies and dealing with complexity, is it possible to take steps to develop practical wisdom? The psychologists Yael Schonbrun and Barry Schwartz believe that it is possible for leaders to take steps towards becoming practically wise by:

(1) starting with the data and focusing on what we do know and what we can control;
(2) avoiding black-and-white, either/or thinking because a practically wise person recognises that many situations involve the nuancing that comes with a paradox mindset[72] of both/and thinking;
(3) using protocols and procedures as a rough guide but being prepared to step outside the rules, bend them, or create new rules;
(4) relying on their internal compass for an intuitive sense of direction when there are no maps or the maps that do exist are out of date;
(5) embracing uncertainty and ambiguity and acknowledging that there are rarely perfect choices especially in circumstances that are volatile and complex.[73]

Practical wisdom is a core capability for leaders.[74] It enables them to exercise morally sensitive judgements that cannot be reduced to a specific guidance, set of rules, or formula. Aristotle's golden mean is simply a metaphor for good judgement. Learning if, when, and by how much a leader should incline towards excess is a product of practice and the particulars of the situation. Practical wisdom helps leaders to manage the risks associated with excesses which left unbridled are the harbinger of hubris and its destructive consequences. A significant implication of this is that there are always going to be situations where inclining to excess and running the risk of hubris may be the right, and sometimes the only, thing to do.

Hubris, Frankenstein, and Artificial Intelligence

Mary Shelley's 1818 novel *Frankenstein; or the Modern Prometheus* cautioned against the hubris that turned a medical doctor into a mad scientist whose creation, an eight-foot tall monster fashioned out of non-living matter, ran out of control causing murder and mayhem. From the perspective of the 21st century *Frankenstein* can be taken as an observation and a warning that: firstly, the bright side of hubris is fundamental to the innovativeness and enterprise of the human spirit; secondly, technologies, such as fossil fuels, nuclear power, and antibiotics, can turn out to be double-edged swords and as such have to be handled very carefully; and, finally, that human societies don't always engage with such technologies in ways that are in their long-term best interests but they may not realise this is the case until it's too late, the use of fossil fuels leading to anthropogenic global warming and climate change is an obvious example.[75]

The sociologists Tom Burns and Nora Machado have argued that the complexity and originality of human innovations sometimes exceeds the capacity of those who developed them, or are charged with regulating them, to fully understand and control technologies and their potential impacts. They describe this 'Frankenstein effect' as human communities being confronted by "systems of their own making that are not fully knowable or controllable in advance and, therefore, are likely to generate negative, unintended consequences".[76] One example of this was the new and, as it turned out, far-too-clever ways of managing risks that were implicated in the global financial crisis (see Chapter 1). Burns and Machado draw our attention to the fact that serious, unexpected problems, near misses, and accidents often indicate that human knowledge and capacity to control such human constructions and their consequences are limited. For example, in 2019 Boeing was forced to cut production of and ground its 737 Max aircraft following two fatal accidents involving Indonesia's Lion Air and Ethiopian airlines. The aircraft's novel and highly complex anti-stall software was responsible for the two crashes in which 346 passengers and crew perished. The *Financial Times'* business and society correspondent John Gapper argued that Boeing's failure combined technical shortcoming in the anti-stall sensing system (it relied on a single sensor which tragically failed in both crashes) with the human error (there hadn't been a fatal air accident for nine years in the USA up to 2018) of being "lured into hubris by its commercial success and safety record. It could not believe it had blundered so badly in trying to avoid harm."[77] Gapper puts this down to some of those involved finding it hard to concede to errors because of the faith that they put in their expertise and not being able to recognise if and when they might be wrong.

In my 2019 book *Hubristic Leadership* I referred to this "hubristic delusion of control" as a 'sociotechnical hubris' which invites unintended negative consequences emanating from complex interactions between people, technology, goals, culture, processes, and context. As alluded to earlier, the most pressing example of interactions between people and technology on a global scale are those which are having potentially disastrous effects on the Earth's climate systems as a result of our collective sociotechnical hubris over the past two centuries. As a species we have shown a collective arrogance towards and contempt for nature and its laws and are now reaping the rewards. Risks arise when the complexity and novelty of innovations exceed the capacity of actors to understand them fully and so are not able to anticipate the 'unknown unknowns' which might come about.[78]

AI is the latest technological double-edged sword which may reveal itself to be complicated beyond our understanding and beyond our capacity to make it fully safe. In 2017 Swiss-based international body, the Financial Stability Board (FSB), warned against the risks from unintended consequences of AI in the financial services industry. It identified major risks of using "opaque models" the complexity of which might mean that firms would find it difficult to predict how actions that are directed autonomously by a model might affect financial markets.[79] New and unexpected forms of interconnectedness could lead to the emergence of new players who fall outside of regulations and of systems for which there is a lack of interpretability and auditability.[80] AI is emerging, not just in finance but across the board, as a complex and dynamic system for which there can never be complete knowledge and within which there will be unintended and only partially understood interactions and unanticipated consequences. Burns and Machado describe a situation such as this as "potentially one of danger or even catastrophe".[81]

At the time of writing experts in the field of AI, including the heads of OpenAI and Google DeepMind have warned that AI could lead to no less than the extinction of humanity as a consequence of a number of disaster scenarios including the weaponisation of AI, AI-generated misinformation destabilising society, the concentration of IA power in fewer hands and in the hand of bad actors, and the enfeeblement of humans to the extent that they become dependent on AI.[82] AI may be the latest product of the hubristic assumption that if we can do something we should, and that the products of our endeavours are within our control and without unintended negative consequences. One of the defining attributes of hubris is to overestimate the likelihood of positive outcomes and the underestimate the likelihood of negative outcomes.[83]

Those who fail to learn the lessons of history are condemned to repeat them. The reckless use of coal, oil, and natural gas and the release of carbon dioxide into the Earth's atmosphere since the onset of the Industrial Revolution is the primary cause of anthropogenic global warming. Seen in this way climate change is a product of "human hubris";[84] in this case a collective over-confidence, over-ambition, and over-zealousness in the use of fossil-fuel-based technologies whilst simultaneously displaying ignorance, arrogance, and contempt towards the negative effects of fossil-fuel consumption on the natural environment. Whether the consequences of AI, intended or otherwise, will be positive or negative remains to be seen.

The Bright Side of Hubris

Throughout this book hubris has been depicted as a negative, dark-side type of destructive leadership.[85] Here and there, however, there have been hints and allusions to the idea that having an excess of ambition—as in Musk's grand vision for humans as an interplanetary species—may not be entirely negative and may in fact be necessary for human progress. 'Nothing to excess' is a useful guiding principle much of the time, but it should not be taken as a cardinal rule. This raises the possibility of hubris having a bright side as well as a dark side, where human ambition is a manifestation of its bright side and human arrogance, contempt, and pride is a manifestation of its dark side. These two sides of the same coin are not unrelated and the relationships between them are complex and not fully understood.

The Ancient Greeks saw hubris in negative terms, and in contemporary politics and business management hubristic leadership it is for the most part considered to be part of the dark side of leadership. In fact, hubristic leadership has been classified as one of a number of types of destructive leadership along with bullying, abusive supervision, managerial tyranny, etc.[86] However, in recent years researchers have come to acknowledge that hubris may have a bright as well as a dark side. For example, a bright-side effect of being hubristic might be that a brash, self-confident, high-CSE leader is prepared to face challenges, accept responsibility, and take control of ambiguous situations.[87] The behavioural scientist Hossam Zeitoun and his colleagues point to an upside of entrepreneurial hubris whereby the 'wins' of a small number of successful hubristic entrepreneurs can add value to an economy whilst harming a substantial number of unsuccessful hubristic entrepreneurs. For this reason they refer to hubris as a "double edged sword that is difficult to handle".[88] Likewise Massimo Picone and colleagues noted that businesses may sometimes benefit from managers over-estimating their abilities, otherwise the fear of losses would stop them from taking the risks necessary in formulating and striving towards inspiring visions that will energise and motivate followers. They argue that visionary hubristic leaders, because they are never satisfied, are able to overcome the attitudinal and behavioural boundaries that constrain run-of-the-mill, mediocre, non-hubristic leaders.[89]

The path between excess and deficiency is a tightrope which leaders have to walk and sometimes it is necessary to incline towards excess. One of the world's most successful investors, Warren Buffett, Chairman and CEO of Berkshire Hathaway, whose estimated net worth is $104 billion, said that good results come from a properly calibrated balance of hubris and humility, i.e. having, in Buffet's own words, "hubris enough to think you can have insights that are superior to the collective wisdom of the market, [and] humility enough to know the limits of your abilities and

being willing to change course when errors are recognized".[90] Douglas
Cairns, Professor of Classics at the University of Edinburgh, argues that the
practical challenge for business leaders is how to minimise the dark-side,
negative effects of hubristic leadership without foregoing the bright-side
outcomes of confidence, ambition, and the will to push the boundaries of
what is possible.[91] Prudence, or practical wisdom (see above), is one way in
which the dark and bright sides of the excesses of 'thinking big'[92] might be
resolved and reconciled.

Managing Exposure to Excesses

The hubris risk factor of excess is in a different category to the other risk
factors discussed in the preceding chapters. The intoxication of power, self-
delusion, irrational exuberance, etc. is to be avoided. Excess, on the other
hand, can be a desirable leader behaviour in certain circumstances, indeed
it may even be essential for humanity to progress. Central to this argument
is the novel idea that hubris can have a bright side to complement its dark
side. A corollary of this is that there may be occasions on which it is necessary not to avoid exposure to excess but to somehow encourage it whilst at
the same time manage its potential down-sides effectively.

Building on the bright-side argument, the Italian sociologist Carlo
Bordoni offers the general observation that the history of humanity is "the
story of boundless hubris".[93] Since the earliest times the persistent desire to
improve and to progress has driven humankind forward. Through incessant experimenting and challenging, humanity has been able to "rise up
on the world and to break all boundaries".[94] Bordoni's view of hubris as the
engine of history[95] involves human beings being oblivious to their limitations and overstepping the boundaries within which they appear to have
been constrained and controlled by nature, as in their inventions which
range from the hand axe to AI. Seen in this way hubris is necessary for
social advancement and technological change. According to Bordoni, those
groups who avail themselves of the "spirit of hubris" will be those who
will "progress and prevail"[96] but doing so necessarily involves both risk
and a disobedience and defiance which is the "salt of life" and constitutes
a form of arrogance.[97] But as the pace of change accelerates so the potential
for hubris is amplified with worries about Frankenstein effects, not least

in AI with fears that we might be victims of our own hubris by creating a monster that will gain autonomy and return to haunt us.[98]

Visionary leaders, by definition, 'think big'. As hubris researcher Graham Robinson has argued, humanity has always needed leaders who have the courage to take significant risks but are also capable of living with the possibility and the consequences of being wrong, and arguably needs them now more than ever. Robinson noted that confidence, ambition, and vision are much sought after when leaders are chosen to lead in the first place, but that one of the great ironies of hubris is that bold risk-takers who were once regarded as heroes are often seen in retrospect to have suffered from hubris "but only in the wake of events that have laid them low".[99] Terry Leahy, the former CEO of the UK's largest supermarket chain Tesco, in noting repentantly in his business autobiography that "hubris is a common fault", remarked that:

> You cannot run a business without making mistakes—and I certainly made my fair share ... [but] business is all about taking risks. Decisions that involve no risks are not decisions that will enable your business to grow. The trick is to learn from mistakes so that they don't prove fatal.[100]

To deliver on a bold and worthwhile vision perhaps leaders do need to have the strength of self-conviction that makes them believe that they're the one, they're exceptional, and it's they who have the capabilities—and the right—to overstep the mark in order to sow the seeds of disruption and change. Leaders such as Musk seek to renew and transform organisations, industries, institutions, and entire societies. If humanity is courting the existential threat of self-destruction as a result of its own hubristic actions—not least in the area of climate change[101]—as Musk believes, then perhaps his vision of colonising Mars is a wise and prudent, rather than an arrogant and foolhardy ambition. Without the visionary hubrist's conviction of what might be achievable humanity itself may never be able to break free of nature's and its own constraints and step forward with confidence into a radically uncertain future. To break free of constraints perhaps we need leaders who have the courage of their self-convictions that is rooted in a self-evaluation which is unequivocally positive and optimistic, and sometimes overly so. Musk's optimism boils down to his 'long-termism';[102] he's reported to have said that "I'd rather be optimistic and wrong than pessimistic and right". Perhaps his long-termism and optimism is the essence of visionary hubris. Whether Musk will be proved wrong and end up being consigned to the hubristic hall of infamy or whether he will be proved right and hailed as a 'saviour of mankind'[103] can only be appraised after the fact. One of the intrinsic problems in making sense of hubris is the inescapable fact that is very much a 'rear-view mirror' phenomenon which makes it an occupational hazard not only for leaders themselves but also for researchers who write about it.

Excess: Signs to Look Out For

(1) Leader develops an excess of self-esteem, self-efficacy, and locus of control;
(2) Leader's strengths are practised to the extreme and become weaknesses;
(3) Leader lacks practical wisdom to do the right thing, at the right time, for the right reasons.

Notes

1 Morgan, K. A. (2009). Philosophy at Delphi: Socrates, sages, and the circulation of wisdom. In Athanassaki, L., Martin, R. P., & Miller, J.F. (eds.). *Apolline Politics and Poetics*. Athens: Hellenic Ministry of Culture, pp.549–568.
2 Frede, D., & Lee, M-K. (2023). Plato's ethics: An overview. *Stanford Encyclopaedia of Philosophy*. Available at: https://plato.stanford.edu/entries/plato-ethics/
3 Hamilton, K. (1963). The false glitter of the golden mean. *The Dalhousie Review*, 437–444.
4 Aristotle. (2004). *The Nicomachean Ethics* 1097b8–11. London: Penguin.
5 Aristotle. (2004). *The Nicomachean Ethics* liii. London: Penguin, p.33.
6 Aristotle. (2004). *The Nicomachean Ethics* 1104a11–12. London: Penguin.
7 Barnes, J. (2004). *Introduction to the Nicomachean Ethics*. London: Penguin.
8 Aristotle. (2004). *The Nicomachean Ethics* 1104a25–26. London: Penguin.
9 Aristotle. (2004). *The Nicomachean Ethics* 1104a20–23. London: Penguin.

10 Furnham, A. (2014). *The psychology of leadership derailment*. Royal Society of Medicine, November 2014. Available at: https://www.youtube.com/watch?v=S0BNIToUFAI

11 Pierce, J. R., & Aguinis, H. (2013). The too-much-of-a-good-thing effect in management. *Journal of Management, 39*(2), 313–338.

12 Chrisman, J. J., McMullan, E., & Hall, J. (2005). The influence of guided preparation on the long-term performance of new ventures. *Journal of Business Venturing, 20*(6), 769–791.

13 Von Bergen, C. W., Campbell, K., & Leird, R. (2016). Too much of a good thing in employment counselling. *Journal of Organizational Culture, Communications and Conflict, 20*(1), 143–152.

14 Bordoni, C. (2019). *Hubris and progress*. Abingdon: Routledge, p.9.

15 Laker, B., Cobb, D., & Trehan, R. (2021). *Too proud to lead*. London: Bloomsbury, p.86.

16 Laker, B., Cobb, D., & Trehan, R. (2021). *Too proud to lead*. London: Bloomsbury.

17 Beltran, L. (2023). Elon Musk has destroyed more than half of Twitter's value in a little over 2 months, investor filing suggests. *Fortune*, January 3. Available at: https://fortune.com/2023/01/03/how-much-is-twitter-worth-elon-musk-fidelity-layoffs-cost-cutting-bankruptcy

18 Yang, M. (2022). Elon Musk makes splashy visit to Twitter headquarters carrying sink. *The Guardian*, October 26. Available at: https://www.the-guardian.com/technology/2022/oct/26/elon-musk-twitter-visit-sink

19 *The Sydney Morning Herald*. (2022). Musk's Twitter play unconventional at best, foolhardy at worst. *The Sydney Morning Herald* (Opinion), April 5. Available at: https://www.smh.com.au/business/companies/musk-s-twit-ter-play-unconventional-at-best-foolhardy-at-worst-20220405-p5abo1.html; Pazzanese, C. (2022). Is there method to Musk's madness on Twitter? *The Harvard Gazette*, November 22. Available at: https://news.harvard.edu/gazette/story/2022/11/is-there-method-to-musks-madness-on-twitter

20 Cunningham, L. A. (2022). Opinion: Elon Musk is hitting 'peak hubris' with his high-risk Twitter and bitcoin plays. Tesla shareholders should be concerned. *Market Watch*, July 27. Available at: https://www.marketwatch.com/story/elon-musk-is-hitting-peak-hubris-with-his-high-risk-twitter-and-bitcoin-plays-tesla-shareholders-should-be-concerned-11658908335

21 Musk, E. (2022). Twitter feed, May 29. Available at: https://twitter.com/elonmusk/status/1530694232251432961?lang=en

22 *Daily Mail* City and Finance Reporter. (2023). 'Chief Twit' knocks £20bn off Twitter: How the social media giant has lost half its value since Elon Musk's takeover. *This is Money*, March 27. Available at: https://www.thisismoney.

co.uk/money/markets/article-11908485/Twitter-loses-half-value-Musk-takeover.html

23 Bove, C. (2022). One chart shows why Elon Musk may be so desperate to back out of his deal to buy Twitter. *Fortune*, July 12. Available at: https://fortune.com/2022/07/12/elon-musk-twitter-deal-stock-price

24 Beltran, L. (2023). Elon Musk has destroyed more than half of Twitter's value in a little over 2 months, investor filing suggests. *Fortune*, January 3. Available at: https://fortune.com/2023/01/03/how-much-is-twitter-worth-elon-musk-fidelity-layoffs-cost-cutting-bankruptcy

25 *Forbes*. (2023). Elon Musk. *Forbes Profile*, May 190. Available at: https://www.forbes.com/profile/elon-musk/?sh=1abf8eb67999

26 Evans, D. (2021). Elon Musk is a worthy person of the year. *Forbes*, December 16. Available at: https://www.forbes.com/sites/daveevans/2021/12/16/elon-musk-is-a-worthy-person-of-the-year/?sh=6af46a427914

27 Vance, A. (2015). *Elon Musk: How the billionaire CEO of SpaceX and Tesla is shaping our future*. London: Virgin Books, p.15.

28 Tesla. (2023). *Elon Musk*. Available at: https://www.tesla.com/en_gb/elon-musk

29 Vance, A. (2015). *Elon Musk: How the billionaire CEO of SpaceX and Tesla is shaping our future*. London: Virgin Books, p.17.

30 Anderson, C. (2012). Elon Musk's mission to Mars. *Wired*, October 21. Available at: https://www.wired.com/2012/10/ff-elon-musk-qa

31 Bilton, N. (2020). Elon Musk's totally awful, batshit crazy, most excellent year. *Vanity Fair*, December. Available at: https://archive.vanityfair.com/article/2020/12/elon-musks-totally-awful-batshit-crazy-completely-bonkers-most-excellent-year

32 Tett, G. (2023). Lunch with FT: Walter Isaacson. *The Financial Times*, September 16.

33 Dove-Jay, A. (2015). Elon Musk biography portrays a brutal character driven by lofty dreams. *The Conversation*, May 20. Available at: https://theconversation.com/elon-musk-biography-portrays-a-brutal-character-driven-by-lofty-dreams-41995

34 Space X. (no date). Mars & beyond: The road to making humanity multiplanetary. Available at: https://www.spacex.com/human-spaceflight/mars

35 Bilton, N. (2020). Elon Musk's totally awful, batshit crazy, most excellent year. *Vanity Fair*, December. Available at: https://archive.vanityfair.com/article/2020/12/elon-musks-totally-awful-batshit-crazy-completely-bonkers-most-excellent-year

36 YouTube. (no date). Elon Musk "If I die on Mars, please not on impact". Available at: https://www.youtube.com/watch?v=wTKuTilFjys

37 Bharmal, Z. (2018). The case against Mars colonisation. *The Guardian*, August 28. Available at: https://www.theguardian.com/science/blog/2018/aug/28/the-case-against-mars-colonisation

38 Space X. (no date). Mars & beyond: The road to making humanity multi-planetary. Available at: https://www.spacex.com/human-spaceflight/mars

39 Vance, A. (2015). *Elon Musk: How the billionaire CEO of SpaceX and Tesla is shaping our future*. London: Virgin Books, p.5

40 Vance, A. (2015). *Elon Musk: How the billionaire CEO of SpaceX and Tesla is shaping our future*. London: Virgin Books, p.5.

41 https://www.reuters.com/business/autos-transportation/tesla-market-cap-eclipses-that-top-5-rival-carmakers-combined-2021-10-26

42 Hull, D. (2021). Elon Musk is his own worst enemy. *Fortune*, November 3. Available at: https://www.bloomberg.com/news/newsletters/2021-11-03/elon-musk-is-his-own-worst-enemy

43 Laker, B., Cobb, D., & Trehan, R.(2021). *Too proud to lead*. London: Bloomsbury, p.87.

44 Laker, B., Cobb, D., & Trehan, R. (2021). *Too proud to lead*. London: Bloomsbury, p.87.

45 Laker, B., Cobb, D., & Trehan, R. (2021). *Too proud to lead*. London: Bloomsbury, p.91.

46 Bilton, N. (2020). Elon Musk's totally awful, batshit crazy, most excellent year. *Vanity Fair*, December. Available at: https://archive.vanityfair.com/article/2020/12/elon-musks-totally-awful-batshit-crazy-completely-bonkers-most-excellent-year

47 Cited in Hiller, N. J., & Hambrick, D. C. (2005). Conceptualizing executive hubris: The role of (hyper-)core self-evaluations in strategic decision-making. *Strategic Management Journal*, 26(4), 297–319, p.297.

48 Bono, J. E., & Judge, T. A. (2003). Core self-evaluations: A review of the trait and its role in job satisfaction and job performance. *European Journal of Personality*, 17(1 Supplement), S5–S18, p.S6.

49 The inverse of emotional stability is emotional anxiety and it's related to neuroticism (i.e. an enduring tendency to experience negative emotional states). Neuroticism is one of the 'Big Five' personality traits (the others are agreeableness, conscientiousness, extraversion, and openness to experience). It's defined as a tendency towards anxiety, depression, self-doubt, and other negative feelings.

50 Judge, T. A. (2009). Core self-evaluations and work success. *Current Directions in Psychological Science*, 18(1), 58–62.

51 Resick, C. J., Whitman, D. S., Weingarden, S. M., & Hiller, N. J. (2009). The bright-side and the dark-side of CEO personality: Examining core

self-evaluations, narcissism, transformational leadership, and strategic influence. *Journal of Applied Psychology*, 94(6), 1365–1381.

52 Pierce, J. R., & Aguinis, H. (2013). The too-much-of-a-good-thing effect in management. *Journal of Management*, 39(2), 313–338.

53 Donald J. Trump, @realDonaldTrump, January 6, 2018.

54 Hiller, N. J., & Hambrick, D. C. (2005). Conceptualizing executive hubris: The role of (hyper-)core self-evaluations in strategic decision-making. *Strategic Management Journal*, 26(4), 297–319, p.308.

55 Owen, D., & Davidson, J. (2009). Hubris syndrome: An acquired personality disorder? A study of US presidents and UK prime ministers over the last 100 years. *Brain*, 132(5), 1396–1406.

56 Hiller, N. J., & Hambrick, D. C. (2005). Conceptualizing executive hubris: The Role of (hyper-)core self-evaluations in strategic decision-making. *Strategic Management Journal*, 26(4), 297–319, p.298.

57 Hiller, N. J., & Hambrick, D. C. (2005). Conceptualizing executive hubris: The Role of (hyper-)core self-evaluations in strategic decision-making. *Strategic Management Journal*, 26(4), 297–319.

58 Urmson, J. O. (1990). *Aristotle on excellence of character*. New Blackfriars, 71: 33–37, p.33.

59 Meyer, M., & Rego, A. (2020). Measuring practical wisdom: Exploring the value of Aristotle's phronesis for business and leadership. . In Schwartz, B., Bernacchio, C., González-Cantón, C., & Robson, A. (eds.). *Handbook of practical wisdom in business and management*. Dordrecht: Springer International Publishing.

60 Pierce, J. R., & Aguinis, H. (2013). The too-much-of-a-good-thing effect in management. *Journal of Management*, 39(2), 313–338.

61 Miller, D. (1990). *The Icarus Paradox: How excellent organizations can bring about their own downfall*. New York: Harper Business, p.3.

62 Miller, D. (1990). *The Icarus Paradox: How excellent organizations can bring about their own downfall*. New York: Harper Business.

63 Hogan, R., & Hogan, J. (2001). Assessing leadership: A view from the dark side. *International Journal of Selection and Assessment*, 9(1–2), 40–51.

64 MacIntyre, A. (1985). *After Virtue*. London: Duckworth, p.154.

65 Ames, M. C. F. D. C., Serafim, M. C., & Zappellini, M. B. (2020). Phronesis in administration and organizations: A literature review and future research agenda. *Business Ethics: A European Review*, 29, 65–83.

66 Shotter, J., & Tsoukas, H. (2014). In search of phronesis: Leadership and the art of judgment. *Academy of Management Learning & Education*, 13(2), 224–243, p.225.

67 Shotter, J., & Tsoukas, H. (2014). Performing phronesis: On the way to engaged judgment. *Management Learning*, 45(4), 377–396.

68 Crossan, M., Mazutis, D., Seijts, G., & Gandz, J. (2013). Developing leadership character in business programs. *Academy of Management Learning & Education*, 12(2), 285–305.

69 Aristotle. (2004). *The Nicomachean Ethics* 1104a20–23. London: Penguin.

70 McKenna, B., Rooney, D., & Boal, K. B. (2009). Wisdom principles as a meta-theoretical basis for evaluating leadership. *The Leadership Quarterly*, 20(2), 177–190.

71 McKenna, B., Rooney, D., & Boal, K. B. (2009). Wisdom principles as a meta-theoretical basis for evaluating leadership. *The Leadership Quarterly*, 20(2), 177–190.

72 Heracleous, L., & Robson, D. (2020). Why the 'paradox mindset' is the key to success. *BBC Worklife*, November 12. Available at: https://www.bbc.com/worklife/article/20201109-why-the-paradox-mindset-is-the-key-to-success

73 Schonbrun, Y., & Schwartz, B. (2020). How practical wisdom helps us cope with radical uncertainty. *Behavioural Scientist*, August 31. Available at: https://behavioralscientist.org/how-practical-wisdom-helps-us-cope-with-radical-uncertainty

74 Küpers, W. (2016). *A handbook of practical wisdom: Leadership, organization and integral business practice*. Abingdon: Routledge.

75 Hård, M., & Jamison, A. (2013). *Hubris and hybrids: A cultural history of technology and science*. Abingdon: Routledge.

76 Burns, T. R., & Machado, N. (2010). Technology, complexity, and risk: A social systems perspective on the discourses and regulation of the hazards of socio-technical systems. *Sociologia, Problemas e Práticas*, 62, 97–131, p.97.

77 Gapper, J. (2019). Boeing's hubris brought failure to the 737 Max. *The Financial Times*, April 10. Available online at: https://www.ft.com/content/2de01914-5ac5-11e9-9dde-7aedca0a081a

78 Sadler-Smith, E. (2019). *Hubristic leadership*. London: SAGE, p.107.

79 Financial Stability Board. (2017). Artificial intelligence and machine learning in financial services. Available online at: https://www.fsb.org/2017/11/artificial-intelligence-and-machine-learning-in-financial-service/

80 Financial Stability Board. (2017). Artificial intelligence and machine learning in financial services. Basel: FSB. Available at: https://www.fsb.org/2017/11/artificial-intelligence-and-machine-learning-in-financial-service

81 Burns, T. R., & Machado, N. (2010). Technology, complexity, and risk: A social systems perspective on the discourses and regulation of the hazards of socio-technical systems. *Sociologia, Problemas e Práticas*, 62, 97–131, p.112.

82 Vallance, C. (2023). Artificial intelligence could lead to extinction, experts warn. *BBC News*, May 31. Available at: https://www.bbc.co.uk/news/uk-65746524

83 Sadler-Smith, E. (2019). *Hubristic leadership*. London: SAGE.

84 Sadler-Smith, E., & Akstinaite, V. (2022). Human hubris, anthropogenic climate change, and an environmental ethic of humility. *Organization & Environment*, 35(3), 446–467.

85 Sadler-Smith, E. (2019). *Hubristic leadership*. London: SAGE.

86 Sadler-Smith, E. (2019). *Hubristic leadership*. London: SAGE.

87 Zeitoun, H., Nordberg, D., & Homberg, F. (2019). The dark and bright sides of hubris: Conceptual implications for leadership and governance research. *Leadership*, 15(6), 647–672.

88 Zeitoun, H., Nordberg, D., & Homberg, F. (2019). The dark and bright sides of hubris: Conceptual implications for leadership and governance research. *Leadership*, 15(6), 647–672, p.662.

89 Picone, P. M., Pisano, V., & Dagnino, G. B. (2021). The bright and dark sides of CEO hubris: Assessing cultural distance in international business. *European Management Review*, 18(3), 343–362.

90 Miller, J. C. (2016). *Ground rules: Words of wisdom from the partnership letters of the world's greatest investor*. New York: Harper Collins, p.170.

91 Cairns, D., Bouras, N., & Sadler-Smith, E. (eds.). (2024). *Hubris: Ancient and modern*. Cambridge: Cambridge University Press.

92 Cairns, D. L. (1996). Hybris, dishonour, and thinking big. *The Journal of Hellenic Studies*, 116, 1–32.

93 Bordoni, C. (2019). *Hubris and progress*. Abingdon: Routledge, p.3.

94 Bordoni, C. (2019). *Hubris and progress*. Abingdon: Routledge, p.8.

95 Bordoni, C. (2019). *Hubris and progress*. Abingdon: Routledge.

96 Bordoni, C. (2019). *Hubris and progress*. Abingdon: Routledge, p.9.

97 Bordoni, C. (2019). *Hubris and progress*. Abingdon: Routledge, p.24.

98 Szollosy, M. (2017). Freud, Frankenstein and our fear of robots: Projection in our cultural perception of technology. *AI & Society*, 32, 433–439.

99 Robinson, G. (2016). Making sense of hubris. In Garrard, P., & Robinson, G. (eds.) *The intoxication of power: Interdisciplinary insights*. Basingstoke: Palgrave Macmillan, 1–16, p.14.

100 Leahy, T. (2012). *Management in 10 words*. London: Random House, p.3.

101 Sadler-Smith, E., & Akstinaite, V. (2022). Human hubris, anthropogenic climate change, and an environmental ethic of humility. *Organization & Environment*, 35(3), 446–467.

102 Main, K. (2022). Elon Musk just shared the guiding force behind his pursuits. *Inc.*, August 9. Available at: https://www.inc.com/kelly-main/elon-musk-philosophy-optimism-longtermism.html

103 Jenkins, H. W. (2015). The saviour Elon Musk. *Wall Street Journal*, May 29. Available at: https://www.wsj.com/articles/the-savior-elon-musk-1432938547

10

AN OUNCE OF PREVENTION

An ounce of prevention is worth a pound of cure.

—Benjamin Franklin

One of the founding figures of the USA, Benjamin Franklin, remarked in 1736 to the residents of Philadelphia in connection with protection from the risk of fires: "an ounce of prevention is worth a pound of cure". Like fire, hubris can be a highly destructive force and therefore Franklin's principle applies: by identifying the early warning signs of hubris and putting effective restraining mechanisms in place, businesses and other institutions can prevent exposure to the hubris hazard and hence no cure is required. By managing the risks it may be possible to keep the hubris "genie" in the bottle[1] and prevent its destructive consequences from coming to pass. But before the risks can be managed and the hazard contained the risks themselves need to be identified. In the words of David Owen, author of *The Hubris Syndrome*, this entails "being alert to the fact that people in positions

DOI: 10.4324/9781003128427-10

of power may not be wilfully reckless, but in the grip of a syndrome that is creating a personality change and affecting their decision-making";[2] it goes without saying as is the case with progressive illnesses, the earlier the diagnosis the better.

A Canary in the Coalmine

In Owen and Davidson's 14 clinical features of hubris syndrome, Symptom 6 ("A tendency to speak in the third person or use the royal 'we'") is a warning sign that a leader may be about to turn hubristic.[3] One of the most famous instances of this was Margaret Thatcher's remark to the waiting press outside 10 Downing Street that "*we* have become a grandmother" on the occasion of the birth of her first grandchild in August 1989. The change in leader's choice of words associated with the development of hubris involves more frequent use of 'we/us/our' or the speaker's own name rather than the first-person pronoun ('I') which might be expected.[4] Thatcher's hubris built up gradually during her prime ministership (she took office in 1979) and reached its crescendo in 1990. It is reported that she 'let rip' at virtually anyone who got in her way, including experienced and respected cabinet colleagues and European political leaders who had the temerity to disagree with her. In November 1990, following a period of fractious infighting, she was removed from office by her own party.[5]

The words that leaders use can be a 'canary in the coalmine' (i.e. an early warning sign) for the emergence of hubris. The identification of these 'linguistic markers' is a promising new line of investigation in that they provide hubris researchers with a source of 'honest signals' which are difficult to manipulate or conceal.[6] In one of the pioneering studies of this type, the neurologist and neuroscientist Peter Garrard and his colleagues analysed the words used by three UK prime ministers, Margaret Thatcher and Tony Blair (who were classified as hubristic) and John Major (classified as non-hubristic) using speech samples from the rough-and-tumble of Prime Minister's Questions (PMQs) in the UK House of Commons.[7] The ratio of 'we' to 'I' was higher for Blair and Thatcher than for Major, and especially so in the case of Blair. This and other research suggests the 'we-to-I' ratio could be a linguistic marker of hubris. A greater use of 'we' compared to 'I' indicates hubristic tendencies. This might sound counterintuitive, more 'we' compared to 'I' could be seen as more other-centric and inclusive. However, this is because a preponderance of 'we' in a leader's speech relative to 'I' is thought to indicate a presumption of power and authority over others and assumes their compliance.[8]

Another example of hubris-speak on the part of a leader were the words used by Donald Trump in the crucial early stages of the Covid-19 pandemic. My colleague Vita Akstinaite and I analysed the speeches made by Trump (a hubristic leader) with those of Prime Minister of New Zealand, Jacinda Ardern (a non-hubristic leader), during the first half of 2020 when the need to contain the disease was paramount. We found that Ardern and Trump scored equally highly on the linguistic category of 'clout', which is an indicator of the speaker's level of power and authority. However, Trump and Ardern differed significantly in terms of three other linguistic categories: Trump was higher on emotional tone but lower on analytical language and authenticity, whereas Ardern was lower on emotional tone but higher on analytical speech and authenticity, see Figure 10.1. Given that the USA under Trump's leadership had one of the worst Covid-19 death rates when we did the research, we concluded that a leader's speech patterns may indicate dysfunctional cognitive and affective (i.e. thinking and feeling) processing and personality style which could have had deleterious effects on

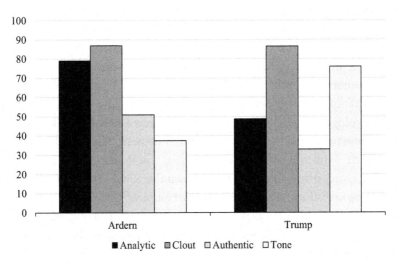

Figure 10.1 Results of Linguistic Analysis of Ardern's and Trump's Early Covid-19 Speeches

decision-making in the early stages of the pandemic. The USA fared badly compared to New Zealand in their respective approaches to the disease and outcomes. The linguistic markers of high emotional tone, low authenticity, and low analytical speech could serve as early warning signs of ineffectual leader behaviours in times of crisis.[9]

The techniques used in this research rely on computer-based methods known as 'computerised text analysis' (CTA) to study the micro-features of leaders' speech, for example counting words in particular grammatical and psychological categories such as how may personal pronouns a leader uses, how many emotion-related or analytical-type words they use, etc. Vita Akstinaite has also innovated the use of machine learning and AI to automatically monitor the words that leaders use; this approach could be used to flag up when danger signals start to present themselves in a leader's utterances.[10] A language-based 'hubrisometer', if ever such a thing were to be developed, could be used to combat hubris through intervention (for example, providing hard evidence as a basis for alerting leaders and those around them to the emergence of a hubris risk) and prevention (for example, using linguistic markers as a screening mechanism in the selection of leaders rather than trying to cure the problem once a hubrist has been appointed). Linguistic analysis is a potent tool in the check-and-balance armoury because leaders' lexical choices (i.e. the words they use) are largely automatic and hard to control, hence they can be subtly revealing of underlying aspects of leaders' personalities which influence their motivations, intentions, and behaviours. This is why they've been referred to as honest signals.

CEO Passports, Selection Processes, and MOTs

In his book *Pariahs: Hubris, Reputation and Organizational Crises* (2016), Matt Nixon makes the case for the innovative idea of a 'leadership passport'. This would be an enhanced version of a traditional CV stored via a trusted third party and made available as and when required to a current or potential employer. In essence Nixon's leadership passport idea is about having:

consistent, objective evidence about an individual, over time, data that under GDPR [general data protection regulation] should be controlled by them, but available more widely. In the hubris context it

> would be highly off-putting to the most hubristic individuals because
> it would be hard to avoid the patterns in that data becoming obvious.[11]

Psychological assessments may also have a role to play in assessment; for example, the Hogan Development Survey (HDS) measures 11 behavioural dimensions that might cause a leader to fail (these are called 'leadership derailers'). The HDS could be used to assess hubris because it taps into a number of hubris-relevant CEO attributes including aloofness, sensitivity to criticism, attention seeking, testing the limits, being overly self-confident, arrogance, inflated feelings of self-worth, etc.[12]

As was noted in the chapter on narcissistic tendencies (Chapter 7), the ultimate way to avoid exposing a business to the risks associated with a hubristic leader is to not appoint one in the first place. This is easier said than done given that dark-side leader traits (such as narcissism and hubris) can often be advantageous to narcissistic and potentially hubristic candidates in the selection process. Such individuals often leave damaged systems and relationships in their wake when they fail to deliver and move on or get fired.[13] Anthony Fitzsimmons, co-author of *Reputational Risk* (2017) which is concerned with how leaders can manage the risks that could ruin their business and their own careers and reputations, points out that "*competencies* determine what leaders can do, whereas *character* determines what they will do".[14] A corollary of this, he points out, is that a leader who balances "confidence with humility, drive with patience, candour with compassion" is likely to be a less risky option and a better performer in the long run than one with an excess of self-confidence allied to aggression and bluntness. This idea aligns with Warren Buffet's advice to balance bright-side hubris with humility (see Chapter 9). Fitzsimmons also points out that outsourcing the recruitment of a chief executive to head-hunters may signify a fundamental weakness at board level. He recommends having "top-class" human resources specialists on board who have a deep understanding of people in executive nomination and remuneration committees. Their specialist knowledge of human personality and behaviour could help committees to get past issues such as heuristics and biases, self-serving behaviours, halo effects, the blinding effects of charm and charisma, the dangers of narcissism, etc., and in so doing help to reduce the risks of unintended negative consequences further down the line as the result of a bad appointment.[15]

When he was CEO of the UK insurance group Equitable Life Chris Wiscarson put in place systems and processes to keep track of his own behaviour, on the basis that asking the right questions could help to identify if he might be inadvertently at risk of being derailed by hubris. Wiscarson has argued for a CEO version of the UK's 'MOT test'. In the 1960s the UK government introduced a mandatory road worthiness test for cars, the so-called 'MOT' (short for Ministry of Transport, the body that administered the test originally). The list of items on the annual test for vehicles over three years old has expanded since 1960; it includes such things as the condition of the tyres, the exhaust system, car body and chassis, seat belts, etc. The MOT, by keeping unworthy and potentially dangerous vehicles off the road, improved road safety immeasurably. Other countries, but by no means all, have similar systems in place; for example, South Korea has the KOTSA (Korean Transport Safety Authority), New Zealand has a WOF (Warrant of Fitness), and in Germany the test is administered by the TÜV (Technischer Überwachungsverein or Technical Inspection Association). As far as the proposed CEO MOT is concerned, Wiscarson suggested that:

> Carried out annually by the senior independent director, an MOT for chief executives could comprise a set of penetrating questions to the CEO, private interviews with the executive team, and visits to key parts of the business without executives present. If a CEO is not comfortable with this, does that not signal hubris?[16]

The Financial Times' Lucy Kellaway's view is that, unlike a car that fails its MOT and has the opportunity for repair and retest, any CEO who fails the hubris MOT test "should not be allowed a second chance, since there is no easy way of fixing a condition that has got so advanced".[17] Some suggestions for questions to be included in a CEO hubris MOT based on Wiscarson's and Kellaway's ideas are shown in Table 10.1.

A similar idea was mooted by Martin Dickson, writing in the Financial Times in 2007 just as the world was about to enter the global financial crisis; he argued the case for a 'hubris index' which could include analyses of CEOs' language (for example, given what we know from the CTA research this might include higher use of 'we' relative to 'I', and the use of words such as 'certain', 'dominant', 'winning', 'unchallenged', etc., see above) as well as gauging how the company acts towards its suppliers, competitors,

Table 10.1 Some Suggestions for Questions to be Included in a CEO MOT Based on Kellaway's and Wiscarson's Proposals

Items to be tested	Pass	Fail	Defects/Comments
(1) Is the CEO arrogant and has their arrogance increased in the past year?			
(2) Does the CEO listen or speak to customers as much as they used to?			
(3) Has the CEO changed their mind willingly on anything in the past year?			
(4) Has the CEO become more reckless and impulsive in the past year?			
(5) How receptive is the CEO to comment and constructive criticism?			
(6) Is the CEO's remuneration commensurate with their achievements?			
(7) Is the CEO's remuneration out-of-kilter with their peers?			
(8) Does the CEO argue for a bonus even when results have gone the wrong way?			
(9) Does the CEO portray company results more favourably than they really are?			
(10) Has the CEO done anything that's even slightly 'dodgy'?			

customers, and investors.[18] Consolidating this idea, the psychologist Adrian Furnham, argued that there are three fundamental questions than ought to be asked ask about a leader so as to discern whether they're likely to fail the MOT: first, "Can they do relationships?"; second "Are they self-aware?"; and third, "Can they deal with change?".[19]

Hubris Health Check

Wiscarson's idea for a CEO MOT is taken a step further in this book with the concept of the 'Hubris Health Check'. The Hubris Health Check (see Table 10.1) is a diagnostic tool for the identification of the early warning signs of hubristic leadership which could pose a risk of negative consequences for the individual and their organisation. Unlike the CEO MOT which focuses mainly on CEOs, the Hubris Health Check also includes relevant organisational and contextual factors such as complicit followers, conducive context, lack of checks and balances, etc. Each of the chapters in this book dealt with a specific hubris risk factor (for example, intoxication with power). At the end of each chapter some of the early warning signs for that chapter's risk factor were listed; for example, for the intoxication of power (Chapter 2) the early warning signs are: increased reliance on stereotyping; not taking others' views into account; decrease in emotional reciprocity; reduction in compassion and empathy; reduction in behavioural inhibition; increase in violations of social norms; increase in self-serving behaviours; and increase in lavish spending. The co-occurrence of several of the early warning signs for a given hubris risk factor suggest that exposure to the hubris hazard is more likely which gives an increased chance of unintended negative consequences arising should the leader be derailed by their hubris. Taken together all of the early warning signs for each risk factor can be consolidated into the Hubris Health Check, see Table 10.2.

Table 10.2 The Hubris Health Check

Risk factor	Signs to look out for	Yes/No
1 Intoxication of power	1.1 Increased reliance on stereotyping by leader	
	1.2 Leader stops taking others' views into account	
	1.3 Decrease in leader's emotional reciprocity	
	1.4 Reduction in leader's compassion and empathy	
	1.5 Reduction in leader's behavioural inhibition	
	1.6 Increase in leader's violations of social norms	
	1.7 Increase in leader's self-serving behaviours	
	1.8 More lavish spending by leader	
2 Complicit followers	2.1 Tacit support for the leader by conformers who are prepared to simply stand by	
	2.2 Explicit support for the leader by colluders who are prepared to connive actively	
	2.3 Leader has become a media celebrity	
	2.4 Leader is given free rein by an ineffective board or cabinet	
3 Conducive context	3.1 'Fake it till you make it' attitude is acceptable	
	3.2 Grandeur of leader's vision overrules ethical concerns	
	3.3 Leading a culture that's conducive to hype, over-claiming and 'greed is good' mentality	

(Continued)

Table 10.2 (Continued)

Risk factor	Signs to look out for	Yes/No
4 Unbridled intuition	4.1 Leader lacks curiosity	
	4.2 Leader is unwilling or unable to appreciate different sides to a problem	
	4.3 Leader's intuition is being used in situations to which it's not suited	
	4.4 Leader's intuition is beginning to crowd out rationality	
	4.5 Increased leader reliance on hard-to-justify gut feelings	
	4.6 Leader lacks requisite experience or expertise to take intuitive decisions	
5 Irrational exuberance	5.1 A long run of uninterrupted successes by the leader	
	5.2 Leader over-confidence and over-ambition	
	5.3 Leader's increased bullishness, recklessness, and risk-seeking behaviours	
	5.4 Preponderance of high testosterone individuals in senior leadership positions	
6 Self-deception	6.1 Leader is unskilled and unaware of how unskilled they are	
	6.2 Leader refuses to seek help or advice	
	6.3 Leader is steadfast and stubborn in the light of obvious shortcomings in performance	
	6.4 Leader welcomes favourable information and rejects unfavourable information	
	6.5 Leader ignores criticisms	
	6.6 Mistakes are increasingly discounted by leader	
	6.7 Other people or circumstances beyond leader's control are blamed for failings	
	6.8 Decisions are taken increasingly from position of in-group solidarity	
7 Lack of checks and balances	7.1 Decisions taken by a small, privileged and isolated inner circle	
	7.2 Members of inner circle have close/conflicting/compromised interests	
	7.3 Organisation overly dependent on high-profile, lauded individual ('key person' risk)	
	7.4 Absence of leader toe-holder/foil	
	7.5 Ineffective governance mechanisms and reporting systems	
	7.6 Lack of financial controls and poor risk management procedures	

Risk factor	Signs to look out for	Yes/No
	7.7 Opaque and inequitable leader remuneration package	
	7.8 Leader purges top team of critics	
8 Narcissistic tendencies	8.1 Leader displays inflated self-view, grandiosity, self-absorption, vanity, incessant need for adulation, sense of entitlement and low empathy	
	8.2 Leader is charismatic and energetic; initially impresses but falters over time and is unable to execute the role over the longer-term	
	8.3 Leader prefers followers to be an echo chamber for their own views rather than a sounding board to test ideas	
9 Excess	9.1 Leader develops an excess of self-esteem, self-efficacy, and locus of control	
	9.2 Leaders' strengths are practised to the extreme and become weaknesses	
	9.3 Leader lacks practical wisdom to do the right thing, at the right time, for the right reasons	
10 Lack of humility	10.1 Leader does not actively seek feedback, is unreceptive to feedback when it's offered, and is oblivious to personal limitations	
	10.2 Leader does not acknowledge abilities and strengths of others, holds stereotypical views of others, and fails to recognise others as role models and sources of learning	
	10.3 Leader lacks open mindedness, has little thirst for learning and curiosity, never asks for help and is unable to say 'I don't know'	

A leader could undertake a Hubris Health Check assessment themself but they may find it difficult to be objective and, if they're hubris-prone or have narcissistic tendencies, they may not be predisposed to consider any negative self-assessment. Others who are well placed to undertake such an assessment include the chair, the board (in business, and in particular non-executive directors), or the cabinet (in politics), senior civil servants, various committees and regulators, other close colleagues, friends, coaches, mentors, family members, and partners, as well as direct reports and subordinates. The Hubris Health Check could be used to calculate a score by adding up the number of indicators that are present (or scoring them on an agree/disagree Likert scale). This score could be used as the basis for the calculation of a hubris risk factor (or even used in a hubrisometer, see above), for diagnosis, and remediation through prevention or intervention at the level of a specific factor as is the case with a motor vehicle MOT. As with any serious illness, the earlier the intervention the better.

'An apple a day keeps the doctor' away is a well-known example of the precautionary principle. In environmental science the precautionary principle is an important idea for the regulation of risk. Environmental scientists use the precautionary principle as a way of managing risk in the highly complex and poorly understood systems such as the ecosphere. The term 'precautionary principle' is thought to have come into English usage from the German word *Vorsorgeprinzip* which loosely translated means 'foresight principle' and emphasises proactivity and anticipation.[20] In environmental science the principle works as follows: when an activity raises threats of harm to human health or the environment, precautionary measures should be taken even if some cause-and-effect relationships are not fully established scientifically. Foresight is important in the precautionary principle because the pace of change, the uncertainty, and the potential consequences of environmental degradation, such as the potential for catastrophe from climate change, have outpaced society's ability to identify the risks and manage and correct the underlying causes. The precautionary principle calls for preventative action, even where there is uncertainty, and places the onus on those who create the hazard. Amongst the downsides of the precautionary principle are that it threatens to paralyse action and stifle innovation. Critics also argue that it is unscientific because it advocates taking action without the requisite evidence. The Hubris Health Check could be one way of putting the precautionary principle into action in business and politics to manage the hubris hazard and prevent its destructive consequences from materialising..

Evidence of impending danger may not always be obvious, if it were preventative action would be much easier. The early warning signs of hubris are likely to vary in intensity from weak to strong. In anticipating future events weak signals can be especially important because they are, on the one hand, potentially useful but, on the other hand, by definition tend to be fragmented, submerged, ambiguous, and difficult to detect.[21] A hubris-resilient organisations is one that is able to identify and make sense of the early warning signs of hubris, and especially those weak signals which may prove to be especially invidious. The important thing to note about a weak signal is that it may not be insignificant; a weak signal could be a strong sign of an impending derailment, especially when several weak signals occur together. Moreover, the signals of an impending hubris-induced derailment might be opaque to the leader and the top team but be more noticeable by subordinates, added to which a weak or ineffective board or cabinet may be unlikely to see, let alone flag up, weak signals and other early warning signs. If this is the case then a hubris-resilient culture would be one in which: first, employees lower down the hierarchy are encouraged to keep their eyes and ears open for the weak signals that might indicate trouble ahead; and second, mechanisms are in place whereby employees can voice concerns to senior managers (including members of the board) who are willing and able to take the necessary action.

At the US technology firm Texas Instruments (TI), which is one of the world's top ten semiconductor companies, employees who see something that isn't right are actively encouraged to talk to a manager, talk to human resources, or contact the Ethics Office. Contact with the Ethics Office can be direct or through an anonymous internet helpline which is managed by an independent third party and is available 24 hours a day/seven days a week and provides users with the option of remaining anonymous. Moreover, employees at TI are expected to hold themselves accountable to the company standards, including "self-reflection where you have fallen short and could have done something different or better … [as well as] your work group holding one another accountable".[22] Systems such as this can help build hubris-resilience into the DNA of a business.

An analogy is the 'Andon' pull-cord system (meaning 'sign' or 'signal') in the Toyota Production System. Every employee is viewed as an expert and everyone is permitted to stop the production line if they spot something that could be a threat to vehicle quality. The principle behind Andon is that highlighting a problem allows immediate counter measures to be implemented to sort the problem out and prevent its re-occurrence. Perhaps organisations need to have a hubris Andon system in place to counter its potentially destructive effects. The Hubris Health Check could be the pull-cord which build hubris-resilience into the culture of a business.

Having flagged up the early warning signals for a specific risk factor in using the Hubris Health Check, action is then needed to reduce the chances of exposing the organisation to the hazards associated with a particular risk factor. For example, intoxication of power can be mitigated by having fixed terms for heads of government and CEOs, subjecting them to cabinet vigilance and top team scrutiny, and holding leaders to account by voters and shareholders/stakeholders. Other possible interventions for each of the hubris risk factors are discussed in the relevant chapters, but none of them are likely to work in isolation and, furthermore, none of them are 'silver bullets' for the hubris hazard.

A Silver Bullet for Hubris?

Chapter 1 highlighted significant remarks made following the global financial crisis by the Governor of the Bank of England, Dr Andrew Bailey: he pointed out the pressing need for financial organisations and institutions to recognise and be prepared to react to the hubris risk. Hubris risk is a very useful concept. Chapter 1 also drew an analogy between the existence of potential hazards, such as sharks and sunshine, and how in such situations risk arises only through exposure to the hazard. Without exposure to the hazard there can be no risk (Risk = Hazard × Exposure), for example, by desisting from swimming in shark-infested waters or not exposing unprotected skin to high levels of ultraviolet light. In each of the cases the ultimate and infallible form of protection is to not swim in dangerous waters or not lie in the sun without protection. It would be helpful if there were some ultimate form of protection against the hubris hazard. This begs the question: Is there a 'magical weapon' in the form of a silver bullet that can protect organisations and civil societies from the destructive effects of hubristic leader behaviours?

Of course, there can never be *a* silver bullet because hubristic leadership is the outcome of complex interactions between hubristic leader behaviours, complicit followers, and conducive contexts, and hubris risk is a composite of the various hubris risk factors discussed in this book. But perhaps the closest we'll ever get to a silver bullet is humility. We've met humility in various guises throughout the book; it made an overt appearance in the remarks from Warren Buffet recounted above above about balancing hubris and humility. For Buffet, humility is the capacity to know the limits of your abilities and being willing to change course when errors are recognised. One of J. M. Keynes' most famous quotes is "When the facts change,

I change my mind – what do you do sir?" When asked, "What makes a great president?" Hillary Clinton remarked that a great leader should have "enough confidence in yourself to make hard decisions, but enough humility to ask for advice from people smarter than you".[23] In his book *Hubris: The Leadership Epidemic* (2018), the neurologist Peter Garrard foregrounds humility as one of the main 'immunity factors' that can prevent organisations from succumbing to hubristic leadership epidemic'. The other immunity factors are: modesty, respectfulness, openness, self-deprecation, and the ability to retain a sense of humour about oneself, exercise self-criticism and self-cynicism.[24] Ultimately, Garrard is arguing that being 'grounded' helps leaders retain a sense of proportion which prevents them from getting too full of themselves.

Humility is traditionally thought of as virtue, i.e. a trait of excellence of character that is considered to be morally 'good'. As a virtue—and the antithesis of hubris—humility has a rich heritage in theology, wisdom traditions, and philosophy stretching back to Ancient Greeks, Taoists, Buddhists, and early Christianity. The Bible's Book of Proverbs contains its own warning against the hubris hazard ("pride goeth before destruction, and a haughty spirit before a fall"). In St Augustine's writings, humility was the foundation of all the other virtues: "in the soul in which this virtue does not exist there cannot be any other virtue except in mere appearance". As a character virtue, humility is relevant to everybody, but especially to powerful and successful people who, because of their undeniable talents, abilities, achievements, and good fortune, occupy positions of significant influence and hence are at greatest risk of succumbing to power's intoxicating effects and the temptation of "thinking big".[25] For individuals who may succumb to the intoxications of power and success, humility can be a tempering influence and help leaders to achieve the right balance between excesses and deficiencies.[26] As such, humility is a moderating virtue which guards against excess, and for this reason it has been referred to as a 'meta-virtue'.[27] For the poet T. S. Eliot humility had a definitive quality: "the only wisdom that we can hope to acquire is the wisdom of humility".[28]

Humility is sometimes taken to signify meekness, modesty, or shyness. When used in this way humility implies deficiency. However, this is a mistaken understanding of what it means to be humble. In its proper usage, and as used in this book in connection with its antithesis hubris, the term humility shouldn't be equated with meekness, inferiority, and lowliness, or subordination and subservience. Rather, humility is better thought of as a character strength which helps to give a proper perspective on life. The term itself is derived from the Latin *humus* meaning 'from the earth' or 'ground', and hence connotations of 'groundedness'. Business ethicist Bradley Owens and colleagues define humility in terms of three core components: willingness to view oneself accurately; an appreciation of others' strengths and contributions; and 'teachability', see Table 10.3.[29]

But does humility have a role to play in business? Jim Collins' bestselling management book, *Good to Great* (2001) was based on a study of 11 companies who'd made the leap from good to great (including Abbott Laboratories, Gillette, Kimberly-Clark, Walgreens, and Wells Fargo) and sustained those results for at least 15 years by having averaged cumulative stock returns 6.9 times that of the general market. Why did Collins and his team find a direct relationship between the absence of celebrity and the presence of great results?

Table 10.3 Core Components of Humility Based on Owens and Colleagues' Descriptions

Component	Description	Practice
Willingness to view oneself accurately	Objective appraisal of one's strengths and weaknesses in order to make sense of, and where necessary modify, oneself	Actively seeking feedback Being receptive to feedback Transparent about one's performance and personal limitations
Appreciation of others' strengths and contributions	Transcend comparisons and competing with others by appreciating what others are able to do and contribute without feeling threatened	Identifying unique abilities and strengths of others Holding complex (i.e. non-stereotypical) view of others See in others valuable role models and learnings
Teachability	Openness to learning, feedback, and new ideas from others	Open-mindedness Thirst for learning and curiosity Asking for help and being able to say 'I don't know'

First, when you have a celebrity, the company turns into 'the one genius with 1,000 helpers.' It creates a sense that the whole thing is really about the CEO. At a deeper level, we found that for leaders to make something great, their ambition has to be for the greatness of the work and the company, rather than for themselves. That doesn't mean that they don't have an ego. It means that at each decision point—at each of the critical junctures when Choice A would favour their ego and Choice B would favour the company and the work—time and again the good-to-great leaders pick Choice B. Celebrity CEOs, at those same decision points, are more likely to favour self and ego over company and work.[30]

Collins and his team found that these good-to-great leaders were all "cut from the same cloth": at crucial points in the companies' growth trajectories they were able to exercise a powerful blend of personal humility and indomitable will allied to a grand ambition that is first and foremost for the organisation and its purpose, not for the CEO's own ego enhancement purposes or as a personal grandiosity project. Collins noted that as individuals CEOs of the good to great companies tended to be self-effacing and quiet, with a reserved demeanour, and some could even be considered 'shy'.[31] Humility is associated with a cluster of positive leadership traits including sincerity, modesty, fairness, truthfulness, unpretentiousness, and authenticity.[32] Moreover, humble leaders understand that they're unlikely to be the smartest person in every room, and if they're truly leading, they might follow in the footsteps of the 6th-century BC Chinese philosopher Lao Tzu and author of the *Tao Te Ching*: "A leader is best when people barely know he exists, when his work is done, his aim fulfilled, they will say: we did it ourselves".

Conclusion

This book began with a discussion of the global financial crisis of 2008, an event that has loomed over economics and politics, and all of our lives in one way or another, for over a decade-and-a-half. During that time Mark Carney, the Governor of the Bank of Canada, was instrumental in helping the Canadian economy to navigate the crisis more successfully than most.

He was Governor of the Bank of England for seven years between 2013 and 2020. In 2018 Dr Carney gave a speech entitled 'Reflections on leadership in a disruptive age'[33] in which he proposed four essential attributes which apply to leaders in all walks of life: ambition, purpose, clarity, and humility.

One of Carney's main themes in the speech was how to create systems that are resistant to shocks; he refers to such systems as being 'anti-fragile'. The concept of anti-fragility can apply as much to CEOs in corporate environments and prime ministers in political systems as it does to the central bankers in the financial system to whom Carney was addressing his remarks. He urged policy-makers to remain humble as they work to build an anti-fragile financial system; the same can be said of CEOs and prime ministers in their endeavours to build anti-fragile corporations and political institutions. For Carney, being humble entails admitting mistakes, seeking and accepting feedback, sharing the lessons that have been learned, being gracious and modest about successes, and honest and frank about failures.

On the other hand, alarm bells signalling a lack of humility are likely to include: a leader who doesn't actively seek feedback, is unreceptive to feedback when it's offered, and is oblivious to personal limitations; a leader who doesn't acknowledge the abilities and strengths of others, holds stereotypical views of others, and fails to recognise others as role models and sources of learning; and finally a leader who lacks open-mindedness, has little thirst for learning and curiosity, never asks for help, and is unable to say 'I don't know'. As Carney's predecessor at the Bank of England, Mervyn King and the Oxford economist John Kay argued in their book *Radial Uncertainty* (2020) there are many questions to which the only sensible answer is 'I don't know' to which they add "we do not make good decisions by professing knowledge we do not and cannot have" but at least by admitting what we don't know we may, with requisite humility, be able to "to do a little to reduce our ignorance".[34]

Perhaps a healthy dose of humility is the ounce of prevention that can help potential hubrists to recognise and accept that they're just like everybody else, that they're on a continuous, life-long path of learning and self-improvement, and that being a powerful and successful person doesn't mean you've made it and have nothing left to learn. Becoming a leader is a process not a destination; it involves undertaking deliberate and stretching practice, being receptive to timely and accurate feedback, and being open to adaptation, change, and continuous learning.[35] Taken together the 'lessons', if they are such, from the tales of hubristic derailment documented in this book might help leaders to learn from history and hence not make the mistakes of their predecessors. Carney's final words of wisdom, especially to those leaders for whom hubris is an occupational hazard, are to "leave before you are asked", [36] to which might be added 'or before you go down in business or political history for all the wrong reasons'. One of the lessons of hubris history is that it is incumbent on business organisations and political institutions to recognise the hubris hazard and in so doing, do whatever they can to avoid its potentially destructive consequences.

Notes

1 Nixon, M. (2016). *Pariahs: hubris, reputation and organizational crises.* Faringdon: Libri, p.103.

2 Owen, D. (no date). *Managing hubris.* The Daedalus Trust. Available at: http://www.daedalustrust.com/about-hubris/managing-hubris-syndrome

3 Owen, D., & Davidson, J. (2009). Hubris syndrome: An acquired personality disorder? A study of US presidents and UK prime ministers over the last 100 years. *Brain*, 132(5), 1396–1406.

4 Sadler-Smith, E. (2018). *Hubristic leadership.* London: SAGE.

5 Owen, L. D. (2006). Hubris and nemesis in heads of government. *Journal of the Royal Society of Medicine*, 99(11), 548–551.

6 Pentland, A. (2010). *Honest signals: How they shape our world.* Cambridge, MA: MIT Press.

7 Garrard, P., Rentoumi, V., Lambert, C., & Owen, D. (2014). Linguistic biomarkers of hubris syndrome. *Cortex*, 55, 167–181.

8 Pennebaker, J. W. (2011). *The secret life of pronouns.* New York: Bloomsbury.

9 Sadler Smith, E., & Akstinaite, V. (2023). Did destructive leadership help create the conditions for the spread of Covid-19, and what are the early warning signs? *Leadership*, 19(1), 7–26.

10 Akstinaite, V., Garrard, P., & Sadler-Smith, E. (2022). Identifying linguistic markers of CEO hubris: A machine learning approach. *British Journal of Management*, 33(3), 1163–1178.

11 Nixon, M. Personal communication, April 24, 2023.

12 Hogan, R., & Hogan, J. (2001). Assessing leadership: A view from the dark side. *International Journal of Selection and Assessment*, 9(1–2), 40–51.

13 Higgs, M. (2009). The good, the bad and the ugly: Leadership and narcissism. *Journal of Change Management*, 9(2), 165–178.

14 Fitzsimmons, A., & Atkins, D. (2017). *Rethinking reputational risk: How to manage the risks that can ruin your business, your reputation and you*. London: Kogan Page Publishers, p.93, emphases added.

15 Fitzsimmons, A. (2018). How to help non-executive directors see through a chief's charms. *The Financial Times*, May 17

16 Wiscarson, C. (2012). We need MOT tests for bad bosses so that boards can spot hubris before it derails the company. *The Daily Mail*, September 23. Available at: https://www.dailymail.co.uk/money/article-2207535/OPINION-Ego-MOT-tests-help-root-bad-bosses.html#ixzz27Z4RobTE

17 Kellaway, L. (2012). Road test CEOs to avoid corporate crashes. *Financial Times*, September 16. Available at: https://www.ft.com/content/doc9bfea-fdb6-11e1-9901-00144feabdco

18 Dickson, M. (2007). Why we need a hubris index. *Financial Times*, September 27. Available at: https://www.ft.com/content/a4fd9044-6d24-11dc-ab19-0000779fd2ac

19 Furnham, A. (2014). The psychology of leadership derailment. *Royal Society of Medicine*, November 2014. Available at: https://www.youtube.com/watch?v=SoBNIToUFAI

20 Online dictionary.

21 P. Wack, P. (1985). Scenarios: uncharted waters ahead. *Harvard Business Review*, September/October, 72–89.

22 Texas Instruments. (2023). *Living our values*. Available at: https://www.ti.com/lit/ml/szzb178/szzb178.pdf?ts=1685763566229

23 The Rest is Politics, Leading (2023). *Hillary Clinton: Fighting Putin, the return of Trump and the killing of Osama bin Laden*, April 24. Available at: https://podcasts.apple.com/ie/podcast/leading/id1665265193

24 Garrard, P. (ed.). (2018). *The leadership hubris epidemic: Biological roots and strategies for prevention*. Cham, Switzerland: Palgrave Macmillan.

25 Cairns, D. L. (1996). Hybris, dishonour, and thinking big. *The Journal of Hellenic Studies*, 116, 1–32.

26 Hare, S. (1996). The paradox of moral humility. *American Philosophical Quarterly*, 33(2), 235–241.

27 Sadler-Smith, E., & Cojuharenco, I. (2021). Business schools and hubris: Cause or cure? *Academy of Management Learning & Education*, 20(2), 270–289.

28 Eliot, T. S. (1940). *East Coker: Four Quartets*. London: Faber. From 'East Coker' one of the *Four Quartets*.

29 Owens, B. P., Johnson, M. D., & Mitchell, T. R. (2013). Expressed humility in organizations: Implications for performance, teams, and leadership. *Organization Science*, 24(5), 1517–1538.

30 Collins, J. (2001). Good to great. *Fast Company*, October. Available at: https://www.jimcollins.com/article_topics/articles/good-to-great.html

31 Collins, J. (2001). *Good to great*. London: Random House.

32 Hyman, G. (2018). Why humble leaders make the best leaders. Forbes, October 31. Available online at: https://www.forbes.com/sites/jeffhyman/2018/10/31/humility

33 Carney, M. (2018). *Reflections on leadership in a disruptive age*. Bank of England. Available at: https://www.bankofengland.co.uk/-/media/boe/files/speech/2018/reflections-on-leadership-in-a-disruptive-age-speech-by-mark-carney.pdf

34 Kay, J., & King, M. (2020). *Radical uncertainty: Decision-making for an unknowable future*. London: Bridge Street Press, p.12.

35 Kouzes, J., & Pozner, B. (2010). *The truth about leadership*. Chichester: John Wiley and Sons.

36 Carney, M. (2018). *Reflections on leadership in a disruptive age*. Bank of England. Available at: https://www.bankofengland.co.uk/-/media/boe/files/speech/2018/reflections-on-leadership-in-a-disruptive-age-speech-by-mark-carney.pdf

APPENDIX

HUBRIS HEALTH CHECK

Risk factor	Signs to look out for	Yes/No
1 Intoxication of power	1.1 Increased reliance on stereotyping by leader	
	1.2 Leader stops taking others' views into account	
	1.3 Decrease in leader's emotional reciprocity	
	1.4 Reduction in leader's compassion and empathy	
	1.5 Reduction in leader's behavioural inhibition	
	1.6 Increase in leader's violations of social norms	
	1.7 Increase in leader's self-serving behaviours	
	1.8 More lavish spending by leader	
2 Complicit followers	2.1 Tacit support for the leader by conformers who are prepared to simply stand by	
	2.2 Explicit support for the leader by colluders who are prepared to connive actively	
	2.3 Leader has become a media celebrity	
	2.4 Leader is given free rein by an ineffective board or cabinet	

Risk factor	Signs to look out for	Yes/No
3 Conducive context	3.1 'Fake it till you make it' attitude is acceptable	
	3.2 Grandeur of leader's vision overrules ethical concerns	
	3.3 Leading a culture that's conducive to hype, over-claiming and 'greed is good' mentality	
4 Unbridled intuition	4.1 Leader lacks curiosity	
	4.2 Leader is unwilling or unable to appreciate different sides to a problem	
	4.3 Leader's intuition is being used in situations to which it's not suited	
	4.4 Leader's intuition is beginning to crowd out rationality	
	4.5 Increased leader reliance on hard-to-justify gut feelings	
	4.6 Leader lacks requisite experience or expertise to take intuitive decisions	
5 Irrational exuberance	5.1 A long run of uninterrupted successes by the leader	
	5.2 Leader over-confidence and over-ambition	
	5.3 Leader's increased bullishness, recklessness, and risk-seeking behaviours	
	5.4 Preponderance of high testosterone individuals in senior leadership positions	
6 Self-deception	6.1 Leader is unskilled and unaware of how unskilled they are	
	6.2 Leader refuses to seek help or advice	
	6.3 Leader is steadfast and stubborn in the light of obvious shortcomings in performance	
	6.4 Leader welcomes favourable information and rejects unfavourable information	
	6.5 Leader ignores criticisms	
	6.6 Mistakes are increasingly discounted by leader	
	6.7 Other people or circumstances beyond leader's control are blamed for failings	
	6.8 Decisions are taken increasingly from position of in-group solidarity	
7 Lack of checks and balances	7.1 Decisions taken by a small, privileged and isolated inner circle	
	7.2 Members of inner circle have close/conflicting/ compromised interests	

(Continued)

(Continued)

Risk factor	Signs to look out for	Yes/No
	7.3 Organisation overly dependent on high-profile, lauded individual ('key person' risk)	
	7.4 Absence of leader toe-holder/foil	
	7.5 Ineffective governance mechanisms and reporting systems	
	7.6 Lack of financial controls and poor risk management procedures	
	7.7 Opaque and inequitable leader remuneration package	
	7.8 Leader purges top team of critics	
8 Narcissistic tendencies	8.1 Leader displays inflated self-view, grandiosity, self-absorption, vanity, incessant need for adulation, sense of entitlement and low empathy	
	8.2 Leader is charismatic and energetic; initially impresses but falters over time and is unable to execute the role over the longer-term	
	8.3 Leader prefers followers to be an echo chamber for their own views rather than a sounding board to test ideas	
9 Excess	9.1 Leader develops an excess of self-esteem, self-efficacy, and locus of control	
	9.2 Leaders' strengths are practised to the extreme and become weaknesses	
	9.3 Leader lacks practical wisdom to do the right thing, at the right time, for the right reasons	
10 Lack of humility	10.1 Leader does not actively seek feedback, is unreceptive to feedback when it's offered, and is oblivious to personal limitations	
	10.2 Leader does not acknowledge abilities and strengths of others, holds stereotypical views of others, and fails to recognise others as role models and sources of learning	
	10.3 Leader lacks open mindedness, has little thirst for learning and curiosity, never asks for help and is unable to say 'I don't know'	

INDEX

Pages numbers in *italics* denote figures, those in **bold** denote tables.

Printed in the United States
by Baker & Taylor Publisher Services